Thirteen Moons

THIRTEEN MOONS

Robert P. Johnson

CAPRA PRESS

SANTA BARBARA

Cover design and book design by Frank Goad, Santa Barbara
Cover woodcut illustration by David Dahl
Author photo on back cover by Dana M. O'Neill
Frontispiece photo by Nick Miloslavich

LIBRARY OF CONGRESS
CATALOGUING-IN-PUBLICATION DATA
on file

ISBN 0-88496-441-8 (alk. paper)

Capra Press
PO Box 2068
Santa Barbara, CA 93120

Moon of the Shedding Ponies

Until one is committed, there is hesitancy,
       the chance to draw back,
       always ineffectiveness.
Concerning all acts of initiative
       there is one elementary truth
       the ignorance of which kills countless ideas
       and endless plans:
That the moment one definitely commits oneself
       then Providence moves too.
All sorts of things occur to help one
       that would never otherwise have occurred.
A whole stream of events issues from the decision,
       raising in one's favor all manner of unforeseen incidents
       and meetings and material assistance,
       which no man could have dreamed would come his way.
Whatever you can do or dream you can,
       begin it!
Boldness has genius, power, and magic in it.

                           — GOETHE

Journal Entry; 30 May 1984:

The best purchase I ever made was the $155 I paid for a 1953 Plymouth Cranbrook. That was when I was a freshman in college. I had hard-bargained the seller down from a "firm" $200. Today, some eight years later, I parked the now rusty "'Brook" on a dead-end spur of the muddy logging road which wanders the spine of Moody Ridge, up here in the northern Sierra Nevada mountains. And it was a good thing there were no parking meters here, because it was my plan to leave it a full year, and I sincerely doubt if my $508 in assets could float that kind of commitment. A year to the day: that was my plan, that was my goal.

Today was an odd day, both weather-wise and otherwise. Strong and unseasonably balmy gusts tumbled off the snow-capped peaks of the Sierra Nevada Mountains, then dragged across this 4,100 foot ridge like a rake. Towering pines swayed and grunted in the eerie wind. The leaves of the California Bay trees spun from their limbs like fishing lures. Firs lifted their skirts and sighed. Indeed, there was something special about the day at which the wind could only hint. The continent was spinning like a record. The whole planet bustled with ennui. Suffice it to say: the time for change was ripe.

I removed the last of my possessions—my snowshoes, mask, and snorkel, my pancake griddle and vegetable seeds, my goldpan and bowsaw and books on Zen and Plato, my manual typewriter and fishing pole—from the Cranbrook's trunk and stuffed them into my bulging backpack. Next, I changed out of my jeans and into a pair of cut-offs, then donned a pair of well-worn Army boots. That task behind me, I hid the Cranbrook's keys in the ashtray, and closed the door without bothering to lock it; one of the advantages of moving from the city; one of the advantages of owning a $155 car.

Today marked my fourth trip into Humbug Canyon this month, this moon. My first was on May fifth, the purpose of which was to find a suitable campsite for my stay. The subsequent two trips were pure and hearty grunt work, to haul in the supplies that would see me through the summer. Today's mission, however, was unique. Not only would it be my first attempt at dragging any of my tipi poles down the three

ROBERT P. JOHNSON

miles of arduous, switch backing trail, but it would also be my official move-in date—Day One of my proposed year in the wilderness.

Last weekend I had stashed the tipi poles behind some brush alongside this logging road. This morning, after shaking last night's rain from the weeds, I found all seventeen poles still there. I dragged four—all I figured I could manage—from the thicket and began to sash them together. As I did a banged-up pickup came splashing up the muddy road, then paused beside me. I knew the driver, he was one of about a dozen inhabitants of the ridge. As it happens, his property shares a disputed boundary with a chunk of property owned by one of my two brothers. In the pickup with the driver was a passenger who I didn't really know other than to say "Hi" to.

"Hi," I said, as the passenger rolled down his window.

"Howdy there, Robert. How's it hangin'?" the driver asked, across his passenger.

"By a thread," I replied. "And you?"

"Not a whole helluvalot."

"How 'bout you?" I asked the passenger.

"Stayin' out of trouble."

"Hey, Robert, is your brother Jim around?"

"Nope, he's a square." They didn't get it. "Why do you ask?"

"Oh, I just kind of owe him an apology."

"For burying your mule on his property?"

"Yeah. He still mad at me?"

"Far as I know."

The passenger couldn't help but to laugh, "Why'd you go and bury your mule on his brother's property?" he asked the driver.

"'Cause it was dead!"

"I see. So how'd his brother find out?"

"Seems he left one of the mule's legs sticking out of the ground," I added.

"A leg!" the passenger guffawed the louder.

"Yeah, well, backhoes ain't for brain surgery." the driver blushed. Then, "Say, Robert, I hear you're living down on the rio these days."

"News travels quick."

"Well, having any luck?"

His question didn't make any sense. "Luck with what?" I had to ask.

"Goldmining!" he and the passenger answered in unison, as if the question would have been obvious—why else would I be living down there?

"Goldmining?" I repeated, before I could stop myself, before I could see the grave error I was committing. For it seems there's just two sources of income for those living down on the river, and if I wasn't doing one—goldmining—I was surely doing the other—cultivating marijuana.

I quickly tried to cover my tracks. "Er, I mean, yeah, sure, I'm mining, only I'm not having much luck, er, yet,"—a most feeble effort.

"Uh-huh." they nodded, as unconvinced smirks began to spread like oil spills across their mugs.

"No, guys, really!" I assured them.

"Don't worry a hair, Robert. Your little secret is safe with us!" And with that they began to chuckle.

*

By now I've learned all too well what those chuckles mean. I've even become quite used to them, for they seem to arise from most everyone to whom I tell my intentions of spending this year in the wilderness—be they strangers, kin, or my closest friends. They are the chuckles of suspicion; the suspicion being that the only reason I've taken this sabbatical from society is to attempt to strike it rich with one heaping and bountiful pot harvest—four hundred plants, one million bucks.

"It's not so!" I try. "It's only a coincidence that this part of the Sierra happens to be in the smack dab heart of one of California's prime marijuana growing regions. And it's only another coincidence that I happen to be moving down here in the spring—in planting season!"

Yet my efforts to set them all straight reliably prove futile. Nobody believes me. At the local bar in the tiny, one-time boomtown up top, friends buy me frosty drafts then ask me how my seedlings are doing. "I'm not growing pot," I tell them. They chuckle. Strangers—strangers no less!—appear from out of the blue on the barstool next to me offering horse manure in exchange for a "bud" come the harvest. "I'm not growing pot. I'm not growing pot," I tell them. They chuckle. Word trickles down the grapevine and to me via one of my brothers that *the*

Man is planning a big bust in my neck of the woods. "Fine with me, I'm not growing pot. I'm not growing pot. I'm not growing pot!" I find myself shouting. To this they merely smile. They pat me on the back and say, "Sure, whatever..." But then, just when I think they believe me, up from the bowels of their bellies... that damn chuckle.

*

The pickup carrying my brother's neighbor and passenger drove off and away up the logging road. In the distance, through the cab's rear window, I could still see them—*chuckling.* As it disappeared around a bend, and the mud puddles had settled from its passing, I shrugged off the incident—*don't dwell in the past, let bygones be bygones, let a dead mule lie, et cetera*—time to move on.

I glanced at by backpack. There, against the Cranbrook it leaned, like a drunk against a urinal. I looked down to the four, sashed tipi poles, lying in the mud like some pummeled boxer. Both seemed perfectly content to spend the upcoming year right where they were. Lazy bastards. I swung my pack atop my shoulders and cinched its belt tightly. I then lifted the lighter end of the bundle of tipi poles to my hip, and began the toilsome trek.

*

So, Bobo—*Jeremiah* Johnson, mountain man—you have all of $508 tucked away in the bank. Is this whopping nestegg supposed to see you through the entire upcoming year—to feed and clothe you, and provide for any emergencies that may arise? And, even if—by some strange gift of Providence—it does, what then of your future once you've completed this sojourn? What then? What will you do? What *change* do you hope for?

*

The trailhead was only another a half mile up the logging road from where I parked the Cranbrook; a slight but steady, uphill climb, exacerbated by the muddy going and numerous brush stumps which snagged the poles. In spite of these opposing forces, I made it to the trailhead: it would be all downhill from here.

I paused at the trailhead to take in the view—the definitive breathtaking view. Yesterday's storm had broken like a vase leaving only cloudy fragments as reminder of its passing. Out across the canyon diaphanous wisps clung to the craggy southern wall. In the airy void in the middle of the canyon, eye-level to me but some 2,200 feet above the river, other clouds dallied in unseen thermals; sucked heavenward for a good thousand feet before being yanked down again by the weight of their sins. Looking twenty-five miles to the east the peaks of Donner Summit stood like a picket fence; "sixty thousand feet tall", if Mr. Twain can be trusted. Floating there, above the Pacific crest, were tightly bunched thunderheads, purple and white—cauliflower ready for the stew.

These highlands—Granite Chief, Devil's Peak, Tinkers Knob—are the headwaters of the American River. Up yonder this mighty river is but an irregular drip from a clump of moss, the irrelevant metamorphose of a single molecule of snow into water. Nevertheless, drip meets drip soon to form drools. Drools join to become trickles, trickles gather into pisses, and the pisses spew forth tiny pukes. In time these pukes fulfill the definition of a creek. Creeks then grow into brooks, brooks into streams, and the streams continue to grow and prosper and horde until we have prepubescent rivers—two of them—*The North Fork* and *The North of the North Fork*.

Each knowing yet nothing of the other, these young rivers begin their descent—tripping down cataracts, teapots over kettles, dipping underground for stretches, out of sight out of mind, meandering from the Sierra like boys unwillingly to school, obedient only to Father Gravity, who lays down the laws, and to their maternal ocean, who nurses and spanks them and sends them off again to distant lands then welcomes them back into her loving bosom. In all, these two rivers will ramble some thirty miles before they meet; through Soda Springs and Royal Gorge, Blue Canyon and Sailors Flat, Mumford Bar, Dream Gap, Rawhide Mine, et al, until they meet finally at Euchre Bar. Here the two become one—*The North Fork of the American*. And near here, some miles down river from the confluence, is the lazy stretch of river that will be my address for the next 365 days—Green Valley.

And below Green Valley, for those who care to know, is a treacherous four

ROBERT P. JOHNSON

mile stretch known to rafters and kayakers and such seekers of misfortune, as Giant Gap. *Alas!*—fearsome Giant Gap; a fortress of crags and cliffs, a colander of boulders, a sieve of logjams, a mere slit through hell. Cruel and wanton, evil beyond measure, here has all that calls itself *wild* retreated for one last stand against humanity's taming, here does nature take her last vehement gasp before acquiescing to the retiring slumber of the Sierra foothills, Folsom Dam, and the senility of the Sacramento Valley.

My eyeballs ached from sensory overload. Like a pig before a sumptuous buffet, I overate. In an effort to make more efficient use of the few remaining hours of daylight, I lifted the tipi poles again to my hip, then stepped from the road and onto the path.

*

So, Robert, whatever made you decide you needed to take this twelve-month sabbatical from society? people invariably ask. But my replies are rarely the same twice. They are as varied as my moods, as varied as the people who ask. *You see,* I might tell some, *I'm a mighty big fan of ol' Henry David Thoreau and I seek to make the American River my Walden Pond.* To those who haven't read *Walden* I might put it this way: *It came down to a choice between two lifestyles: one wherein I paid $500 per month rent for a noisy apartment, commuted an hour through traffic to work, punched in at a job I hated but kept only so one day I might retire so to enjoy a brief time pondering how I had wasted my one and only life. The alternative being this: a life of repose and adventure, of pretending that our time here is to be enjoyed and explored, of trout fishing whenever I am so inclined or of sleeping in until the tipi glows warm with the morning sun, a lifestyle wherein my only chore is to breathe and my only hobby to witness the sun hurdle the horizons and the moon be nibbled through its phases by that unseen mouse.* To others, especially family members, I lie directly: *I'm here to write my book!* But I have no such intention, it's just a ruse to pacify them. Indeed, I can't recall telling anyone the true reason for my endeavor.

*

Once on the trail winding down into the canyon the punishment of my task turned to pleasure. The combination of the steep downgrade, the slick and rain-soaked poles, and the damp oak leaves littering the trail, made for about as frictionless a glide as physics would allow. As the pitch of the canyon grew steeper the trail crimped into dozens of tight, zig-zagging switchbacks. Some of these switchbacks had hairpin corners too tight to navigate the twenty-foot poles around. As a result I often had to trust the bundle to slide by itself down steep washouts. Whereupon I would hike the switchback, catching up with the bundle somewhere below where the washout again crossed the trail.

My first big fright came about two miles down the trail, for it was here that I happened upon The Ambassador—a big, fat rattlesnake who looked as if he had just swallowed Pavarotti. From first glance it was obvious that this was no ordinary rattler. For whereas most from his species will quickly coil the moment a threatening presence is detected, then switch to "on" that horrid *buzz* (known to be every bit as invigorating to the human heart as thirty minutes of brisk aerobics), The Ambassador deigned to nothing so banal. Perhaps he was too fat. Perhaps he was too old. Or, perhaps, as I chose to opine, he was just too damn cool.

Not about to tread on him, The Ambassador and I stared at one another for several minutes with the kind of bitter respect shared by emissaries of warring nations across a bargaining table. Soon, however, he lost interest. Hissing once, he slowly pulled himself into a rocky crevice, pausing just long enough for a customary wag of his rattles before disappearing altogether.

By then it may have been noon. The sun hung in the sky like a white-hot fireplace poker, just waiting to jab you in the eye. Trying not to let it, I pressed onward. After another dozen switchbacks I came at last into the welcoming shade of The Halfway Cedar—a billowy evergreen which signaled, approximately, the trail's midway point. I dropped the poles, ripped off my backpack, sat against the cedar's trunk, and settled into a deserved rest.

With the clatter of the dragging poles temporarily muted, I could hear I wasn't the only one out of breath; the canyon too was winded. When the wind swept one way across the arid canyon slope it dragged with it the thick, musty scent of California poppy. And when it swept back the other, pungent pennyroyal.

ROBERT P. JOHNSON

Knowing a thing or two about goals and the getting there, I knew the sooner I ended this pleasant respite, the sooner I could enjoy a more lasting one. Hence, I stood over my beaten legs, slung my pack onto my back, lifted the bundle of tipi poles again to my hip, sighed, then trudged into the second half of the hike.

After another forty minutes the steep slope of the canyon wall yielded to the valley floor. Here the agony of the knee-buckling descent became the torture of the flesh-tearing manzanita. Fallen trees littered the trail. These I would step on top of rather than over, having heard as a boy scout how rattlesnakes love to hide beneath such logs and play *inny-meeny-minny-moe* with our young ankles. A second or two after stepping off the logs I would feel the dragging ends of the tipi poles drop over the same.

After tunneling through the brush for what could have been a half mile, the trail eventually opened into a lush meadow. Sweet hints of honeysuckle and wild azalea glazed the ham. The trail bisected the meadow, passing me between blossoming pear and apple trees rising like pearly gates.

Near the top of the meadow I stumbled upon a grave. By all means a simple grave, a mound of stones, gathered from as far away as ten yards; and a crude cross, fashioned from two survey stakes uprooted, no doubt, from some subdivision miles away. Wedged between some stones at the base of the cross there sat a small mayonnaise jar containing a sun-stained note. I wrestled with the jar's rusty lid, then extracted the typed note:

"Joe Steiner lived a great part of his life here on the American River. He arrived in San Francisco in the early 1900's as a young man in his mid twenties, coming from Europe via a four-masted sailing ship. He was a native of Switzerland and felt right at home here in these beautiful mountains, a prospector in search of gold, he made his living with pan and sluice box. Later in life he dug a mine not far from here. The opening faced the river and the mine extended several hundred feet into the hillside. It was complete with blacksmith shop and ore cart. His home in summer and winter was a good sized tent complete with wooden floor and woodstove. He lived on produce from his garden, honey and staples purchased in the town of Towle no longer in existence. A cup of his coffee consisted of two thirds strong coffee. He had many friends who visited the area from time to time. In later life his hair and full beard turned a snow white and would make a perfect Santa. He died in his camp as he wished and when his remains were discovered he was buried here in this spot.

"Please honor him by not disturbing the grave site. One of his greatest accomplishments was the construction of a suspension bridge downstream. This was done almost single-handed."

R.I.P.
Joe Steiner
1880 to 1950 approx.

I folded the note back into the jar and, mumbling an ad libbed prayer, carefully placed it back atop the grave. However reverent my behavior may seem, its motive was purely selfish, for I was well aware that the terrace upon which I planned to pitch my tipi was the very spot where Joe Steiner had lived his last forty years. I had no need for an irate ghost nagging me for the forthcoming year, even if he *did* look like Santa.

From Steiner's grave it was a quarter mile straight to the river, a route which the trail followed directly. Through the lower end of the meadow my boots began to sink through the lush grass and into the muddy bog beneath. This action gave rise to a veritable symphony of sounds—

ROBERT P. JOHNSON

squishy notes as my heels sunk in, sucking crescendos as they pulled out again—noises offensive to women or persons of feeble natures.

The meadow ended at a spring choked with vernal flora: columbine, tiger lily, yarrow, blue camas, watercress, moss, and rush. Ladybugs, seemingly millions of them, massed on the rocks and tree trunks at the spring and along the creek which flowed from it. In another twenty yards the creek ended as well, yielding obsequiously to the river. Splashing through the creek and stepping upon the dry and level terrace, I was home.

*

Journal Entry; Historical Digression:

As recently as one hundred years ago this canyon was the stomping grounds for the Maidu Native Americans. Then, in the mid-1850's, Europeans, riding the tidal wave of the California goldrush, swooped into the valley by the hundreds. Soon thereafter Chinese slaves—emancipated now that construction of the transcontinental railroad up and over Donner Pass was complete—poured into the valley, anxious to adopt the American dream as their own. In the late 1880's the population of this three-mile stretch of canyon peaked. 2,500 men worked side by side in those years, laboring either for large companies employing hydraulic mining technologies, or else doing it on their own with shovels, sluice boxes, and goldpans on twenty-foot square placer claims. By day the miners tore up the river banks as fast as they could, ever cautious not to roll a boulder into their neighbor's digs—due cause for a killing. By night they chewed whiskey, smoked beans, drank roll-yer-own cigarettes, and cheated at Pinochle. When they slept they did so atop their pistols and pouches of gold, and dreamt of Mister Nugget and the booty the morrow would surely bring.

Then came the end. Regarded as California's first environmental legislation, a state-wide ban on hydraulic mining went into effect that same decade. This came about after Sacramento Valley ranchers complained about the rivers of silt pouring from the foothills, too thick for their cattle to drink. The ban tore through the goldrush like a hollowpoint bullet. The big hydraulic operations turned belly-up and retreated from the canyon leaving their rusting hardware to the grasshoppers and the rattlesnakes. The canyon sighed, its nagging itch had passed.

Still, a few men remained—"stragglers", "holders-on". Since the turn of the twentieth century these same personality types have tumbled into the canyon each spring, their packs stuffed with provisions, their buckets overflowing with ambition. But come each fall, out from the canyon they crawl, whimpering, with little more to show for their efforts than the notches taken in on their belts and the new holes in their jeans. Calling these men *prospectors* is giving them the benefit of the doubt. Sure, they spend their days mining, but gold is not why they're here. For they are society's lepers—drunks, fugitives, ex-cons, ex-sanes—who have fled the real world to come cower for a time beneath Mama Nature's petticoat. Why here? Because life here is as simple as life gets—not *easy*, just simple.

*

JOURNAL ENTRY; EVENING, DAY ONE:

Dusk slid overhead just a bit ago, rendering the sky a placid puddle of turquoise and lime, rimmed along the eastern horizon with indigo and along the western end with the golden remnants of the expired day. The few clouds were now high, blazing streaks of crimson and orange. Above and beyond them, the night reached down through the firmament—bright Venus here, not-so-bright Saturn there, the moon new and hidden.

Whereas the world verifies itself with sight by day, by night it seems to do so with sound. Crickets come immediately to mind—a billion in each ear, fiddling their part of an insomniac symphony to the incessant *sssrrrssshhh…* of the river.

I balance a pot of water atop three uneven stones. Into the pot I heap a fair measure of coffee. Building a fire around it, the pot is soon consumed by flames, the water boiling. I remove the pot and set it upon the cool earth beside the fire. To coax the grounds into settling I add a splash of cold spring water. *Cowboy coffee*—it's all the rage. Pouring

ROBERT P. JOHNSON

myself a mug, I lean back against my sofa—actually, a log—gaze into my color t.v.—actually, the campfire—and lose myself in its hellish chaos—actually, a perfect and logical order.

Suddenly, a gunshot. .22 caliber, I determined as the bullet whizzed through my mustache. I heard it too, but not until much later. Perhaps it wasn't all as close as it seemed; as with light passing into water, the truth is known to bend as it passes through panic. My head swung towards the creek where, there, a shadow lurked.

"Didn't startle ya, did I?" the shadow asked, friendly-like, as it stepped towards the faint light of the fire.

"*Startle me?*—how?" I replied, through my cucumber-cool countenance.

The shadow splashed forth through the shallow creek. Features emerged: a gun barrel pointed harmlessly downward, a man—scruffy and slight, his hair black, his beard long and graying, his face a deep bronze.

"Howdy, name's Slim," he said.

I nodded. At the time I was munching some trail mix. I felt obliged to offer him some. I held out the bag.

"Don't mind if I do," Slim said, reaching into the bag. It was then that I became aware of another of his distinguishing features, he smelled like a Calcutta sewer.

Through the clear plastic I watched Slim's hand sink towards the goodies. Then, like the jaws of a boa constrictor dislocating to swallow a pig, so too did his hand seem to expand around the bag's contents. The simple but calculated act seemed to take the better part of the evening. When Slim finally retracted his loaded meathoof, not so much as a sunflower seed remained in the bag.

"So, that shot you fired off —" I began, pouring him a mug of joe.

"Just announcin' my presence. Had you a door I would've knocked," he chortled.

"Mighty polite of you."

"Yeah, I think so. I appreciate a warning shot or three before folks come stomping through my camp," he said, accepting the mug.

"Oh, me too. Shoot at my feet if you're passing through. Shoot at my head if you're staying, I always say."

"Yep, a courtesy all but lost in this cold day and age."

"Care for some coffee?"

He sipped then grinned, "Don't mind if I do."

He then pulled a flask from his hip pocket and poured a shot of its syrupy contents into each of our mugs. "Care for a lump of sugar?"

"Depends, what is it?"

"Piss."

"In that case, two lumps, please."

Slim smiled and poured us each another shot. I caught the fruity whiff of apricot brandy as I sipped—a fitting nightcap.

As we sat there nursing our coffee royales we tossed fragments of chit-chat across the campfire until we knew all that a couple of misfits need to know about one another, which wasn't much. As we talked, or talked not, the dusk drained from the sky allowing the heavens to pour overhead like a milkshake of diamonds.

An hour slipped past. Slim was concluding a partial recounting of his years, "... and the next fifteen I spent in San Quentin prison."

"What for?—if you don't mind my asking."

"Hell, I ain't got nothing to hide. For burning down the house my pa willed to me."

"Can't a man burn down his own house?"

"Not if it turns out his pa never owned it to begin with."

"Tough luck, bum-steered by pa. Then what'd you do?"

"Moved down here. Been here twelve years now."

"Twelve years!"

"Yep," he nodded, staring into the fire.

I began adding up his adventures in terms of the years they consumed: two in Korea, four in Nam, two as a New York City junkie, seven spent locked up in marriage, et cetera. The tally came up to forty-three years.

"Geez, Slim, you've packed a lot into just one lifetime. How old are you?"

Slim straightened his back proudly, "Forty-two."

"Forty-two!"—I could now deduce one of two things about Slim: either he had a penchant for embellishing the truth, *or*, he was first drafted into the military at the tender age of negative one. I decided to

ROBERT P. JOHNSON

keep my findings to myself.

"So, Slim, how are the winters in this neck of the woods?"

"*Winters?*—hell, I may be dumb but I ain't stupid!"

"You don't stay the winters, I take it."

"Hell no; not even much of the fall if I can help it. I pull up 'round September and head down to Frisco to do termite work 'til about May. No siree, Bob, this place's no place to be come winter!"

Slim must of seen the color drain from my face, for he then asked, "You ain't plannin' on stayin' the winter, are ya?"

I nodded my head.

He shook his.

We lapsed into another silence.

"So, are we the only ones living down here?" I asked, as I refilling our mugs with joe and changing the subject.

"Far from it," Slim replied, recharging our drinks with brandy. "There's two old brothers—twins. They live 'bout seven miles down-river, just beyond Giant Gap. They got themselves a couple of dredges workin' the canyon's only legitimate claim. Then, of course, can't forget to include my partner, though I'd sure as hell like to."

"Why's that?"

"'Cause he's full of shit; thinks he deserves two-thirds of our gold just because we're using his piece-o-shit sluice box. Hell, I'm convinced the damn thing loses half the *color* we run through it. And he has the nerve to call himself *The California Goldminer!*"

"*Hah!*—The California Goldminer livin' down here now?"

"You know him?"

"Sure, ever since I was a kid. My great grand uncle was a goldminer in the little town up top. We lived in Oakland but my family used to come up here a lot. I always remembered The California Goldminer crawling out of the Bear River and into town to cash in his gold and to tie on a drunk. Must've known him thirteen, fourteen years. Don't ever recall seeing him sober though."

"You know him alright."

"So, it's you, me, the two old brothers, and California. Well, I gotta admit, that's four more than I thought there'd be living down here."

"Oh, and there's another—" Slim began, before pursing his lips suspiciously.

"Another what?" I pried.

"Er, another goldminer."

Slim was doing some particularly bad bullshitting. I decided to press. "Another goldminer, huh?"

"Yeah, well, kind of. A *part-time* miner."

"A *part-time* miner?"

Slim nodded meekly, "That's right."

"Well, what's he do with all that *free* time?"

Slim retracted at my inquiry. He swung his eyes to my own and narrowed their focus until they burned like beams into my frontal lobe. He was attempting to see through to my motives. Was I an undercover Placer County sheriff, a DEA "narc", a CAMP (Campaign Against Marijuana Proliferation) snitch, or any other such manifestation of *The Man?*—this is what he was trying to divine from my skull. The stare down lasted longer than some marriages. Finally, Slim relaxed his gaze, then smiled.

"Let's just say he's in the agriculture business," he winked.

"In a big way?"

Slim nodded. "In a very big way."

"Where's he growing it?"

Slim retracted again, thinking I was clearly overstepping my bounds.

"Just so I know where not to wander," I assured him.

Slim seemed satisfied with my explanation. Then, with an ever so subtle tilt of his head, he alluded to a tall hill rising abruptly from the river's south bank, just across the river from my camp.

I knew of this hill. There's quite a legend about it, a legend that's been haunting me since I was thirteen.

"So, he's growing his stuff up on Snakehead Point?"

Slim nodded, then nervously downed his coffee with one rushed gulp.

That mysterious legend: I wondered if Slim knew about it. Or this Marijuana Grower; surely, if anyone down here did, it would be him— he's camped right on top of it! I had to find out. Employing the same beam-like stare Slim had used on me, I took a calming breath then asked:

"On the pyramid?"

Observers of hydrogen bomb detonations have noted the utter

silence of the event. It was this same utter silence which lead me to suspect that such a bomb must have just then hit my camp. For all the canyon's din—Slim, the fire, the crickets, even the river— all seemed to fall instantly and inexplicably mute. And yet, from the silence, one thing rang loud and clear; Slim knew the legend of the pyramid.

*

Since puberty just two things have been on my mind, and this pyramid was one of them. I first learned of the legend way back when I was thirteen, from a pair of archeologists from the University of Pennsylvania. They had driven all the way from there in a beat-up Rambler station wagon full of picks and shovels and such. They were planning to excavate. The hot summer day they rolled into our little goldmining town, I happened to be sitting on the shady porch of the general store, enjoying a rootbeer popsicle and minding my own business.

"Hey, kid, do you know where Snakehead Point is?" they asked. That was all it took: our paths met and their obsession became mine.

By the time I turned fifteen I truly believed my life's mission, my *raison d'être*, was to discover this enigmatic edifice. To that end I searched for it summers and off-season holidays, often enlisting friends, willing or not, into my service, placing in their tender and disbelieving hands the harpoon for my Moby Dick. Despite my years of earnest expeditions into this canyon, I never found it. With the passing of youth so too passed my fervor for the pyramid. At first I merely reclassified its status from *real* to that of *legend*—impossible to either prove or disprove. Then, soon and thankfully thereafter, I stopped believing in it altogether—*thankfully* for I was now entering high school, and high school was no place to be different.

As for the present, I didn't want this year in the woods to have anything to do with the pyramid. True, I've only the pyramid to thank for my ever being introduced to this lovely canyon, but it is *not* why I am here. I am twenty-seven and I want now to keep my mysticism pure and simple and only about as deep as a proper cast of a dry fly upon a calm and troutless pond. I don't need anything arising from the murky depths and pulling me under...*again.* I had purposely retired the legend of the pyramid, I didn't need it flying back in my face. And yet, here it was.

*

"So, what about it, Slim?—do you think this Marijuana Grower knows—" I began, before Slim exploded.

"You steer clear of him *and* his hill full of wacky tobaccy!" he warned with stern finger. "That fat asshole's crazy as a bug. Got's himself an assault rifle and a mean-as-hell dog!"

"Those are some good reasons, Slim. I appreciate the warning."

We sat in silence for a few more minutes. I purposely didn't add anymore wood to the fire. End of the show. Slim caught the hint. He stood, stretched, and groaned, then picked up his rifle and bade me goodnight...

"Well, goodnight. What did you say your name was?"

"Robert."

"Hey, that's the pothead's name too!"

"Common name."

"Small canyon!" he retorted. "Well, goodnight, anyway."

"Goodnight right back at ya, Slim."

With that, Slim turned from the fire's warmth and began the dark commute back to his camp, as he described it, nestled in an invisible gulch about a mile and a half up river.

I watched as his image faded into the shadows from whence it had come, then listened as his boots sloshed through my creek. But, suddenly, somewhere there in the middle of the creek, his sloshings stopped.

"Oh, by the way," he shouted, with a subtle but obvious chuckle in his voice, "the soil's pretty acidy down these parts. You'd be wise to mix some of that fire pit ash into the dirt before you plant," he warned, adding, "Oh, and keep in mind that August and September is helicopter season. Sky's full of 'em! Nightie-night."

So that was it—he too suspected I was here to grow pot!

As he turned away again I could hear his sloshing continue across the creek, his chuckles soon blending with those of the creek, crickets, and river—the whole planet, chuckling.

I decided I wouldn't waste my breath trying to convince Slim that I wasn't here to grow marijuana. He'd never buy it. Besides, it might behoove me to let him think I was. At least that would be easier for him to grasp than my *actual* reason for being here—whatever it was.

I fumbled with my pack in the dark until I managed to find my sleepingbag. Kicking away the sticks and stones covering one of the terrace's more appealing spots, I unfurled my bag, stripped, and crawled into it.

Lying flat on my back I tilted my gaze across the river towards towering Snakehead Point, rising above the black horizon like an obsidian arrowhead; eclipsing the stars behind it, stabbing the night with a night all its own. Taking in its ominous silhouette I could feel the weight of the long-dormant obsession returning. And I didn't like it one bit. However much I had hoped to leave the pyramid buried in my past there was no denying the fact that it was *I* who had come back to it. *Why?* No, I retract that question for I don't believe in predeterminism, I don't believe in fate, I don't believe in destiny. *And yet, here it was!*

I returned my gaze to the starry dome straight above. A shooting star tore through the firmament. Its life brief.

Moon Of Making Fat

Where is he, this natural man who lives a truly human life? Who, caring nothing for the opinions of others, acts only in accord with his impulses and reason, without regard for the praise or blame of society. In vain do we seek him among us. Everywhere only a varnish of words; all men seek their happiness in appearance. No one cares for reality, everyone stakes his essence on illusion. Slaves and dupes of their self-love, men live not in order to live but to make others believe they have lived!

—JEAN-JACQUES ROUSSEAU

The sun hung over the noon-hour sky like a fried egg, sunny side down. It was too hot to hang around camp so, packing along the last two cans of beer from my move-in-day six-pack, I set upon a leisurely stroll up the river trail. About fifteen minutes later I found myself at the bank of a particularly calm and beautiful stretch known as Mercury Pool. There, beneath the forgiving shade of a lush alder tree on the north bank's stony sandbar, I sat and popped open a beer. A dozen steps away the river slipped past, down its mottled gold and olive riverbed like an endless serpent of clear silicon. I had sat there for some time before I noticed the goldminer and his hound hunched over a sluice box directly across the river from me, not thirty yards away. Likewise, the incessant din stirred by the rapids just below the pool had kept them oblivious of me. By Slim's description—*fat*—I knew at once who this lowly tatterdemalion was—the assault rifle-toting, crazy as a bug Marijuana Grower. And there by his side, his mean as hell dog.

My first instinct was to put an egg in my shoe and beat it. But, instead, for some strange reason, I found myself—hands cupped around my mouth—shouting across to him: "Howdy!"

Like a distant gong, my call rang within The Marijuana Grower's brain. I watched it happen. Casually he straightened his aching vertebrate, tipped back his worn prospector's hat, and began a methodical 360º pan of the area. Somehow his sweeping gaze passed over without detecting me, possibly because of my being tucked beneath the shade on the otherwise glaring sandbar. He even stared straight up into the wide, blue sky for the source of the shout, divulging a candid glimpse into his character.

I shouted again, "Over here. Straight across the river!"

This time he found me. For some time he only stared. Then, finally, he shouted back, "Twat?"

Twat?—I didn't know if I had heard him correctly. I returned the shout, "What?"

Again, it was some moments and a visible head scratching later before he shouted back, "Ay kant 'hi(e)r ewe!"

I tried to make sense of what he had said: *I punt deer pooh* , or possibly,

I chant voodoo? Either way, Slim's warning was appearing more valid by the syllable—*crazy as a bug!* I shouted again, "I can't hear you!"

Obviously frustrated now, The Marijuana Grower began ripping off his shirt, hat, and pants. He then pulled on a baggy pair of cut-offs and, sans hesitation, dove into the frigid river. By the time he surfaced the current had swept him five yards downstream. He waited another second until his drift brought him to a taut nylon rope he had stretched across the river. Reaching up and grabbing the rope, he began pulling himself, hand over hand, towards my bank. This rope device gave this stretch of river reason enough to be called, The Mercury Pool Crossing. And had The Marijuana Grower lost his grasp of the rope while crossing it was probable he would have been sucked into the rapids below. And had that happened it was probable he would not have survived. When The Marijuana Grower emerged on my side of the river he was shivering like one of those hardware store paint-shaker machines, his already Irish-blue skin now dropping off the visible light spectrum and well into the ultraviolet range.

"Now, what the hell were you shouting about?" The Marijuana Grower implored.

"Just shouting *howdy*," I replied.

"That's all? I risked life and limb just to say *howdy?* Wouldn't a simple wave have sufficed?"

"Why didn't you just pull yourself across in your raft?"

"Because—hey, how'd you know I had a raft?" he asked, suddenly suspicious.

"I spotted it parked over on your side a couple weeks ago."

"*A couple of weeks ago*—how long have you been camping down here?"

"Just two days, but I've been packing down supplies since the fifth of May."

With each new detail I offered, The Marijuana Grower grew ever more suspicious. "How long are you planning on staying?" he ventured.

"Kind of nosy, aren't you?"

"A man of my occupation has got to be."

"And what's your occupation?"

"I grow marijuana."

"Suddenly you seem pretty trusting. How do you know I'm not a cop or something?"

"Are you?"

"No," I replied.

"That's how I know. The name's Robert," he said, producing his rope-clenching, earth-plowing, nose-picking, dick-whacking, cracked and callused meathoof.

"So's mine," I said, extending my own to his. We shook. "Would you care for a beer?"

"First place, all-time, dumb-question award. Congratulations."

I gave him a beer.

As we sat there chatting and sipping The Marijuana Grower repeatedly tossed a stick into the river for his half black Labrador, half who-knows-what dog.

"What's your dog's name?"

"Bud."

"As in *marijuana* bud?"

"No, as in *buddy*—you know, man's best friend."

Despite whatever shortcomings Bud may have had as a show dog or rocket scientist, one thing must be recorded in his favor; namely, there isn't now, never was, and forever never will be a better stick-fetcher in all the world. And that's a fact. And if any hubris-pumped dog owner tries to tell you otherwise, just politely shake your head and assure them, "Nope, Bud's the best." They deserve to know. And another thing about Bud's character: whereas Slim had described him as *mean as hell,* I found that to be as far from the truth as here is from there.

"So where's your assault rifle?" I asked The Marijuana Grower.

"Assault rifle?" he squeaked, his eyebrows twisting in confusion. "Are they required now?"

Judging by the facts that Bud wasn't *mean as hell,* The Marijuana Grower wasn't *crazy as a bug,* and neither owned an assault rifle, I deduced that Slim must only have said those things to scare me away from Snakehead Point and The Marijuana Grower's plantation.

"Yeah, but I won't say anything," I assured him.

As time passed, our conversation stumbled back to the subject of the raft:

"I lost the raft to the river gods one night," The Marijuana Grower began as he tossed Bud's stick, for about the twelfth time, into the exact same spot of the river—the smooth but swift tongue of the rapids.

Bud barked excitedly, leapt from the sandbar, flew for some yards with legs tucked aerodynamically, splashed down, surfaced, snorted out a snootful of water, then began his dogged pursuit as The Marijuana Grower continued:

"It was about a minute after midnight, about a minute into April Fool's Day. Bud and I were in the raft along with half our supplies as I ferried us across the river by means of the rope. Then, right out there— right in the goddamned, smack-dab middle—the current caught the raft's upstream tube and just sucked it from beneath me. We were right out there, right where Bud is now."

By now Bud had caught up with the stick and was negotiating his turn around. What may not have been apparent to him by then, but was certainly so to us, was the sad fact that he was now caught in the tongue's inescapable current, soon to be swallowed down the angry gullet of the rapids ten yards below. Nevertheless, The Marijuana Grower continued nonchalantly.

"Next thing I knew I was clutching the rope, my back surfing on the current, the river running then at about twice the volume that it is now. As I lay there, staring up at the full moon and enjoying the most frigid experience of my life, I could hear Bud, still in the raft, yelping as the current dragged him away, his barks becoming fainter and fainter until altogether drowned beneath the roar of the rapids."

The Marijuana Grower's story was graphically enhanced by the fact that Bud was presently being sucked down those very same rapids. *And violent rapids they were!*—first they twisted through a tight right bend, dragging Bud against a sheer rock wall, then they straightened out for forty yards of choppy, haystacking froth, then they bent left and disappeared around another bend, leaving any further horrors to the imagination. Amidst this tumult all we could see of Bud was his snout and stick, bobbing up and under like a particle of flotsam in a hurricane, before disappearing altogether around the bend.

The Marijuana Grower seemed unfazed: "Yep, I recall dragging in the water there, staring up at the full moon and thinking to myself, *Bud is*

ROBERT P. JOHNSON

history. Soon, however, it would be my turn. You see, I weighed 304 pounds at the time, rather than the trim 240 I do now, and I just couldn't hold on to the rope. So, like Bud, I took my ride. After what seemed like an eternity of tumbling down the icy darkness, a whirlpool snagged me and eventually spit me out against the bank. I promptly named that pool *God's Pool.*"

"What about Bud?"

The Marijuana Grower chuckled, "If only he could talk! Bud showed up back at camp a few hours later."

Right about then, some fifteen minutes after he first leapt into the river, Bud, the idiot/savant stick fetcher, returned—shivering but wagging, worn, torn, tattered, soaked, and battered, but unmistakably proud of the fact that he had indeed fetched the stick. He dropped it on the sandbar and shook all over us.

"Fuck you, Bud!"

The mutt barked, begging for another toss. This time I obliged him, tossing the stick, as had The Marijuana Grower, onto the tongue of the rapids.

"So, how'd you come to hear about the pyramid?" I asked The Marijuana Grower as Bud took to wing.

The Marijuana Grower's ears perked. "*Ah*—the pyramid!"

"Let's see…" he began, "As I recall I had just been kicked out of the Bhagwan Shree Rajneesh's ashram up in Oregon —"

"You were one of those *orange people?*" I asked.

"Please, *sanyassins.* But, yeah, I was one. Anyway…"

Not one to answer a question without proper prefacing, The Marijuana Grower went on to tell each significant beat of his life which played any role in steering him towards our canyon and the legend of the pyramid. The *Readers Digest*'s condensed version of the same might read so:

Born and raised in middle-class, upstate New York, he snatched his diploma from the hand of his high school dean, raised it like a spyglass to his eyeball, and promptly set sail for California. He is twenty-eight, though he would say *fourteen,* insofar as he sees no reason to count his prepubescent years. What most of us might admonish as failures he hails as triumphs: dropping out of more colleges than he can count on his digits, growing pot between runways at a major metropolitan airport, frequenting prostitutes (often choosing the least desirable ones out of a complex interplay of lust and charity), and, perhaps his greatest accomplishment, a record-setting sixty-two continuous weeks on the unemployment dole.

As a Sanyassin he and his then-girlfriend lived at both the Oregon ashram and the one in India. Whereas she was attracted by the Bhagwan's spiritual teachings, The Marijuana Grower admits it was the cult's practice of tantric orgies and free-love that had hooked him. But after three heart-breaking years of devotion it was becoming ever more apparent to him that *free-love* basically meant he now had to share his girlfriend with everyone else. "She didn't seem to mind."

To no one's surprise the girlfriend became pregnant with another man's child. In accord with the ashram's no-children policy, she was asked to leave. Good to the last drop, The Marijuana Grower migrated with her. Hitchhiking down the highway of their intuitions, they rolled to a stop in Santa Cruz, California, where they dug in for the birth of the child. The baby was born healthy and happy and The Marijuana Grower loved it as if it were his own. Then, sometime around the baby's first birthday, the girlfriend whisked off into the sunrise, babe in arms, in an attempt to secure more stable environs. "Can't blame her," The Marijuana Grower said, and he meant it.

In spite of all his "failures", The Marijuana Grower maintains a snobby pride of his life thus far. He sees his as a life lived bravely rather than one of whimpers and curtsies, a life sans compromise, the moody painting hung off in a dark corner of the museum, a life he describes with one word, *bittersweet.* "Anyway," he continued, "I was attending a wedding down in Santa Cruz last year where just about everyone present, except for me, claimed to be some sort of psychic. At the time I was lying on my back, guzzling champagne directly from the fountain's spigot. That's when I overheard some fuzzheads talking about taking a field trip up to the Sierra to search for "the pyramid". I suggested it would help their karma immensely to take along a card-carrying Sanyassin. They bit.

They brought me here: right up to the top of Snakehead Point. After a few days of much meditation and extra-sensory masturbation, the psychics were reasonably convinced they had found the pyramid. I, on the other hand, was reasonably convinced I had found the world's premier place to grow pot; pot I could sell at a premium on account of it being *pyramid pot*. Naturally, I kept my findings to myself, then returned here on the last day of March of this year."

Bud returned again after having retrieved the stick I had tossed for him. "Let's go, Buddy," The Marijuana Grower muttered as he stood to leave. He then quickly snatched the stick away from Bud and, prudently, tossed it all the way across the river—the only way he'd get Bud to cross. Bud was already half way there by the time the stick landed.

"Well, probably see you around," The Marijuana Grower said as he began towards the river's edge.

"It's likely."

"Cheerie-o." he said finally, then dove back into the chilly water, then drifted with the current, then grabbed hold of the yellow nylon rope, then began to ferry himself, hand-over-hand, across Mercury Pool Crossing.

JOURNAL ENTRY; 8 JUNE 1984:

Obese—that's how big the day was. Long before the sun popped out of the toaster I was already scampering up the ridge trail leading from the canyon, hacking away at the overgrown brush with a machete. The reason: up on the ridge I still had ten tipi poles and its four sections of canvas yet to drag back down. Such a haul might normally translate into four or five arduous trips, but my conquering the 2,200 foot ridge in record time had my veins pumping with dangerous levels of machismo and my better judgment switched to "off". So, I sashed together six poles and began wrestling them back into the canyon.

A switchback or two below the Halfway Cedar I happened upon The California Goldminer, returning to the American River after a week-long sabbatical up in Amador County. Now, the mere fact I caught up with him—while dragging tipi poles, no less—should suggest something about his hiking pace. We're talkin', *slow*. So slow, in fact, that, to my knowledge, no one or no thing has taken longer to hike either in or out of the canyon than he. Potato bugs included. Whereas your average, healthy human can make the trek in two to four hours it often takes The California Goldminer that many *days*. The reason for this has deep psychological roots; he hates the hike. As a result he has to be shit-faced drunk before he can even coax himself into the endeavor. And for its completion to come to fruition he must maintain a port-pickled stupor throughout the journey's duration, necessitating many mid-trip refuelings. For this reason whenever anyone hiking this trail stumbles upon a tattered heap of smelly hair and denim, nestled near the vestiges of a small campfire and hugging a teddy bear-shaped rock, thumb in mouth, snoring like a chainsaw, and head resting on a jacket draped over a gallon jug of cheap wine, that anyone can be reasonably certain he has stumbled upon The California Goldminer in the middle of his work-day commute. Hence, when I stumbled upon just such a tattered heap this morning, sprawled face-down in the dust and pine needles, I too was reasonably certain of its identity.

"California, how goes it?" I asked.

The tattered heap hiccuped, implying that all was going according to plan.

"I heard gold dropped to $327 an ounce today."

The tattered heap hiccuped again, implying this time that, Yes, that may be so, but the price is certain to go up again so long as third-world nations continue to default on U.S. loans, congress continues to spend more than it receives through tax revenues, and our trade imbalance remains negative.

If there's such a thing as being born under a lucky star, then there must be such a thing as being born under an *un*lucky star, The California Goldminer's being just such a case. If not, then perhaps his rotten draw can be blamed on numerical superstition; id est, the fact that he was born the last of thirteen children. To hear Slim tell it: *Cal was born into a hillbilly family so dirt poor the only clue all them kids had that Christmas had come was the steamy pot of possum stewin' on the woodstove.* And though it's difficult to imagine that anyone could sink below such an abject start on life, The California Goldminer must be credited for accomplishing just that.

With a few coughs and groans he fought his way back to that all too rare state—*consciousness*. Cracking open an eye to barely the width of a

ROBERT P. JOHNSON

squint, he allowed a few rays of sunlight to seep into the swamp of his slumber. Noticing that he had "come to", I tried again to communicate:

"Good morning, California."

His lips began to twitch, as if speech was some old jalopy that needed bump-starting. "Morning?" he mumbled at last.

"Well, here in the Pacific Standard Time Zone anyway."

"Morning," he repeated, as if the word were vaguely familiar.

"That's right," I averred, trying to be patient in spite of the heavy load of tipi poles tugging at my arms. "Hey, I'm trying to get these tipi poles into the canyon before summer's out. So if you'll kindly roll either to one side of the trail or the other I might be able to squeeze on by."

"Morning," he said one last time, as he turned himself, ugly side up, and contracted his body to a fair imitation of a sitting position.

Surmising that The California Goldminer wasn't going to move off the trail for me until his blood alcohol count dropped below 60 proof, I grabbed the bundle of tipi poles at its balance point and hoisted them to my waist. "Don't mind me," I said, as I began to tip-toe gingerly over him.

"Okay," he replied, meaning every word. Then, "Hey, that's a darn good idea!"

"What is?"

"Dragging those poles down the trail."

"Yeah? Why's that?"

"They'll make a hell of a racket!"

"Yeah, so?"

"Sure to scare off every rattler in the county!"

"But snakes can't hear."

"They don't know that."

I pondered The California Goldminer's ratiocination for a bit, until it ran me into a cul-de-sac. "Ain't that the truth," I said finally, patronizingly, as I continued with my hoisted load. Then, safely beyond him, I set down one end of the bundle and resumed my dragging them down the trail. "See ya, California."

"Hey, wait up!" he shouted.

"For what?"

"Fur me. I'm comin' whiff ya!"

With that declaration, The California Goldminer tried earnestly, three times, to climb to his feet. Failing with each, another option came to him: "Hey, join me for breakfast. Hell, look at all the stuff I got crammed in my pack here—seventy-two dollars' worth, a whole month of food stamps. I can't eat it all myself!"

"So feed it to a bear. I'm a busy man."

"Then promise you'll come on down to The Outlaw Camp for dinner sometime!" he demanded, referring to his cubical cabin fashioned from black plastic stretched tightly over a framework of fairly straight tree limbs, and tucked up a ravine a few miles downstream from my camp.

"Alright, I'll be sure to R.S.V.P.," I shouted, as I entered the switch-back below.

Three silent moments followed before he decided he could not bear the loneliness. "Hey, hey—hold on. I'm comin' with you!" he shouted.

"I ain't waitin'. You'll just have to catch up."

"Ah, c'mon—just give me a sec' to sling on this mothersuckin' pack."

Without slowing I glanced back up the trail at The California Goldminer. He had hoisted his hopelessly overstuffed pack to one shoulder and, in a futile struggle for balance, was spinning crude pirou-ettes beneath its awesome mass.

"C'mon, California. I ain't here to watch a ballet!"

Being, as there were, far more laws of physics working *against* rather than *for* him, he fell. Pity forced me to stop and wait. By the time he stood again and finally caught up with me, he was sporting and ear-to-ear smile. He was happy; happy to be back in the canyon, happy to be drunk, happy to be a goldminer, happy to be alive. With me in the lead, *scarin' off all the rattlers,* we moseyed on down the trail.

"Hey, hey, just look at all these trees! Ain't they somethin'? Ain't they pretty? Ain't they why you're here?"

"In a way —" I began to say, with every intention of saying more, perhaps even something profound, had not The California Goldminer cut me off. The problem lay in his unique way of conversing: *he* does all the talking.

He paused to take in the grandeur the view proffered. "Yep, these trees is why I'm here—these trees and these mountains. They're why I ain't no flatlander anymore. Know that? Yessiree, this here's my crib.

Hey, hey, ain't those ridges somethin'?—the way they're stacked up, one behind the other, like waves on an ocean. How many miles we tawkin' here—a hundred square? Hell, if that ain't a big enough crib for this ol' baby then I just don't know what to tell myself!"

After he had absorbed all the splendor from the view he could hold, he shook his bowed head and sighed, his a joy too personal to convey. He then pulled a brown paper bag (hiding a liter bottle of something) from under his belt, unscrewed its metal cap, then took a deep swig from it. He sighed contentedly then offered it to me: "Care for a sip of vino?"

"Ah, no thanks, California."

"Good, 'cause I won't have known what ta tell ya!" he guffawed, removing the empty bottle of Maddog 40/40 from the bag and showing it to me. Always the optimist, he inverted the bottle high above his begging uvula in an attempt to suck one last drop of God from its rafters. Succeeding, he licked his sated lips then tossed the bottle into the manzanita bushes. We moseyed further.

"Hey, hey, wanna know somethin'? I've kept drunk all this month!" he announced sincerely proud, as if the feat was a credit to his self-sufficiency.

"That's great, California."

"Yeah, I know."

After some switchbacks more we came to a split in the trail; where I turn upstream and he turns left.

"So, you be sure to stop by for lunch one of these days. Hell, $72's worth of food—we'll be a couple of fat ol' miners 'fore summer's out!"

"Alright, we'll do lunch."

"You bet'cha," he said.

As I plowed into my last mile, I glanced back up the trail. There, at the shady fork where I had left him, The California Goldminer had already shed his pack and uncorked another bottle of something. And there, I would wager dimes to donuts, would he settle for the remaining nine hours of day and the night as well—there on his safe though noticeably tumbling Earth.

*

In spite of it being my most difficult haul yet, I made it into camp before noon. After a jumbo pancake and egg breakfast, I wandered down to the river, dove in, and began swimming upstream. I'd estimate the river's flow to be around 900 cubic feet per second, and the temperature still chilly 54º F-ish. At Mercury Pool, the third pool up from my camp, I swam out to a large, flat rock in the center of the river. And there, in the sun, napped for the better part of the afternoon. The days are just packed.

*

Some six yards from where I envision the tipi to stand, a spring pours from out of a shady bank. A goldminer of years past—very possibly Joe Steiner himself—tapped a rusty, six-inch diameter pipe horizontally into the bank, thereby allowing himself civilized access to the spring's cool clear water. The pipe spills the water into a foot-deep, three-foot diameter pool, rife with ladybugs, tadpoles and water beetles. From the pool begins one of the shortest creeks on the planet, meandering no more than twenty yards before it spills off the edge of the camp's terrace and flows into the river.

By dusk I had cleared a curvy (because it borders the creek) six by forty foot patch of rush and grass for my garden. *In the weeds I found a garden*, though not quite the work of art as the *David* which Michaelangelo had managed to "find" in that massive hunk of marble.

JOURNAL ENTRY; 10 JUNE 1984:

Since early yesterday it's been raining hard enough to prevent my hiking back up top and retrieving those last four tipi poles. The rain is delaying the setting up of my tipi. The rain is hampering everything I want to do, which includes moving out of this piece-o-shit, black plastic tarp, under which I am currently hunkered.

I'm sorry. I shouldn't be calling this "shelter" a piece-o-shit. No matter how temporary the situation, one should resist biting the hand that feeds you. And the tarp: it deserves better. For here it is, trying its darnest to protect me from Pluvius's slobber. On a Sunday, no less! That it happens to be failing utterly is probably not so much its fault as my

ROBERT P. JOHNSON

own: my fault that I chose to give up those four sturdy walls and water-proof roof, built to code, for this unruly wilderness endeavor; my fault that I don't enjoy being cold and wet and miserable. Indeed, whatever shortcomings I perceive in this piece-o-shit shelter's character may well be my own. Isn't that how misdirected anger works? And isn't this real-ization one of the first essential steps towards a comprehensive grasp of the Truth? I sure hope so, 'cause I'd hate to find out all this suffering was for naught.

*

Some hours have passed since the above entry, but nothing has really changed. Nothing *physical,* that is. For I am still hunkered here beneath this glorious tarp while the life-bringing rains still sprinkle Providentially down from Heaven. *Emotionally,* however, I am trying to adopt a more optimistic attitude… there, it's working… I feel wonderfully miserable. After all, things *could* be worse... I am fairly certain of that.

I've only re-opened you, dear journal, because I think I've stumbled upon yet another verity of life; this one being, what I shall call, *the innate human need to work.* For what else could explain this anxious, irrepress-ible urge of mine? Why else am I eyeing my fledgling garden like a cat eyes a mouse—hand shovel in one hand, a dozen packets of vegetable seeds in the other—salivating almost while I patiently wait for this frickin', *blessed* rain to let up so I can pounce?—so I can work!

So far today, between cloud bursts, I've planted rows of: radishes, carrots, and green onions. Still to come: spinach, corn, beets, peas, bush and pole beans, broccoli, tomatoes, chard, acorn and crookneck squash, pumpkins, ornamental gourds, and sunflowers. I'm well aware that it's an ambitious assortment for such a tiny garden. Hence, I'll probably have to expand the acreage once the storm breaks, if not so much for the garden's needs as for my own—to work.

JOURNAL ENTRY; 11 JUNE 1984:

Grasshoppers really don't emerge until the sun has had ample time to dry the dew from the meadow. This, my studies have found, requires approximately forty-five minutes of direct morning sun. This gave me forty-five minutes to kill. To do so I heaped a small pile of pine cones and sticks onto last night's campfire's embers, blew on the subsequent smolder until it burst into a small flame, replaced the cooking grill atop the ring of stones, then brewed a small pot of coffee. That done, I climbed back into my sleepingbag and, reclining against the sofa-log beside the fire, sipped from the mug until the sun had purged the morning of its chill. Life's a bitch.

The respite gave me time to ponder the nightmare I had last night. Like 99% of all my nightmares, this one starred a rattlesnake. I was alone inside a large grocery store, a Safeway store. It was the middle of day and all the frightened customers and clerks were staring in through the ad-painted windows from outside. They were frightened because of the vicious rattlesnake that had somehow wormed his way into the store and was slithering about the food racks—nipping at ankles pushing shopping carts and hissing at faces reaching high for nine-packs of toilet paper. *I* was frightened because I was armed with only a broom and wore only a pair of cut-off jeans. Apparently I had been summoned to the store for the express purpose of exorcising it of the beast. A modern-day St. Patrick. The broom my flute. The store's cool linoleum floor my Ireland. Over the course of the dream I caught only one glimpse of the rattler; he came at me across an aisle. I leapt atop an open freezer to narrowly escape him. He then craftily hid beneath the freezer and waited; there to hold me permanent captive, there to slowly freeze me to death while straddling an assortment of ice creams and ice milks and ice pops, my mission a failure.

And so last night's was not unlike many of these recurring rattlesnake nightmares; corny but terrifying. At two points in my life these dreams came with great frequency. One was the period of months in which I kept a rattlesnake as a caged pet in my apartment. This was while I was in college. Some friends and I were picnicking at a river above Santa Barbara. The snake (only about fourteen inches long then) swam right up to me as I stood in waist-deep water. I flicked it into my daypack with a stick and carried it, gingerly, home. Thereafter, I dreamt of it most every night, that it had escaped its cage and was wandering freely within my messy bedroom. The other occasion was the four

ROBERT P. JOHNSON

nights of a five-day solo hike I took three years ago in this very river canyon; hiking from Lake Tahoe, up and over the Sierran summit—the trickling headwaters of the American—all the way down to here. En route I happened upon an average of three rattlers a day. Insofar as most of the trek had no trail to follow, I often encountered the snakes in awkward places proffering difficult retreats. During these nights the dreams were particularly horrifying, probably because I knew morning would bring no relief. In a way it was like a soldier dreaming of war; awaking from his nightmares only to begin, again, to live them.

If a psychiatrist were to interpret these nightmares, I'm sure he or she would explain that these dreamed-up rattlesnakes symbolize my fear. That is, when the emotion of fear creeps into my dreaming mind I readily assign the form of a rattlesnake to represent it. In this same way a Jew might dream of Nazis, or a surfer might dream of sharks, fear being the common essence of these monsters of the id.

I recall from one of Carlos Castaneda's books an exercise wherein Don Juan instructs him to try to look at his own hand while dreaming. From this model I've decided the next time a rattlesnake slithers into my dreams, I will try my darnedest not to run screaming or leap atop a freezer. Rather, I'm going to try to muster the nerve to *piss* on it! What could happen? I could wet my sleepingbag. Alright then; I will try to calmly reach out and *pet* it—ever so affectionately. What could happen?

*

Grasshoppers are the world's finest trout bait and the meadow readily produced two of them. Within ten minutes the two grasshoppers produced two trout which I promptly cooked and ate for the world's finest breakfast. Towards noon I was feeling a bit lonely, so I decided to wander upstream to the Comfort Zone and pay Slim a visit. Maybe even run my new canyon alias by him, my *nom de plume*.

I call Slim's camp the *Comfort Zone* only because of a certain, small thermometer he has tacked up—along with a half dozen rattles from rattlesnakes—on a thick fir growing just outside his cabin. Slim had swiped the thermometer from a freight train he had hopped a few years back, or so the story goes—you know Slim. The place happened to be a railroad depot yard in Detroit. The train happened to be stacked with virgin automobiles. The month happened to be late November. And Slim happened to be cold enough to do most anything just to stay alive. And what he did was to break into one of the virgin autos—a Cadillac, of course—and ride on its backseat all the way to Truckee, California—heater blasting (he claims) and radio blaring. The trip had been pleasant; so pleasant, in fact, that Slim felt a wee bit blue when it was over. He searched the car's interior for a memento of the experience. The thermometer caught his eye.

Now, what I find so interesting about this thermometer, if not irksome (enough so, apparently, to warrant my naming the hobo gold-miner's camp after it), is that the manufacturer had the gall to paint a thin blue band between the gradations 68° F and 72°, and to declare this 4° margin the "Comfort Zone". *Why?*—that's all I want to know. Would not Cadillac owners, of all people, know if or not they were comfortable? And what happens at 73°? Do beads of perspiration break out on our noses and cause us to keel over of heat stroke and perish? And at 67°, what happens then? Do we become more frigid than we already are? And what is to come of humanity? Are we fated to be perpetually bounced between heaters and air conditioners, protected but essentially imprisoned within this minuscule comfort zone—a mere four degrees? Let us hope not. Let us pray! For just as certain as we've built this fragile, *comfortable*, electronic, oil-based, plastic palace economy up from the scorching, frosty, *un*comfortable world it will someday crumble to dust again, tossing us, unprepared, back to the rudimentary dog-eat-dog hell of our origin. When? Within our lifetime.

I apologize, dear journal, for the diatribe. I lost my cool. I got heated. At least you now know how Slim's camp got its name, despite the fact that I've yet to see the mercury in that thermometer come within 15° east or west of its thin blue margin—The Comfort Zone.

*

Like a small two-street town, our canyon has just two main trails: the *ridge trail*, the four-mile path which climbs 2,200 feet and out of the canyon; and the *river trail*, which roughly follows the meandering

ROBERT P. JOHNSON

course of the American for six or so miles before devolving into deer paths at either end. Like an upside-down 'T' the ridge trail terminates into the river trail's mid-point. My camp happens to be located smack-dab in the middle of this intersection, granting me both the advantage and disadvantage of seeing everyone who tumbles in or out of the canyon.

An easy twenty minute stroll up the river trail from my camp brought me to the intentionally camouflaged spur trail leading down into the Comfort Zone's wooded gulch. From where I stood I could just make out Slim's boxy, black plastic hovel—looking like one of those old 110 Brownie Instamatic cameras—through the firs, oaks, bay trees. You really had to know what you were looking for to see it. It is at this point that Slim likes his visitors to announce their presence, preferably by a gunshot. I gave an Injun whoop.

Soon a muffled retort arose from the gulch, "Who goes thar?"

I decided it was time to get him use to my new canyon name. "Rattlesnake!" I shouted.

"Rattlesnake?" he shouted back.

"That's right."

For a second there was utter quiet throughout the gulch. Then, like a kernel of popcorn from a hot skillet, Slim kicked open his cabin's door and popped from it. Soon he had mustered a full-steam, uphill charge from the gulch and straight towards me—his .22 rifle in hand, his .38 pistol in hip holster, hate in his eyes, fiery purpose snorting through flared nostrils. As the yards between us shrank I tried to recall what I might have said or done over the past two weeks to upset him so. I tossed a bucket into my memory's well but it came up dry.

"Well, where is it?" he asked, gasping from the sprint.

"Where's what, Slim?"

"*Where's what*—the rattlesnake, dummy!"

"Oh..." I began, feeling kind of bad for making Slim run all that way for nothing, and kind of stupid for not having predicted this misunder-standing, "... er, it slithered off in that direction," I lied, pointing to an impenetrable thicket of manzanita.

"Well, sure as hell ain't gonna chase it inta there. Damn it anyway. Frickin' things give me the heebie jeebies."

"Me too."

"Goldminers just like only one kind of rattlesnake—the kind that ain't rattlin' no more!"

JOURNAL ENTRY; 13 JUNE 1984:

While trout fishing these past few days, I've crossed paths with The Marijuana Grower time and again, at either his mining digs on the south bank of Mercury Pool or a new, more promising spot he's testing on a sandbar down river.

"You seem to be putting a lot more into goldmining than into growing your pot," I told him a couple days ago.

"An astute observation, Rattlesnake," he told me back. "And my crops are sucking the proverbial *big one* from the neglect."

"So, why're you doing it?"

He shrugged, "A couple of reasons, I reckon. For one, Bud and I are shit outta bucks and teetering on the precipice of starvation. For another," he paused to find the words, "I don't know. Goldmining just feels... honest."

"Thoreau claimed the Irish went about life with a *moral boghoe*."

He paused to ponder. "I fail to see the correlation."

Over the course of our conversations he and I have excavated many parallels between our lives. Already knowing we shared the same first name, *Robert*, we've now come to learn we have the same middle name as well, *Paul*. Other coincidences include: We both are the fourth child of Catholic families; both with two older brothers and one older sister. Seems too these brothers all share the same first names, with our eldest brothers even sharing the same birthday. Furthermore, both of us drive old Plymouths, both are avid chess players, both our mothers were eaten away by cancer, and both of us like to fancy ourselves as would-be writers—*would-be* if we had any kind of perseverance. Though this list goes on and on, the most startling similarity between us is not so much physical but, rather, a matter of character. That is to say, were there such a thing as a mirror which reflected only one's soul, then, I would swear, when looking at him, that I was looking at my own image—at my own philosophies, values, and phobias. Topping this curious list of similarities is the most curious fact of all; that of all the places in the world, both he and I should be drawn to this same remote canyon, on the very same summer, *and* for the same, very unlikely reason—the legend of the pyramid.

"What do you make of all these coincidences, Bob?"

"I don't know, Bob. Could be they're not so coincidental after all."

"Meaning we're *supposed* to be here?"

"We're talkin' the age-old conundrum: predeterminism vs. free will."

"You said it; I didn't."

"*Why?*—is the next question that comes to mind."

"Why are we both supposed to be here?" we pondered, "Probably has something to do with this pyramid legend," we surmised, "it seems to be our common link to this snakepit."

"But neither of us believe in it."

"Beliefs are malleable. Besides, it's not altogether impossible. After all, the Mayan pyramids down in Mexico aren't so far away, especially relative to the distance separating them from the pyramids in Egypt."

"So, do you think it's our *raison d'être*, our common destiny, to discover this enigmatic edifice?"

"You said it; I didn't."

*

Yesterday was the full moon and, being so, The Marijuana Grower and I decided we should spend the entire day searching for the pyramid. It seemed silly, but we did it anyway. Our expectations, though completely insane, were modest: first, excavate the pyramid's entrance (using his handle-less shovel and loose-headed pick); second, enter it's main chamber (he had a vague recollection of the Cheops pyramid's floor plan from a book he read as a child); and, third, loot it.

*

The crude trail, as blazed by The Marijuana Grower, winding to the top of Snakehead Point begins at the Mercury Pool Crossing. As planned, we rendezvoused there at daybreak. As expected, we were each a couple hours late.

"Didn't keep you waiting, did I?"

"Nope, just got here myself."

Squinting into the brilliant silver dawn flooding down from the canyon's southern ridge, we pushed aside boughs of fir and cedar and plowed headlong into our ascent. As we climbed we tried to prepare ourselves for the ordeal which lay ahead:

"*Tons* of gold?"

"Probably. And silver and sapphires and rubies, ad nauseam—your common trash treasures."

"Might make good fishing lures. How are we going to carry all of it?"

"Might have to make a few trips."

We reached The Marijuana Grower's camp atop Snakehead's truncated summit around nine in the morning. There we scrounged up the loose-headed pick and the handle-less shovel, managing to whittle a fair enough handle for the latter and wrap a fair enough amount of baling wire around the former to make both safe and efficient. We then set out from the camp to scratch and pick at the Earth's crust for the remainder of the morning and some of the afternoon, hoping to strike upon something aeons old and sculpted of stone. We were six feet into our fourth test hole when The Marijuana Grower recalled an apropos bit of gossip:

"Last week, when I went to town to cash in my gold, I decided I'd try a different assay office, seeing how the one I usually go to only pays 77% spot (77% of the current price of pure gold). A nice, old lady runs the place. When she noticed the unusual purity of my gold she asked me where I had mined it. When I told her she went kind of pale in the face with eyes about as wide as typewriter ribbon spools. Then, with trembling voice, she asked, "Near the pyramid?" After I confirmed her suspicion she told me of a miner who had come into her office a few years back, also "pale as a ghost".

"Why was he pale?" I asked.

"I'll tell it as she told me: 'With the fall storms brewing and the river cold and muddy and on the rise, this miner fellow decided to migrate from his sandbar and climb a ways up the hillside. He was looking for a rich enough spot to justify his staying in the canyon through the

ROBERT P. JOHNSON

winter. With his crevice pick and a goldpan he began taking test pans from creeks and abandoned digs here and there, scooping up mud and panning it down to check for *color* (specks of gold). He followed one such creek up to the entrance of a mine tunneling horizontally into the hillside, not an uncommon thing in these parts. He took a test pan from the gravel spilling out of the mine's mouth and, after panning it down, came up with about twenty specks of color (about the minimum amount of gold that should show in a test pan if mining there is going to be worth a damn, according to The California Goldminer). This was a good enough showing to tempt the miner a few steps into the tunnel to see what might turn up there. Lo and behold—twenty-two specks. He decided to plunge a bit further in... twenty-five. Further... thirty. Further still... *thirty-five!'* The assay lady reckons the miner was probably some forty yards into the tunnel by this time. Then... " The Marijuana Grower took a dramatic pause.

"Then what?"

"Then something very strange happened to the miner. It was great, Rattlesnake, you should've seen the assay lady's face as she was telling this part. Talk about pale!"

"You're looking a little blanched yourself," I told him.

"Yeah? Well, it stands to reason; 'cause this miner fellow—now all hot and bothered 'cause his test pans are showing thirty-five specks of color—all of a sudden runs into a barrier!"

"A barrier?—like a wall or something?"

"Yeah, 'cept it's an *invisible* wall!"

"*Invisible*—meaning glass?"

"No. Meaning something vastly high-tech!"

"Meaning *plexi*glass?"

"No. Meaning something right out of *Star Trek!*"

"A force field?" I asked, incredulously.

"Exactly. Apparently, whatever it was, he could shine his flashlight beam through it just fine. But when he tried to push himself through it he met something that felt like magnetic resistance!"

"He should have checked his dental fillings at the door."

"You think I'm bullshitting, don't you?"

"No, I *know* you're bullshitting me."

"I swear to God, Rattlesnake, I didn't make this up."

"Then the assay lady did."

"No way, this lady is as pure as can be. Turns out she's a devout Pentecostal. Why, afterwards we had a great chat about religion. She even tried to save me. And though my gold weighed in at just under six dollar's worth, she gave me a ten anyway, then paper clipped some Pentecostal pamphlets to it."

"Then the miner fellow made it up."

"Snake, you just don't want to believe this pyramid exists, do you?"

I pondered his hypothesis as he went on:

"I really don't give a shit what you think; I think I believe it. And know what else? I think the tunnel that miner stumbled into is the entrance to our pyramid!"

Weighing the "evidence" of the miner fellow's story, we decided to move our exploratory digs from Snakehead Point's truncated summit and, rather than digging at all, begin to search its heavily foliaged slopes for a mine opening—hopefully the very one the miner fellow had stumbled into. But after five fruitless hours of this we decided to give it up. We had searched probably a hundred acres of steep hillsides; through thickets of ticks and potential rattlesnake lairs so adverse that it is more accurate to measure the task in terms of blood, sweat, and tears shed, rather than in acres and hours squandered. And though we scoured Snakehead's surface area fairly well, I cannot say, beyond reasonable doubt, that we scoured it so thoroughly that there *doesn't* exist such a tunnel leading into the hill's belly, or even a dozen such tunnels. But I *can* state, sans doubt, that if there is such a tunnel, The Marijuana Grower and I failed to find it.

"Know what I think?" The Marijuana Grower asked, as we sat, dispirited, on a rock ledge and gazed with sweat-stinging eyes towards the river's silent rapids far below.

"No... what?" I asked, too tired to stop from uttering the rote response.

"I think we should build one!"

"Build one what?"

"A pyramid, shithead"

I rolled my eyes.

ROBERT P. JOHNSON

"I'm serious, 'Snake. I don't mean a full-size pyramid, just an econo-model; just big enough for one person—*me*. And we'll put it right over there," he exclaimed, pointing to the center of Snakehead's football field-sized flat top, "—smack-dab center stage!"

We constructed the pyramid from hefty oak logs, some more than a foot in diameter. The log ends we joined with twenty-penny nails and baling wire, plenty of both. Its square base measured fourteen feet a side. It's altitude might have measured ten feet had it not been truncated to accommodate a three-foot-square platform. We even took care to align the structure to the true, not magnetic, points of the compass. And it was this last attention to detail which ate up most of the time, for each time we thought we had the pyramid accurately aligned the compass needle would suddenly show an err of $7°$ or so. This happened so often we became convinced we were the butts of some cosmic prank—the gods up there *chuckling*. I finally took The Marijuana Grower's battered, piece-o-shit compass from him and tossed it, forcing us to forego exactitude and settle for eyeball alignment. *Let's see, the sun sets in the west, right?... There—aligned.*

For dinner, Bud, The Marijuana Grower, and I scooped steamy rice past our grubby beards with our grubbier meat hooves. By then it was night. Out beyond the campfire's orange tongues the pyramid structure danced with the faint and flickering light, appearing all the more undecided as to which realm it belonged—reality's or imagination's.

"What should we name it?" The Marijuana Grower asked through a mouthful of rice.

"We should name it what it *is*—Eros's Pyramid."

The Marijuana Grower looked puzzled. "And who might Eros be?"

"The builder of the pyramid," I cryptically explained.

"But *we* built the frickin' thing."

"No, we only provided the labor—the slave labor," I said, finally.

The Marijuana Grower let the matter drop. Despite knowing each other for so short of a time we had become used to letting such things go unsettled, sometimes for days. We found the practice humorous in a very wry way.

Soon the full moon was creeping up behind the canopy of oaks which cover Snakehead's pate. Insofar as both The Marijuana Grower and I are somewhat open-minded to the mystical possibilities of pyramids and full moons and such, we agreed that one of us must sleep within our creation. For reasons I would learn later, I was chosen.

I unfurled my sleepingbag and aligned it, by the rising moon, so my head pointed east. During this time The Marijuana Grower had scurried off into the darkness towards his tent (perched some fifty yards off out on the knoll's rim). Though I had assumed he had turned in for the night, I soon saw his flashlight beam bouncing back towards me. And soon thereafter he was kneeling beside me within our oaken pyramid framework. Beaming sadistically he switched the flashlight off. Then, by the light of the full moon, he fanned a deck of cards out in front of me.

"Pick a card, any card," he said.

"I know this trick."

"Just do it, shithead."

I selected a card; one he couldn't possibly trace.

"Let me see it."

"Some trick," I said, turning the card over for him.

To my surprise the card wasn't an ordinary playing card—not an *ace* or *king* or *five* or even *joker*. Instead, it pictured the rather pathetic portrait of an aged and lonely peasant man dressed in a hooded cloak and holding a shepherd's crook.

"Hit me," I told The Marijuana Grower.

"These are tarot cards," he explained. "We're just taking a little peek into your future."

"But I don't want to take a peek into my future."

"Oh. Well, too late now. Let's see what it's gonna be," he said, snatching the card from my hand and holding it up for the moonlight to catch. "Ah, very prophetic—very prophetic, indeed!"

"Why, does it say something about me beating the living tar out of you?"

He ignored my threat, "You've chosen *The Hermit!*" And with no more explanation than that—if that even qualifies as an explanation—he stood, slipped the card back into the deck and, whistling merrily, followed his bouncing flashlight beam back to his tent.

ROBERT P. JOHNSON

For the next several hours I tossed and turned, unable to sleep, unable to think of anything but the Hermit card. Even counting sheep proved futile. For every third or fourth one to leap over the fence would be followed closely by the raggedy Hermit. *Was it possible? Was the tarot card accurately foretelling the solitude which lay ahead for me come autumn— once the river became too cold or too high for Slim, The California Goldminer, and the two brothers downstream to continue their mining efforts, and once The Marijuana Grower finally reaped his harvest? Or was my selection of The Hermit card purely a coincidence—one out of fifty or so? Or might any of the cards, if selected, have seemed appropriately prophetic?...* These are the questions which tossed darts into my insomnia as I lay there within the pyramid's shadowy embrace and watched the moon roll across the felt sky like an icy cueball.

As restless as the night may have seemed, I eventually fell asleep only to be roused an hour or so before dawn by scores of mosquitoes enjoying a quaint breakfast buffet on my face. Off in the distance I could hear the contented snores of The Marijuana Grower, the kind of snores that can only emanate from a mosquito-proof tent. Only then did I realize why *I* had been chosen to spend this first night in our pyramid.

Without waking The Marijuana Grower I dressed and broke camp. The full moon hung over the western horizon where the sun had half a day before, its light making the hike back down Snakehead Point a simple task. By the time I reached the Mercury Pool Crossing the sky was turning the pale shade of champagne, bubbling with the eminent dawn. I forded the icy, belly-deep river holding my pack overhead.

Moments ago I stumbled back here into my camp. The first thing I did was to rinse my swelling, mosquito-bitten face in the spring. Presently I'm building a small fire for a pot of coffee. The first direct sun ray of the dawn glints down the ridge. It warms my skin and drags my attention back up to the summit of Snakehead Point. I settle into my sofa-log. The fire's smoky start bursts finally into a small, smoke-less flame. The water boils. I remove the pot, add coffee grounds, and set it aside to brew. I then open you, dear journal, and spread you across my lap, and then return my attention to the sun taking to wing over Snakehead. How shall I put this, dear journal? What shall I scribble upon your pristine pages to capture what it is I'm feeling? How about: I have learned some strange things these past few days—coincidences, we call them—which are coaxing me to believe that, for reasons as yet unclear, I am meant to be here, that I am meant to spend this year in the wilderness.

But don't we all suspect this at some point in our search for meaning? Isn't there something in the way the universe grows fuzzy out around its edges, or the way time becomes equally vague as we gaze beyond this present moment towards either the past or the future, that makes our experience here in the world feel so *solipsistic*? Isn't it obvious to us by now that the only irrefutable verity is that there are no verities? Can't we all just lay down our Bibles and Korans and Bhagavad-Gitas and admit that the "Truth" is unknowable, and that life is, at best, an insolvable mystery?

JOURNAL ENTRY; 22 JUNE 1984:

Spring died today. Or, maybe, yesterday; I can't be sure.

My progress with the tipi's raising stands as such: all seventeen poles are now down in the canyon, lying here in camp; but all four sections of its canvas skin (the three small inner liners, and the one large outer cover) remain on top of Moody Ridge, stuffed in the Cranbrook's trunk. Insofar as today promised a blue-skied reprieve from the past few days of thunderstorms, it seemed a good time to begin wrestling the canvases down the ridge trail. Still, I promised myself I wouldn't over-do it; not as I had when hauling in the poles. I would limit myself to just one section of canvas per trip, a trip or two a week. No hurry, my piece-o-shit tarp can still muster fair resistance any weather the fledgling summer cares to throw at me. Perhaps by the Fourth of July the tipi will stand.

That was my plan; a good plan, as plans go. But just as fences are made to climb so too are plans made to unravel, as did mine when *The Bros* attacked. It happened at about three o'clock this afternoon. I had just slammed shut the Cranbrook's trunk and was in the midst of cinching my backpack's belt when they snuck up from behind.

ROBERT P. JOHNSON

"Hi, Bob. We're spending the weekend."

The Bros—short for *The Brothers*—are what you might call my "friends", for they are the litter with whom I was raised, the pack with whom I caroused and bumbled my way through the Oakland public school system. Together, we learned how to guzzle beer down and puke it right back up again. Together we learned to communicate in belches similar to the way charismatics speak in tongues. Together we learned how to light our farts, hang B.A.'s, and hide five or more in the trunk of a car when sneaking into a drive-in movie. And together we watched, with curious magnetism, as our coed's breasts sprouted then grew—from mere salmon eggs to fried eggs to sculpted stacks of Eggos to hanging eggplants. All of which brings us to this present point in time where, although scattered by colleges and careers about the west coast like chaff in the wind, we remain the closest of buddies, the miles between us bridged easily by the propinquity of our hearts.

But more than mere friends, The Bros are my peers; the set-screws of my values, the windcocks of my aspirations. This I must admit however much I fancy myself as a free-thinker; my independence of them is only geographical. Outwardly, I hate peer groups. I see them as harmful to humanity. I believe peer groups are the dinosaurs of our era; fated to buckle beneath the weight of evolution, destined to think wrong, vote wrong, and bring wrong upon others. And all because the individuals within peer groups don't really think at all. Rather, they merely court and patronize one another in such a way as to maintain their frail social contract. I suspect this is why philosophers and monks often seek solitude, for only when freed from society's tethers can a mind be individualized. For this reason successful philosophers are somewhat like cavemen toting big clubs, cavemen who set out bravely into the wilderness of their minds to slay such dinosaurs. I had hoped to do this—to slay dinosaurs—but my friends are forever interrupting my solitude. I had hoped to slay dinosaurs, like some sort of modern-day Alley Oop, but the beast is forever trampling my wilderness before I can even whittle a club. I had hoped to slay dinosaurs, but more and more I see myself as part of one; *my* dinosaur—The Bros.

"So, did you guys bring any beer?" I asked Vid, Karp, Blaze, and Mac—

the four Bros who showed up at my canyon's doorstep this visit.

"Of course we brought beer."

"Not too much, I hope."

"Of course too much. Why?"

"It's just that you'll need plenty of room in your packs for my tipi canvases."

The color drained from their faces.

"*Tipi canvases?* Hell, Bob, we figured you'd have all that crap packed down and set up for us by now."

"Welp, you figured wrong. Like the wise man said, There's no hope when you're a dope."

"But you've had two months!" they whined.

"Sure, I could've done it all by myself. But I knew you guys would want to share in this grand endeavor, so I waited. Think of it as an honor."

I opened the Cranbrook's trunk again and lifted from it the tipi's heaviest canvas. I then turned to Vid—who, no doubt, organized the raid—and, shoving the sixty-pound, folded bundle into his chest, said, "And think of this, Vid, as the *biggest* honor."

"*Ugh!*—what's this?" Vid grunted, weighing the canvas in his arms.

"It's the tipi's main canvas."

Vid shoved the canvas back into my chest muttering something to the effect of, "Kiss my ass, Bob. I'm already carrying all the food."

"So let Karp carry the food," I said, shoving the canvas back into Vid's chest.

But, again, he shoved it right back. "How 'bout just bequeathing this *honor* onto him?" Vid said, before turning away, leaving me no place to shove the canvas next *but* into Karp's chest. So I did.

Similarly, Karp weighed the heavy canvas in his arms, shook his head, and said, "It ain't my cross to bear." Then shoved it back to me.

"Karp, it's no cross; it's my *home*—my shelter 'gainst the rain, sleet, and bitter cold, without which I will surely wither and perish!" I said, pushing the canvas back at him.

"So, wither and perish. Look at my pack—it's stuffed!"

"But look at your arms—they're free!"

"Thaaz right, and thaaz just the way they're gonna stay!" Karp smirked, allowing the canvas to drop to the dust with an earth-shaking *thud!*

I lifted the canvas, brushed off the dust, scowled at my cruel ex-friend Karp, then carried it over to where Blaze was trying to find room in his pack for one more can of beer.

"You know, Blaze," I began quietly, "about my terminal disease and the large sum of money I have tucked away —"

"I wasn't aware of either," Blaze said, exhibiting surprisingly little concern.

"Yeah, well, I'd kind of like to keep it that way... until I get my will made out, that is."

"Your will, huh?"

"Yep. I'll be starting a rough draft of it tonight, just kind of taking notes—you know, to remind myself who my *real* friends were," I said, handing the tipi canvas to Blaze.

But before the weighty bundle could even leave my arms, Blaze was already shoving it back, saying—with, I suspect, feigned regret—"Well, then remember me as the one who *wouldn't* carry that."

"I must have failed to mention the *very* large sum of money —" I began, as I tried again to shove the canvas into Blaze's chest.

He, again, shoved it right back, shaking his head and stating with fair confidence, "No, I think you did."

Holding the canvas in my arms, I *tsk-tsked* Blaze with a solemn wag of my head, "Well, men probably have kicked themselves harder... but, then again, maybe not." I then carried the main canvas over to the open tailgate of Mac's truck, against which Mac was presently lacing his boots, then tying the laces with a double knot.

"Say, that's a good idea, Mac—tying a double knot. Would ya mind holding this a sec' while I double-knot my laces?" I asked, handing the canvas to him. He fell for the ruse, holding the canvas while I pretended to re-tie my shoes. I decided to lay on a thick coat of verbal insurance:

"Have you ever noticed, Mac, how it always seems to come down to just you and me? When all the other Bros have given up hope and tossed in the towel, it's always you and me who give it that extra erg, who go that extra mile. Like the first time we bought rubbers —"

"Bob —" Mac tried to interrupt.

"... Remember that?—ninth grade. None of the other Bros would even step foot in the drugstore."

"Bob —" he tried again.

"Yep, just you and me—trying to pronounce *prophylactics* while the druggist kept shouting, *Do you boys mean rubbers?*"

"Bob —"

"Just you and me, Mac—the chips down, the money on the table, when push came to shove—none of the other Bros. I think they looked up to us for that; you know—us out there on the fringe, taking all the risks, willing to dream that impossible dream. Just like that afternoon in the drugstore buying rubbers—you counting on me, me counting on you —"

"Bob, I ain't carrying this tipi canvas."

"You and me and the druggist shouting, *Rubbers? You boys want rubbers?*"

"Save your breath, Bob. I won't do it," Mac declared, trying to hand the canvas back to me.

"Then your aunt waltzes into the drugstore and you got all scared and ran out the back door and left me, all alone, red as a beet in front of your aunt and all those strangers, trying to pronounce *prophylactics,* and the druggist still screaming, *What'd'ya want? Rubbers? Spit it out, boy! You wanna buy rubbers?...*"

By this point Mac had clean and jerked the tipi canvas above him and was gently balancing it upon my head.

"... Yep, just me, Mac—just me in front of your aunt and the whole world!"

"We kinda looked up to you for that, Bob!"

"But you owe me, Mac!"

"Fine. I owe you," he said, turning coldly away and leaving me standing there by the tailgate, canvas atop my head—it spinning ever so slightly in the breeze.

Yes, and these were The Bros: my "friends." Who has heard a dinosaur whine and snivel so?

*

ROBERT P. JOHNSON

The final edge of daylight was just taking flight from the tips of the highest ridges when we stumbled into camp. We had conquered the trail in good time, somehow managing to find room enough in our already stuffed packs to haul down a case of beer, my manual type-writer, and all four sections of the tipi's canvas. I was pleased. And by the time those same ridgetops began to blush with the alpenglow, thirsts had been quenched, trout caught, dinner prepared, and the tipi erected. I was *very* pleased.

Presently it is about as nigh to night as dusk can dare. Our bladders have tired of beer and I see a tall bottle of Jack Daniel's is winding around to my side of the campfire again. And I see that it is far from full. Whiskey—how the west was won. The Bros are chattering away at high volume; Vid with Karp, Blaze with Mac. Me—the odd man out for the moment—with Jack. A wilderness honky tonk. Leaning back against my sofa-log I listen to them. Their conversation seems tied by a short tether to the topics of salaries and real estate—things they all have. The talk stirs mixed emotions within me; of envy and pity. Karp has caught his first two trout ever and is frying them in a skillet of corn oil. Vid caught something and is frying it as well. He claims it's a cutthroat trout but it's only about the size of a herpes virus.

"Yeah, it may *look* small," he tried to assure us, "but, let me tell ya, this little fucker put up one hell of a fight!"

"Sure it did, Vid."

The sparks rising from the fire carry my attention skyward. The song of the crickets replace the chatter of The Bros. Fleeting silhouettes of bats dart, hither and thither, overhead. I can feel, through the seat of my pants, the river's rumbling. I can taste, against my skin, the coolness of night. Like vines hanging in a jungle, all these sensual distractions are, and like a curious monkey, my mind swings from one to the next.

My wandering eye settles upon the tipi. Before a landscape of wan-ing daylight it stands; proud yet humble. Like a retired Indian chief, it seems to be content to be off by himself in a quiet corner of the saloon—leaning warily against the bar, sipping patiently at his sarsaparilla. And all that surrounds him seems to become him: the grassy terrace serves well as his moccasins, the kerosene lamp glowing through his canvas skin alights him from within like a soul, and the dusk-lit sky—of turquoise and crimson, skewered atop the spindly tips of his poles—his feathered headdress. And though he must hear our conversation, he chooses to ignore it. And though it will soon be just him and me—out here on the fringe, where push comes to shove—he chooses to ignore me as well. *Why?* Probably because he still sees me as part of the dinosaur; chattering away ambitiously about geosynchronous orbits and stock market trends in the very same, self-centered, short-sighted way the brave dinosaurs of his day chattered about counting coup and bison hunts. To him must I make amends. But for now he looks over my head; his hopeful gaze fixed on the eastern horizon, his lonely eye squinting beyond towards the saloon doors of time.

ROBERT P. JOHNSON

Moon When the Cherries are Ripe

Men make the truth serve the pursuit of appearances,
while appearances are given them for the pursuit of truth
—CLAUDE DE SAINT-MARTIN

So where's this "solitude"? I can tell you where it *isn't*—the wilderness. That's for sure. For if it's not Slim, stopping by for coffee on his way to or from goldmining, then it's The California Goldminer tumbling back into the canyon after a hearty binge, tiring my ear with bullshit until he sobers enough to recall whether his Outlaw Camp is upriver or down. And if it's not California then it's sure to be The Marijuana Grower and his wonder dog, Bud; the former kvetching about the latest low-hovering helicopter, neglecting his crop, the girl who left him, the body lice that won't, and the pot bust he feels is inevitable; the latter hyper-charged with stick-fetching energy. "Bud, git!" And if it's not any of these "locals" then it's likely to be some happy campers or kayakers or fishermen or fuzz-headed, weekend mystic in search of some lost pyramid—*Have I heard of it? Nope, sorry, can't say that I have....* Indeed, people seem to be stopping in at my tipi with such frequency that I sometimes feel like I'm manning the only open information desk at Chicago O'Hare Airport.

I don't know why this should bother me. I mean, it's company. And each visitor is usually good for a beer or Snickers bar or the dehydrated food they didn't have the stomach to stomach. I guess it bothers me because I'm no closer to accomplishing what I had set out to accomplish—my secret agenda. Nor am I any closer to completing the piece-o-shit novel; stuck over there in my "clackle-clacker" (Slim's name for my *very* piece-o-shit typewriter), like some house pet caught in the ringer of an antique washing machine. I guess it bothers me because I can only foresee failure arising from of this year in the weeds.

It is for this reason that I have the following announcement to make, dear journal: I quit. Yep, as of right now this wilderness experience, this "year of solitude" is officially terminated due to sudden and unexpected sanity. *Wham-bam thank you, ma'am*—I'm outta here!

Furthermore, I feel the word *solitude* should now be struck from every language. For there's no such thing anymore—not for lepers or criminals or even astronauts. And while we're at it, *Walden Pond* should be banned from our libraries. For it is to blame planting the seed for this wilderness endeavor in my too-easily-led brain. And Mr. Thoreau?

ROBERT P. JOHNSON

Why, he should be posthumously vilified, at least until he confesses that all those "solitary" Walden nights were actually spent eating lasagna and crashing on the couch over at Emerson's toasty-warm house.

And *life?*—yes, I now fully grasp the meaning of life: life is the condition wherein every plan we make unravels, every intention mistaken, and every vase we cherish breaks. And *truth?* Why, truth is easy too, as easy as the three-worded-mantra sandwiched between the shrug and the tobacco spit of any cowboy existentialist—*It don't matter.*

*

So good was I feeling about my decision to abort my wilderness sojourn that I hiked out this morning, packing along my first of many retreat loads. "Go to town, buy yourself a popsicle!" my inner voice told me.

On the ridge I stopped in on a friend, to tell her the good news. Mary is her name, and a small, primer pink and gray trailer is her home. She was working, in the buff, in her garden when I drove up. I reckon I surprised her, for a harmless toot from the Cranbrook's horn sent her scurrying for her trailer's door like a sinner for a Bible on Judgment Day. Much to her chagrin and embarrassment the door had somehow locked itself. Hence, Mary was forced to sit naked on her doorstep while I climbed through one of the trailer's windows and opened the door for her from the inside.

"Oh, hi, Mary," I said, opening her door, "C'mon in. Is that a new dress? You didn't happen to buy it at the emperor's garage sale, did you?"

Mary bore the humility admirably, kicked me out of the trailer, dressed, emerged with a pair of ice-cold Lucky Lager beers, then started the greeting anew:

"Good morning, Robert. What a surprise."

"Good morning, Mary."

The sky was a vast sea of blue salsa, with the sun simmering in the middle of it like a jalapeno pepper. We unfolded a couple chaise lounge chairs and set them beneath the shade of a behemoth fir.

A "chat" with Mary is like strapping into one of those carnival Tilt-O-Whirl rides. That is to say, her mind uses evolution to support theories on physics to support theories on religion to support theories on politics to support theories on National League expansion to support theories on creation... and so on. That is to say, her wit wanders wondrously.

In the midst of some profound subject, she handed me some sheets of her latest poetry. I read them, then asked:

"Now, is this good poetry or bad poetry?—I can never tell with poetry."

"Oh, a notch above great," Mary averred.

I nodded; fully trusting Mary's opinion on literary matters, if only because Ernest Hemingway once patted her mother's belly when she was pregnant with Mary. Reason enough.

"So, Robert, how's the year in the woods coming along?" Mary asked, out of the blue. The query took me aback.

"Er, great. In fact, I've finished it."

"Compressed twelve months' adventure into just twelve weeks? I'm confused."

"Think of it as parole for good behavior."

My statement shocked Mary. I dare say, it kicked her in the balls.

"You gave up?!"

"No, Mary, I *wised* up."

"And what about the book you were writing?"

"Suffice it to say, it ain't gonna happen."

If my decision to pull out of the canyon hadn't kicked Mary hard enough, my decision to give up writing the novel certainly did. The smile that rode so sweetly upon her lips just moments ago turned suddenly to a twisted frown. Veins, where no veins should be, began to throb across her brow. Her face began flipping through every shade of red like a fire captain through paint store samples. Steam spewed from her ears and flames from her nostrils. Her eyes glowed like the cores of nuclear reactors. And the Earth around us began to tremble. I held tightly to the chaise lounge's armrests, sensing that I was in for a scolding.

"NO-O-O-O!!!" she cried, she wailed, she boomed.

"But, but, but —"

She bolted upright in her seat, "NO-O-O-O!!!"

"But, but, but —"

"For heavens sake, NO, NO, NO, NO, NO...!" she reiterated, now driving home her point with several stiff-fingered jabs to my sternum— so stiff-fingered, in fact, that I felt she was close to jousting me over backwards in my chair. "NO, NO, NO!" she continued, "You *have* to finish your year in the wilderness! You *have* to finish your book! Completion is vital!"

"Geez, Mary, I don't see what the big deal is."

"That's obvious, for if you *did* you wouldn't be calling it quits!"

"I wouldn't?"

"Hell no, for two reasons; the first being the benefits it bestows upon society as a whole."

"Yeah, but —" I foolishly tried to interrupt, until Mary rolled over me:

"Our society is basically a cowering bunch of narrow-minded sissies, boiling with adventurous urges but lacking the courage to live them. Meanwhile, here—all around them—a universe, vast and boundless, is exploding into life; stars collapsing into themselves, nebulas growing at beyond the speed of light, a single cell evolving from slime, armies raping and pillaging, cultures and history, eternity, consciousness, infinity and God. All this, happening right this very second. But what are ninety-nine percent of us doing with the brief, one-in-a-trillion opportunity we call *life?* We're squandering it, that's what!"

"Yeah, but —"

"This is why when someone like you gets a wee bit brave and drags a tipi into the woods, or walks across the continent, or just stands out on the street corner handing out photocopies of doughnuts, it makes the rest of society a wee bit more free. It liberates us by prying, a wee bit wider, that narrow slit of acceptable behavior. This is why it's vital for you to complete your year in the woods!"

"Yeah, but —"

"Now I'm going to tell you why it's vital that you finish your book; i. e., the benefits it brings to *you* and to you alone."

"Yeah, but —"

"*Thought efficiency.* You see, presently your mind is an amorphous sea sloshing to and fro, thoughts and theories swirling in chaotic eddies as if caught in the wake of a passing steamer—an ocean of notions, notions of the absolute."

"Yeah, but —"

"But the process of writing forces you toss a lasso around all those notions; to rewrite and rethink them, to discard faulty premises and to weave a tapestry of the sensible ones thereby whipping your brain into an ever more efficient thinking machine. Whether or not the book is ever published is beside the point for, ultimately, not a single erg spent writing is ever wasted!"

"Yeah, but —"

"On the other hand, should you abort the book and your endeavor— *tsk-tsk!*" Mary paused to wag her finger at me.

"Then what, Mary?"

"Mush!"

"Mush?"

"Yes, gray matter mush: that's what will become of your mind. And all because you will forever look upon your decision to call it quits as a failure and, identifying with that failure, you will have no choice but to look upon yourself as a failure as well. Penultimately you'll blame the dreamer within you for the failure, since it was he who dragged you into the endeavor. Then ultimately, to protect yourself from future failures, you'll force yourself to stop dreaming altogether. Conformity. It will be at this point that your mind will become mush. And although the universe will still be exploding with awe-inspiring things all around you you will no longer possess the tool with which to ponder it. And so, like so many of us, you will have squandered your one-in-a-trillion opportunity."

"Yeah, but —"

"Yeah but what?"

I had to scratch my head... "I forget what I was going to say."

"See there—*mush!* It's happening already!" To then drive to heart her point, she renewed the attack on my sternum, punctuating each stiff-fingered joust with, "Completion is vital! Completion is vital! Completion is vital!..."

*

ROBERT P. JOHNSON

It is evening now and, needless to say, I am back at the tipi. Never even made it to town today. Never bought myself that congratulatory popsicle. Just kind of turned around right there at Mary's trailer and came back.

A few things have changed since this morning. For one; my sternum aches. For another, I now feel committed to see through this year in the wilderness. Completion is vital. And for still another; I now have a new clackle-clacker; "new" to me, that is, but old by any other standard. Lugging it into the canyon proved one of my greatest challenges to date, it's mass being equivalent to that of a '39 Packard's engine block. Mary gave it to me to replace the piece-o-shit I had been using. It looks ancient enough that I half-expected it to type out hieroglyphics. But, to my surprise, English spewed out instead—smooth as baby's pooh. In fact, these very words are spewing from it as we speak, culminating with the phase that seems to sum up everything that I am at this point: "notions of the absolute."

I pause to let the chill drain from my spine. I gaze out beyond the page... towards the river, slipping past. It takes a few minutes, but then it dawns on me—*Hey, I'm alone! Solitude at last!*

JOURNAL ENTRY; 4 JULY 1984:

The sandbars glow in the cool, somber light of the quarter moon. A bath of platinum. By harsh contrast, the river is a bottomless black—an endless, beginningless ribbon of ink cleaving the pale voids. As I sit out here beside my tipi, this midnight hour, I smile. *Why do I smile?* I smile because, today, whether you were aware of it or not, humanity took another bold step forward—a quantum hop, in fact. For on this day the most efficient method of fishing for river trout had its debut; *Amphibious Drift Fishing.*

*

Insofar as today was to be Independence Day, and insofar as all of us residing down here in Humbug Canyon are outstanding patriots, and insofar as this was, after all, the *American* River, we decided to hold a trout derby—*The First and Only North Fork of July Trout Derby.* The teams were chosen and the river divided; Slim and The California Goldminer would fish that section of the river between the tipi and the Pacific Ocean (i.e., *downstream*), The Marijuana Grower and I would fish that section of river between the tipi and the Pacific Crest (i.e., *upstream*). Thereafter, at sundown sharp, we were to lug our stringers of fish back here for the awards ceremonies and for what promised to be a grand fish-fry.

After Slim and The California Goldminer stumbled off into the darkness and towards their camps, "to get an early pounce on the derby", I revealed to The Marijuana Grower the secret technique that would win us the derby:

"Amphibious drift fishing!"

"Amphibious drift fishing?"

"When you fish with Rattlesnake, you fish with science."

*

Amphibious drift fishing is to angling what the assembly line is to the automobile industry—efficiency. It was designed specifically with wild, narrow-canyoned rivers in mind, to be fished solo or with, at most, one companion. Since I've been fortunate enough to have had access to such places, amphibious drift fishing has been evolving towards perfection within me, mellowing like a fine Bordeaux—I its humble and unsuspecting agent, its Henry Ford.

The logic behind amphibious drift fishing is based on the understanding that the first cast into any pool is the most likely to land a fish. Thereafter, with each subsequent cast, the probability of success diminishes proportionately. And, of course, should one fish be caught, the odds of pulling another from the same, terror-ridden pool drops geometrically. Hence, the prudent fisherman learns over time that the most efficient way to fish a river is to take only a few casts per pool and then move on to the next.

*

ROBERT P. JOHNSON

After resigning a third game of chess to me, The Marijuana Grower rose from my table in a somewhat less than communicative mood. I felt I should warn him anyway:

"As the name implies, amphibious drift fishing involves a bit of swimming. So resist the temptation to bring more than the bare essentials; hooks, an empty, water-tight salmon egg jar to carry live grasshoppers, tennies for comfort, cut-offs for modesty, and your fishing pole—nothing else."

He grunted as he glanced skyward to guesstimate the hour by the position of the moon—2 a.m.

"I forgot my flashlight," he hinted.

"Take my lantern."

"Thanks," he said, as he unhooked the kerosene lantern from its accustomed spot—a limb on the three-trunked cedar growing in the center of my camp.

"Nightie-night."

"Righty-right."

For the next three-quarters of an hour, I watched intently as he and the tiny lantern, flickering like a firefly, ascended Snakehead Point; *intently* in case he tripped and subsequently set the whole Sierra ablaze—wouldn't want to miss that. But he didn't.

Thereafter, I pushed past the tipi's door flap, stripped and settled into my cot. Staring up at the stars through the tipi's open smoke flaps, I fell asleep counting the fish I was surely going to catch, come the morning.

*

It was close to ten in the morning by the time The Marijuana Grower and I rendezvoused at the Mercury Pool Crossing in order to begin our half of the derby. Slim and The California Goldminer were, no doubt, well into the contest by then, which didn't bother me—it's a myth that trout bite better at dawn. Besides, only we possessed the secret weapon.

As The Marijuana Grower forded the crossing (by now just waist-deep) to join me on the north bank, I could see he hadn't heeded my advice to travel light. Quite to the contrary, with pockets bulging and backpack overflowing, he looked about as superfluously accessorized as a westbound dustbowl Oakie. Aside from being over-packed he was over-dressed as well: army boots, thick wool socks, baggy full-length jeans, a long-sleeved sweatshirt worn beneath a long-sleeved army shirt, his leather prospector's hat, and a red bandanna for flair.

"You know, it's been over a hundred degrees every day this week. Probably be over a hundred again today," I mentioned, as he and Bud sloshed up the sandbar to where I waited. Bud shook.

"Yeah, so?"

I shrugged, "Just making conversation."

We turned and began up the river trail.

For the next three hours we hiked, stopping not even once to fish or swim. We couldn't have even if we wanted, for the trail here rides four hundred feet above the river, along sheer rock cliffs precluding any access to the water. Though this trail was chiseled and blasted out of the solid serpentine between fifty and a hundred years ago, most of it remains in good shape. Some sections, however, have broken away, leaving just slim remnants of the trail. Such stretches can make one wary of even their closest friend—"You can go first," "No, I insist, after you!"—or scornful of a hyperactive hound with a large stick in its mouth—"Bud, git!"

At last we reached our goal—Euchre Bar, the confluence of the North and the North of the North forks of the American. From here we would begin fishing back downstream, but not before a much-deserved skinny dip.

"Shit!" The Marijuana Grower shouted, for no apparent reason, as he lay sunbathing over a large boulder.

"Why the testy invective, your dudeness?" I asked, as I tossed Bud's stick into the river for the umpteenth time.

"'Cause I'm famished! 'Cause I *need* a salami and cheese sandwich, right here and now, or I'll die!"

"Did you pack any food?"

"Hell no, you told me not to!"

"Yeah, but I told you not to pack a lot of things. I probably could have forgiven a few salami and cheese sandwiches."

"Actually, I'd settle for a big bowl of curdled water buffalo's milk —"

"Always *my* second choice."

ROBERT P. JOHNSON

"... and a mango smoothie! That's what we'd have after an orgy at the ashram in India. While the girls were still going at it, us guys would jog down to the marketplace where, for about three cents, we'd pig-out! *Shit*—what I wouldn't do for a mango smoothie right now!"

All this food talk was having its effect on my own salivary glands. In the clear water beneath my dangling feet I could see several trout: some grilled over mesquite, some sandwiched between sourdough and smothered in catsup, hell, some even sushied.

"Ah, but here's the irony," The Marijuana Grower continued, "you've heard me rant and rave about how great India was, but do you want to hear the sincere, absolute truth?"

"Bud does."

"The truth is that I was *miserable*. Not all the time, of course, but easily half the time. No, *exactly* half the time!"

"So why were you miserable at all?"

"Because that's just how life is; with only our own experiences to draw from, we must arbitrarily draw a line down the middle of them all and call those over there *happy* and those over there *sad*. It's just like living down here; people must think we reside in Heaven—fishing, gold-panning, reading, and swimming all day, playing chess all night—no worries, right? But the truth is, we still get depressed, right? And probably just as often as anyone else, which is exactly *half* of the time! Mark my words, sometime next decade you'll look back upon these long, boring days as if they were nothing short of bliss. You see, time does that."

"Time does what?"

"Time heals! Time mends together everything we assumed were opposites. *Love* and *hate*; they aren't separate emotions you know. Rather, they're the extreme conditions of the same thing—*lovehate*, one word. *Goodevil, warpeace, agonyecstasy, blissbummed;* all opposites blend into themselves with time."

"Speaking of time..." I said, suggestively reassembling my fishing pole.

Taking the hint, he climbed to his feet, "Alright, fuck you. Time to win us a trout derby."

*

The etiquette of amphibious drift fishing dictates that no one partner gets first crack at each new pool. Wouldn't be fair. Rather, each fisherman alternately lags behind, allowing the other ample time to fish the pool below. Afterwhich, the upstream partner may pass the downstream partner (exchanging a joke of tasteless nature in the process) and proceed to the next and untried pool. This is the type of courteous behavior with which humanity could live in peaceful co-existence indefinitely. *Do unto others… Take but one virgin…* But, alas, never yet has the lion lay with the lamb but in death.

*

We fished the lazy pools of Euchre Bar with fair enough luck. Progress through this stretch was easy since the canyon here is wide and banked, on one side or the other, with long sandbars. Yet further downriver, along at least three of the five miles we had ahead of us, the canyon narrows formidably. This is the stretch of river we call, *The Gash.*

Down there there are no sandbars to make the going easy. *Down there* the only mode of travel is to toss yourself into the wild river and allow it to swallow you down its angry gullet. But one does not just do this for the masochistic pleasure derived, but for something far more rewarding. For, as with clouds, so too does The Gash have a silver lining; here we're talkin' trout—trout as big as tugboats, trout as plentiful as umbrellas on the Italian Riviera, trout as wild as Bangkok hookers. Yet this trouty girth and plenitude is no accident, but due solely to the fact that, prior to today, there existed no plausible method for fishing such tight stretches. Indeed, a fly fisherman would only frustrate himself (further) by either beating his $500 rod to little pieces against the sheer rock walls, or by snagging his #4 humptulips hellions in a water ouzel's nest. And your basic bait fisherman, sans sandbar, would surely drown. Hence, there's really only one way to fish *down there*—amphibious drift fishing.

*

By the bottom of Euchre Bar I had violated etiquette by wandering several pools, perhaps a mile or more, downriver of The Marijuana

Grower. But this was as much his fault as my own. For though I admit to being an impatient fisherman, he is as every bit *over*-patient. Over-dressed, over-packed and now over-patient—as patient as a fossil! Indeed, his method seems less an attempt to appeal to the fish's appetite than to simply bore it into a deep sleep and hope it inhales the hook while snoring.

In the early pools, Bud had been running continuously back and forth between his master and me in an attempt to mend the gap between us. But now that the schism had widened so, the hound was growing noticeably distraught, not to mention, dog-tired. So, for Bud's sake, I rested on a sunny rock where the canyon pinches in on the river and the first pool of The Gash begins. Soon I was napping, dreaming of things that hardly matter. It was probably five o'clock before The Marijuana Grower caught up. I awoke to find him sitting cross-legged beside me, rolling a cigarette, his edible plant book open over a leg.

"How many fish?" he asked.

"Four. And you?"

"Five."

He licked the edge of the rolling paper and twisted it.

"It's getting kind of late. Think we'll make the awards ceremony?" he asked, passing the pouch of tobacco to me.

"Nope."

He lit his cigarette then passed me the match so I could light mine.

"The canyon seems to get pretty narrow down here. How do we hike it?" he asked, this being his first visit this far upriver.

"We can't."

"What'd'ya mean, can't?"

"From here on down we have to swim it."

"What about the trail we hiked up here on?"

I pointed skyward. There, etched across the face of the rock wall several hundred feet above us, the trail gleamed in the afternoon sun like a scratch on the window of a skyscraper. The Marijuana Grower squinted up to it for some time before acquiescing:

"Agreed, we swim it."

With our fishing poles clenched in our jaws to allow us use of our hands, we edged around a buttress of bedrock as, inches below us, the swift rapids tugged at our ankles. This feat brought us to the bubbly headwaters of the first pool of The Gash.

Here we paused to let The Marijuana Grower impale a grasshopper over the length of his #10 fish hook and lower it to its turbulent fate. The current ran with his line.

*

Most anglers will use 2 lb. test line when fishing for trout in streams and small rivers. I use 4 lb. test if only because that's what my father had around the basement. The only time I might use a heavier line would be in rivers, such as this one, known to contain fish larger than trout.

At least three other species of fish call this fork of the American *mi casa*. One is the Western Sucker, a horrendously ugly creature God created to use as an argument against His own existence. The sucker earns its name by virtue of its function in life—sucking algae from rocks. As boring as this task might sound there is no arguing it is lucrative, for any sucker worth its fins is certain to reach lengths in excess of twenty-four inches. Also lurking in these waters is the Sacramento Squawfish; another large, carp-like loser that can be eaten in a pinch, though it is not known by what. The only other non-trout I know to reside here is the bizarre Sculpin.

The first time I laid eyes on one of these spiny creatures, I was certain it was some pre-Pleistocene species that had somehow survived the great freeze. Regardless of its origins, in that the Sculpin never grows much larger than a Hostess Twinkie, I don't lose a whole lot of sleep worrying about one snapping my line. This, unfortunately, is not the case with the other aforementioned trash fish. For often have I cast a shiny-new roostertail into a bubbly pool, chock-full-o trout, only to have a behemoth Squawfish swallow it whole, or to have a sucker somehow manage to snag it on his hip, either event rendering me $1.29 the poorer by the loss of the lure. Another theory is that these trash fish *purposely* steal our lures; it being chic—*ala* self-mutilation—amongst their ilk to be seen with a spinner or two hanging from a lip. So, to deny them this honor, I'll often forego 4 lb. test line for 6 lb. test. But today, here in The Gash, I'm using 8 lb.

ROBERT P. JOHNSON

*

The second pool of The Gash was good for a thirteen inch brown trout.

"Time to move on," I told The Marijuana Grower as I reeled it in, "amphibious drift fishing, you know."

The Marijuana Grower squinted up to the towering cliffs again, hoping to find a detour around the next pool. Finding none, he sighed. It was going on six o'clock and considerably cooler now, especially down here in the shadow of the canyon. Both of us were chilled and wet and not cherishing the prospect of becoming more of either. He lowered his frown downriver, trying to see where the river would carry us next.

"So, what's it going to do to us around that bend—toss us off Victoria Falls or something?" he asked.

"What's it to ya?"

"Oh, just this silly preference I have for life over death."

"*Lifedeath*—one word."

"*Eat shit*—two words."

Against better judgment we jumped into the river and allowed its effervescence to sweep us away. Around the bend the river straightened into a long, languid pool—its bottom black and nowhere to be found. Here the current slowed until its downstream progress was imperceptible. In some parts of the pool the water even back-eddied upstream. Insofar as the serpentine walls here were too sheer to scale and the bottom far below the reach of our toes, a sandbar at the pool's far end offered the first and only rest. To this end I sidestroked, holding my pole above the water with the other hand.

Climbing out upon the sandbar, I turned to check on The Marijuana Grower's progress. I was concerned about him; the swim had been hard enough for me, dressed only in tennis shoes and cut-offs, but here he was—veritably dressed for winter, not to mention what all he was carrying in his rucksack. Searching upstream I now had a damn good reason to be concerned; he had disappeared—sunk apparently. All that evidenced his prior existence was a litter of flotsam: fish bobbers and tubes of sunscreen, a rusty canteen and some jars filled with moldy salmon eggs, plastic film containers filled with the black sand of test pans taken upstream, a peanut butter jar hopping with apprehensive grasshoppers, his pouch of tobacco and pack of rolling papers, the edible plant book and a natural history guide, and, in the center of it all, his leather prospector's hat. All this bobbed gently on the still, black pool as if mourning the fate of their owner, and somewhere beneath it all I imagined The Marijuana Grower to be. But where? Had he truly drowned? I couldn't be certain, as neither could Bud—judging by the worrisome circles he was swimming around his master's possessions.

I thought about diving in and trying to rescue The Marijuana Grower, but then frowned, recalling that my lifesaving certificate had expired some years back. Besides, there was fishing to do—a derby to win! *Honor. Glory.* And, most importantly, *survival of the fittest*: I owed my genes to our progeny.

I exchanged my soggy grasshopper for a fresh one, then stepped out onto a rock jutting into the next stretch of rapids. I released the catch on my reel. The grasshopper was taken by the galloping froth. Loops of line ran down through the eyelets of my pole and away. The pool looked promising.

About then I heard a terrible gasp, not unlike that of a spouting whale. Bud started barking excitedly. I turned my attention upriver to check the disturbance. To my surprise the sound had emanated from The Marijuana Grower who had just then surfaced and, fittingly, right beneath his hat. Yes, he surfaced but tarried there only long enough to suck in a quick bite of air, and before submerging again.

"What's his problem?" I asked Bud.

But Bud could only whine his response. Time and again, the hound poked his snout into the water in an attempt to see to where his master had sunk. I, on the other hand, returned my attention to the task at hand—my line, now forty yards into the next pool and entering what seemed to be a likely spot for a strike.

Soon again The Marijuana Grower surfaced, sucked in another lungful, and submerged. As he repeated this procedure over and over I began to discern a pattern, a method to his madness. He was obviously suffering from negative buoyancy and had devised this strategy to prolong his misery. Nevertheless, his progress towards the sandbar exhibited a slow but commendably steady persistence. As he began surfacing much closer I could make out the stringer of fish he clenched tightly in

Robert P. Johnson

his teeth—a half dozen trout, all cleaned and gutted and tangled in his beard.

I couldn't help but laugh. And each time he sunk again, or flailed at the surface with his arms, or sucked another hissing breath through his clenched teeth, or lunged for Bud (who wisely kept a safe radius away), or tried to shout, *It's not funny... cough, gasp... I'm drowning!* the harder still I laughed. After all, it was a beautiful sight; modern man confronting nature and losing miserably.

After what seemed like hours, The Marijuana Grower finally dragged himself onto the sandbar and promptly beached himself, head between his knees and heaving for oxygen.

"Just out of curiosity, Rattlesnake, did the thought of rescuing me ever cross your mind?" he asked, after he had caught enough of his breath.

"Sure."

"When might I have expected it?"

"When you communicated that your situation was indeed dire."

"And how might I have communicated that?"

"Well, jettisoning your fishing pole and crevice pick and whatever's in that rucksack would have been a good clue," I replied, beginning to reel in my line.

"Good point," he said, noticing his rucksack as if for the first time today. He pulled it off to take inventory of its contents: "I reckon I could have gotten by without some of this stuff. Like this collapsible shovel or goldpan or spyglass." He then waded back into the river to round up the floating debris, "Or this magnetic chessboard, or these Louis L'Amour books, or this or that or these..."

"I'll tell you again, amphibious drift fishing is a discriminating sport."

"I'll know better next time."

"There may be no next time, we've still got a couple miles of this to go." I felt a tug on my line, "Hey, I got one!"

After I reeled in what proved to be a dandy twelve inch rainbow and stuffed him into my creel, The Marijuana Grower and I exchanged a pained grimace then jumped back into the swift current.

For the next two miles we were continuously hopping in or out of pools—some swift, some slothful, some abysmal, some superficial, some sieving through a colander of busted bedrock, some slipping like fine-grade oil through alleys of serpentine so perfectly smooth and symmetrical they seem beyond even the expertise of the Army Corps of Engineers. Tiger lilies, ferns, columbine, mosses, *ad infinitum*, line the banks of The Gash; their roots stretching, like a rock climber's limbs, in all directions just to cling to the slightest hint of a crack; their nourishment derived from the mists of freefalling creeks and the sun which but blinks in these deep fissures.

We hopped into one of The Gash's final pools. Much to our glee, its bottom was just within reach thus permitting us the luxury of tiptoeing lightly over its bedrock while the current carried our bobbing heads along at the pace of a brisk jog.

"Lord, have pity!" The Marijuana Grower ejaculated with no physical provocation. "Lord, have pity on me; your loyal servant, to whom you cannot spare a penny, nor pocket to hold one, nor home but that plastic hovel, nor income but that eked from your piss-poor sandbars, nor promise of prosperity but that which grows from yonder hillside, nor wine but these sacred waters, nor song but that which chirps from your insects and fowl, nor mate but the palm of my hand.

"Lord, have pity on we who have no means nor choice but to trust your river to carry us where it will, our hands resisting not the wisdom of its course, our feet traipsing but lightly across its bedrock crust, our minds bobbing at the surface where fear yields to mystery."

I turned towards The Marijuana Grower. His head—big and hairy and beaming blissfully—bobbed along like a runaway beachball with no body attached. And Bud's too, which licked our faces and swam figure-eights around us. Three bobbing heads with the world slipping past was all we seemed to be.

"Well said, Bob."

"Thanks, Bob. May we have an *amen*, Bud?"

"Amen," said Bud.

*

By the time The Marijuana Grower, Bud and I made it back to the tipi, all that remained of the daylight was a cool blush in the western sky.

ROBERT P. JOHNSON

Around my campfire pit Slim and The California Goldminer had left clues of hours of waiting: a stack of firewood, a cold pot of coffee, an empty six pack of Buckhorn beer, and a few fish skeletons smoldering in the ashes of the dying fire.

"Reckon we missed the fish fry."

"Reckon so."

I exchanged my wet duds for dry ones, offering The Marijuana Grower a loaner set of dry clothes. He graciously declined the offer. I knew why—his crabs.

"Slim's probably got a fire going. Want to head up there?"

"Sure."

I grabbed my flashlight. Its beam dragged us the mile or more up the river trail to The Comfort Zone.

*

"Well, kiss my ass. If it ain't the amphibious fuckheads!" Slim cussed, pretending to be mad. We slid down the trail leading into The Comfort Zone's gulch and stumbled into the light of his campfire. "Did you two just now finish up fishin'?"

The Marijuana Grower straddled the fire in order to dry his clothes. "Shit, Slim, it was terrible. Rattlesnake dragged me clear to Utah and back then tried to drown me!"

Slim laughed as he poured us each a mug of his infamously thin, thrice-boiled "cowboy" coffee. He then pulled the pot from the grill so we could cook our fish. We rolled the trout in a mixture of flour, salt, and pepper, then lay them in a skillet of oil. Slim rolled everyone a cigarette. Minutes later we were eating trout after trout while more sizzled in the pan.

"So, who won the derby?" The Marijuana Grower asked.

"Welp, I caught four. California caught two and a healthy drunk," Slim answered. "How 'bout you fellas?"

"Seven to six: Rattlesnake took me in the back nine."

"Sounds like the First Annual North Fork of July Trout Derby done ended in a draw, all the way around," Slim opined.

"Reckon then we'll have to schedule a rematch," The Marijuana

Grower said as he wrestled with the skillet and spatula—trying to keep the fish from curling away from the heat. "Damn, these fish are too fresh!"

Slim chuckled, "As if our lives ain't hard enough!"

*

JOURNAL ADDENDUM; MIDNIGHT-ISH:

Although this Fourth of July is the 208th anniversary of our nation's independence, I like to think of it as being the 139th anniversary of the day Thoreau first pitched camp on the shores of Walden Pond. For his was a desperate lunge for a loftier independence—for a *true* independence.

The reasons as to why any of us move to the wilderness is, no doubt, personal and varied. Yet what we each find here is common to all; the uninsulated pains and unbuffered pleasures of life. Everything here is the same as it was in the days of Thoreau or Christ's or Peking Man. Nothing changes where nothing changes. What can be accomplished instantaneously in modern society with either a flip of a switch or a stomp on the gas pedal, out here must be gnawed at and grunted over for hours. And yet there must be reward in all this extra effort. For what else can explain why my neighbors pour buckets of gravel through their sluice boxes for eight hours a day for fourteen dollars of beans and beer? I don't know why. That is, I can *sense* the reason but I doubt if I could put it into words. Heaven and Earth: I suspect they too may be merely the extreme conditions of the same thought. *Heavenearth*—one word.

Am I drifting? Is my point vague and my route there nebulous? Probably… I don't know… I'm sorry. The river too meanders yet manages to find the ocean.

Amphibious—existing in two mediums.
Drift—going with the flow.
Fishing—for what?

It's kind of funny when I look back on it; just two days ago I was wondering if I could bear to stay another week out here in the wilderness. Whereas tonight—sitting out here against the tipi's canvas and staring up into the wide and inviting heavens—I'm wondering if I could ever bear to leave.

JOURNAL ENTRY; EXCUSES, EXCUSES:

Naturally, one would think that any self-imposed exile to the no man's lands of the wilderness would bring with it a certain emancipation from the strings and red tape of governmental bureaucracy. But not so. For even the wilderness is managed by the government these days, despite the fact that the two are, essentially, a contradiction of terms.

The management of my particular wilderness is the overlapping responsibility of the United States Forest Service, The Bureau of Land Management, and numerous private property owners. By the maps I've been sent it appears that most of this region falls under USFS jurisdiction as part of the Tahoe National Forest. Since camping within a national forest is limited to just two weeks I, in order to be legally able to stay for a whole year, had to find a site that was located on either BLM land or private property.

First I tried the feds.

To receive BLM approval for my endeavor it was necessary to convince them that I had come in search of gold, then to beg them to issue me a mineral claim. (In my case a *placer* claim, for rivers, rather than a *lode* claim.) After many months, letters, fees, triplicated documents, and faded Xeroxed maps with red circles on them, I was finally issued a claim.

The claim came with two stipulations, the aforementioned red tape. The first stipulation required me to extract at least $100 worth of mineral from the claim, or to make improvements to the land—building structures, cutting roads, felling trees, digging mine shafts, hosing away topsoil, etc.—to the tune of $100 per year. Should I fail to provide documented proof of such at the end of each fiscal year, my claim would lapse. It is nothing short of laughable that this $100 figure is the same today as it was back when the Mining Act of 1872 was first adopted; back when $100 meant something, back when $100 made grown men pant and drool.

The second stipulation of the Mining Act of 1872 is rather nebulous and, in a philosophical way, intriguing. For it mandates that the claimant (*moi*) satisfy what its legalese calls, "The Prudent Man's Rule." Below is a partial description of this rule, as sent by the BLM with my mineral claim forms:

> "... the test has been satisfied where minerals have been found and the evidence is such that a person of *ordinary prudence* would be justified in spending more money and doing more work with a reasonable prospect of success in developing a valuable mine...."

Now, what I find so intriguing about this Prudent Man's Rule is its allegorical implications. For although its text ostensibly concerns itself with only the tangible wealth of minerals, its *soul* hints of something transcendental of worldly treasure—of something above and beyond "the yellow metal that make white man crazy". To me this Prudent Man's Rule seems to pose the question, Is there anything to be gained by living a year in the wilderness? Beyond that, the Prudent Man's Rule goes so far as to demand *evidence:* "Is the *evidence* such that a person of ordinary prudence could be justified in spending more time and doing more work with a reasonable prospect of success?" *Evidence?*—what evidence? Where would I find evidence supporting philosophical success? Judging by the ex-cons, current-cons, drunks and crazies that people my wilderness, I doubt if the *evidence* is very strong that a year of solitude is a "prudent" at all. But then again, what about the great recluses of old: Thoreau, Mohammed, Buddha, Christ, etc.? Was not one of them *prudent?*

I don't really know. Only time can show and tell if there is anything truly prudent about this endeavor above and beyond learning how to cook beans, tap-dancing around buzzing rattlesnakes, and perfecting the art of trout fishing.

JOURNAL ENTRY; 17 JULY 1984:

Again today, for about the fourteenth in a row, it was quite warm; *quite*

ROBERT P. JOHNSON

warm being that point where pines burst into flames and boulders melt to molten, like fudgesicles on Mojave asphalt, at the mere mention of noon. And today was quite warm. Let's hope it doesn't get hot.

The Marijuana Grower stopped by the tipi late this afternoon after spending the day goldmining with Slim a couple miles downriver. He was depressed again because, for about the fourteenth day in a row, he's neglected to haul water for his pot plants. "It's just too fuckin' hot!" he lamented. As he then went on to describe about how most of his plants have either withered or died from thirst and famine, I couldn't help but notice that the austerities of his occupation seem to be taking the same toll on him. For in just the four months that I have known him his mass has been whittled from his 304 lbs. maximum, to his present 190. Except for the highways of white stretch marks mapping his former gutline he's looking pretty good.

Dusk. A dinner of fresh squash, beans, peas and spinach from the garden, lentils and rice, a pot of cowboy coffee of indeterminable acidity due to indeterminable insect and ash content, a best-o-five chess match, moths smash-dancing against the kerosene lamp's mantle, mantra chanting crickets, Bud dashing off into the night after each stick tossed off the terrace, the waning moon shouldering through the starry night like an Irish cop through an unreputable pool hall—*Go home, fellas. Tell yer mudda she wants ya!*... a typical night on the rio.

"It was a day not unlike today—quite warm," I mumbled, cryptically, as I shoved my queen's pawn forward two spaces to begin our final chess game of the night.

The Marijuana Grower looked up and waited patiently for me to elaborate. The crickets chirped. Bud whined beggingly as he trotted to and fro beneath the table, his stick-in-mouth beating against our knees.

"Do you mind telling me what you're mumblin' about, 'Snake?" he asked, shoving his king's bishop's pawn out two spaces.

"*Quid pro quo.*"

"*Quid pro quo?*"

"Yep. You told me how you had come to learn about the legend of the pyramid. Now it's only fair that I tell how I had."

"Oh...you're right. *Quid pro quo.*" He then settled back in his seat and clasped his hands behind his head to fully savor the recounting. "Fire away."

I began: "It was a day not unlike today—quite warm. At the time, I was minding my own business as well as a thirteen year old can; working hard on a popsicle and sitting all by my lonesome on the bench out in front of the general store in the tiny goldmining town up top. That's about when I heard their station wagon roll into town. Though it was still around a bend and a good half mile away, it's missing muffler pre-announced its arrival like cheap aftershave. In another couple minutes the beat-up Rambler pulled up in the middle of the deserted street twenty feet from my outstretched tennies, there to idle and backfire in a cloud of blue smoke as its two occupants—hippies both—tried to shout to me. But I couldn't hear a word they said. Championing the problem, the driver turned off the motor and shouted again,

"'Howdy!'

"True to native protocol, I said nothing.

"Now the passenger would try. Climbing out through his window—I take it his door didn't work—he shouted across the wagon's roof to me, 'Say there, big guy, we're archeologists from the University of Pennsylvania and we need some friendly local to give us directions. 'Mind helping us out?'

"'Why should I?'

"'Well, it's for the advancement of science.'

"Obviously this passenger fellow was as adept in psychology as he claimed to be in archeology—probably had a Ph.D. in manipulation of thirteen-year-olds—for in the course of two sentences he had rendered me putty in their hands.

"'Scientists?' I asked, awestruck—scientists being tantamount to baseball heroes to a fledgling teenager.

"'That's right. And we're trying to find the North Fork of the American River. In particular, a place called Snakehead Point. You wouldn't happened to know where that is, would ya? We could sure use us a guide.'

"At the time I didn't know the North Fork from Oxnard, but I sure as hell wasn't going to let that small matter hinder the march of science, 'Sure, I know it like the back of my hand!' I lied.

"'Great, could you point it out to us on this map.' the driver said, as he hopped from the Rambler and began unfurling a 7.5 minute topo-

ROBERT P. JOHNSON

graphical map across the car's dusty hood.

"Before I knew it, I was rubbing elbows with the hippie scientists, the three of us bent over the map intently following every move my index finger made across the map's intricate swirl of gradation lines. From my mouth poured an unnaturally sagacious voice. Whether it was clairvoyantly channeling knowledge from some mysterious place or merely bullshitting us all, even I didn't know: 'This here's where the North of the North Fork joins the North Fork... this here's Humbug Canyon... and this here's Snakehead Point!' I said, finalizing the aerial tour by tapping my finger on the spot.

"'Well, that's great. We sure appreciate your help!' the passenger said, as we stood up straight again and the driver began re-rolling the map.

"'¡De nada!' I added casually, but knowing they owed me, at least, an explanation. 'So, what interests you fellows about that part of the canyon.'

"Obviously, the hippie scientists weren't expecting this. They looked at one another as if asked to break some solemn vow. One shrugged. The other nodded. The passenger then elaborated: 'We have reason to believe there's a pyramid somewhere in that canyon.'

"'A *pyramid?*' I asked, incredulously.

"'That's right, a bona fide, aeons-old pyramid. Here, let me show you a textbook that mentions it,' the driver said, diving then back into the Rambler and rooting around for the text.

"As he searched, I used the opportunity to peek into the back of their wagon. There, amidst a heap of fast food trash, were all the tools one would expect of an archeological expedition: picks, shovels, cots, lanterns, even those mining hats with lights. And on the car's roof rack; more of the same. I even glanced at their license plate: *The Keystone State.* They seemed on the level. The driver emerged with the textbook, opened it to a dog-eared page then handed it to me, 'Here.'

"Do you remember what it said?" The Marijuana Grower asked.

"Almost verbatim!" I assured him, then recounted the words:

"'On the North Fork of the American
River near Snakehead Point stands a
pyramid built by Eros and his family.

To protect it against pillaging natives Eros is said to have cast a hex over the immediate area before leaving the canyon. As a result, Indians who come into the pyramid's presence become dizzy and disoriented.'"

The Marijuana Grower pondered the quote. *"Hmmm…*so that's why you wanted to name our little dinker wooden pyramid *Eros's* Pyramid, eh?"

"That's right," I said as I made my second move of the already fifteen minute-old chess game, sliding my queen's bishop's pawn forward two.

"Did the book say anything else about the pyramid?" The Marijuana Grower asked.

I shook my head, "The hippie scientists said it didn't."

"Hmmm… do you recall the book's author or title?"

"I don't. But, oddly enough, The California Goldminer does. It seems he ran into the archeologists too, shortly before they were run out of town."

"Run outta town?—for what?"

I shrugged, "For being hippies without any, as they called it, *resources*. At least that was buzz about town. Nobody ever saw them again. They probably took one trip into the canyon here, camped up on top of what's now your pot hill, scratched at it for a few days with their picks and shovels like we did, concluded the pyramid was no more than a legend, lost interest, then pulled out of the canyon and drove back to the University of Pennsylvania whereupon they promptly changed majors."

"Humph—probably to Poly Sci," The Marijuana Grower speculated. "So, was that the last you heard of the pyramid before moving down here?"

"Actually, no. About two years later the legend bit at me again. I was fifteen, and a friend and I were on a day hike down to here just to go swimming. While we were still near the top of the trail we came upon two boy scouts, the first of a troop hiking out of this canyon. Before we even had the chance to say *hello* to these guys, one of them starts shouting all-excitedly, 'There's a pyramid down there! There's a pyramid down in this canyon!'"

The Marijuana Grower looked up from the chess board. "No shit? He really said that?"

"I swear to God. And at least three times. Then the second scout starts boasting about how the whole troop of ten or twelve of them had marched right across the pyramid and how it had four sides and all but was kind of covered with a lot of loose rock and gravel. He said also that there was nothing growing on it except for some manzanita on the very top."

"How big did they say it was?"

"About a hundred feet tall."

"Doesn't sound like they were describing Snakehead." The Marijuana Grower scratched his beard," *Hmmm...* did they mention which side of the river it was on?"

"That's where I screwed up. I either forgot to ask them, or else *did* ask but just forgot what they said. In either case, I got the impression that they never crossed over to the south side of the river."

"Which would definitely rule out Snakehead." The Marijuana Grower mused silently for a bit then asked, "What did their scoutmaster have to say about all this?"

"Well, that's an interesting side note. I kept looking down the trail for him as more and more of the scouts hiked up, but he never came. So I asked them where he was. They said, 'He's sick. He was having fainting spells so he and some of the guys stayed down at the river for a while.' That's when I decided to take a wild stab in the dark, 'Does your scoutmaster have any Indian blood?'"

"*Ah,* testing to see if he'd been struck down by Eros's hex!" The Marijuana Grower rightly surmised. "And what did they say?"

"They were surprised I had asked. So was my friend, who hadn't heard of the pyramid or Eros before then. Then one of the scouts says, "Yeah, Ben (the scoutmaster) is half Cherokee!"

The Marijuana Grower thought for a minute then stood and walked from the table. I followed him to a corner of my camp's terrace, to a spot which was beyond the light of the kerosene lamp and offered a wide view of the surrounding canyon's black ridges and wide, star-speckled sky.

"The archeologist's textbook said the pyramid was *near* Snakehead Point, right?—near it but not on it." The Marijuana Grower asked as he searched the silhouetted ridges.

"That's right."

He then pointed to a peak about a mile and a half northeast of my camp. Its sharp black tip bit a perfect triangle out of the starry sky. "See that peak? The psychics I came here with called that hill *The Temple of the Moon*. Know what else? Slim says that the fellow who first brought him to this canyon, twelve or so years ago, used to tell Slim that he'd see UFOs flying in and out of it from time to time."

"And I believe *everything* Slim says," I scoffed.

"The point, Rattlesnake, is *not* Slim's credibility, but the sad fact that we may have been searching and scratching for the pyramid on the wrong side of the river. One of these days we're gonna have to launch an expedition up The Temple of the Moon."

"How about tomorrow?"

The Marijuana Grower shook his head, "Can't."

"*Can't?* What could possibly be more pressing than looting a pyramid?"

"My pot plants—they're beginning to sex. I have to start yanking out all the male plants before they have the chance to pollinate the females. If I don't, all my toil will have been for naught."

"I see. How long will that take?"

"The next few weeks at least."

"Well, the pyramid has waited this long for us, I suppose it can wait a fortnight longer."

"I hope so," The Marijuana Grower said as he pulled on his worn prospector's hat and then turned to leave.

"'Night, David."

"'Night, Chet."

After a few steps he turned back, "Hey, why don't you come up Snakehead next week or so: I'll take you along on a sex tour of my crop."

"Sounds good. I'll mark my calendar."

"Alrighty. *¡Buenos nachos!*" he said, walking off into the moonless dark.

"*¡Hasta me loogie!*" I shouted after him.

Clenching a huge stick in his mouth, Bud began to whine, torn between staying or leaving. But the hound's indecision lasted only until the Marijuana Grower's shout shot in from the dark afar, "C'mon Buddy!" and towards it Bud dashed.

Moon When the Cherries Turn Black

"Eros, worshipped by the ancient Greeks as a
cosmic force and divinity of fertility, as well as
the personification of the power of love. Hesiod,
8th century B.C. Greek poet, depicts Eros as the
first of the gods, the offspring of Chaos, or of
Heaven and Earth."

— FUNK & WAGNALL

Journal Entry; 4 August 1984:

The California drought was having one of its best years and I wanted to take full advantage of it, especially while the water was still warm enough to swim. I had two items on my Things To Do Today list. The first was to fish previously unexplored (by me) Giant Gap; the particularly ornery stretch of rapids downriver where the canyon pinches in on the valley like a huge sphincter. The second item was to finally meet Frank and Benny Hutchinson; the goldmining twin brothers who work one of the canyon's few legitimate placer claims and live, year-round, just on the other side of the "Gap." Because my mission involved an arduous twelve mile round trip, most of it swimming and scrambling over trail-less bedrock, I set out from camp a good hour before sunrise.

The first two miles were easy, a simple matter of following the river trail down to the far western end of the valley. En route I passed The California Goldminer's digs. As expected for this hour, he was nowhere in sight. The only evidence of him was a sluice box dragged up onto the river bank, a goldpan set atop a five-gallon plastic bucket with a rock holding it all down in case of a flood or gale-force gusts, and his summer's work to date—a 5' x 5' x 5' hole dug into the sandbar. If he was in the canyon at all he was, no doubt, sleeping off a drunk up at his infamous Outlaws' Camp, tucked up yonder draw a good quarter mile off the river.

I walked beyond The California Goldminer's digs for another half mile until I reached the point where the valley runs out of trail, and where the trail runs out of any terrain short of sheer. This was the entrance to Giant Gap, about as subtle and inviting an entrance as the pearly gates of Hell itself. During the spring this place must redefine the word *terror*. Evidence of this is found in the high water marks rising more than fifty feet above me, where the serpentine cliffs are polished almost to a luster by vernal run off. And so it flows; not for just one pool or two, but for *miles* of pools—two or more solid miles of the most pissed-off, class-five white water in the Sierra. Yes—in *high* water. But, fortunately for me, this month has seen some of Giant Gap's lowest flow levels to date—running presently at about 300 c.f.s.

In the left rear pocket of my cutoffs, an empty, airtight salmon egg jar, astir with a dozen very nervous grasshoppers. In the other rear pocket, another salmon egg jar, this one stuffed with spare fish hooks, rusty super duper lures, and a shiny-new rooster tail. On my feet, a pair of seen-better-days tennies, portholes worn through fore, aft, starboard and port, on the bridge and in the hull. In hand, a Mitchell 300 open-faced spinning reel screwed to a does-the-job fishing rod. On my shoulders, a shaft of morning sun, perched there like an abalone in heat. And all around me, the crystalline, cool, hazel, tranquil, effervescent, tumbling, twisting, tugging, gurgling, cleansing and eternal river. That's right—amphibious drift fishing.

*

Suffice it to say, I survived my passage through Giant Gap. Four hours, four miles and eight trout later, I washed ashore near the Hutchinson brothers' digs. Insofar as they've held title to the claim since before this stretch of canyon was granted Wild and Scenic River status in 1975, the brothers are permitted to use internal combustion engines to abet their goldmining efforts. This gives them the unfair advantage of using power dredges over the canyon's other miners' sluice box techniques. Throughout the low water months, from early June through late September, Frank and Benny spend a few hours each day submerged, from depths ranging from mere inches to twenty feet. A floating compressor feeds air down to their regulators, half-inch wetsuits protect them against the river's chill, and a five horsepower Briggs & Stratton two-stroke engine sucks (through 4", 6" or 8" hoses) from the riverbed any and all sand, gravel, lead, iron and gold up to the surface where it is processed through a powered, floating sluice box. With two such dredges in operation, it is not uncommon for the Hutchinson Mining Co. to reap $200 a day—a $100 per man per day compared to the manually laboring miner's $14. Come fall, they take off their wetsuits and hang them up until the next summer. They work four months and sleep eight. At last, the Prudent Man!

I split my stringer of trout, leaving four down in the river and carrying the other four up to the Hutchinson's cabin. The spacious, 16' x 20', one-roomer is one of the very few permanent structures in the canyon, hauled in a couple planks at a time and completed in 1961. With wooden floor and walls, glass windows, two twin beds, electric lights, refrigerator and (brace yourself) an 18″ black & white television, the abode is the veritable Taj Mahal of the canyon. To power all this opulence the brothers merely hook up one of the Briggs & Strattons to a portable generator, which then trickles amps into the dozen 12-volt car batteries hooked up in series. A three hour recharge can supply their domestic electricity needs for a few days.

The sun struck noon by the time I dragged myself to their doorstep. Frank was just then coming out through the cabin's screen door before I had a chance to knock. My unannounced presence startled him. For some time he just stared at me, squinting and refocusing as if I was the biggest enigma he'd encountered all week. I decided to help him out.

"Hello, Mr. Hutchinson. My name's Robert Johnson. I live about six miles upriver."

Slowly, as reason returned, Frank began to smile. *"Hah!* For a minute there I thought you were my brother Benny. Heck, we get visitors only about every hundred years or so. But then I couldn't figure out if he had lost thirty years or if my eyes were finally going bad!" he said, now laughing.

"Fortunately neither," I offered.

"Here, have yourself a sit, Johnson," he said, pointing me towards their dirt-floored patio, proffering a particularly fine view of a wide bend in the river. "I'll grab us a beer."

"Just what the doctor ordered." I moved to the patio and sat in one of its three civilized, aluminum and nylon, lounge chairs. From within the cabin I could hear the refrigerator door slam several times as Frank tried to get the latch to catch. After threatening the appliance with sufficient epithets, he finally got it to do as told. Soon thereafter he emerged with three cans of cold beer; namely, Hamms.

"Here ya go," he said, handing me my beer, "to you 'from the land of sky blue waters.' By the way: name's Frank—Frank Hutchinson," he added, shaking my hand.

His grip was firm, hardened by years of wrestling mining equipment. His sixty-year-old frame was tanned and strong but not beaten, like those of most other miners. And it didn't take much chit chat to learn that his mind was as sober as the river and crammed with kind and honest thoughts.

"There's my little brother," he said, pointing towards the far end of their sandbar some forty yards away. "He's just panning down the last of his day's gold. He'll be up here in a minute."

"*Little* brother? I heard you two were twins."

"Oh no-o-o, we was born a good eleven minutes apart. Different fathers too. You'll see," Frank teased.

Everything about the Hutchinson's little slice of heaven suggested that theirs is a happy camp; not drunken like The California Goldminer's Outlaw Camp, not paranoid like The Marijuana Grower's atop Snakehead Point, not sinister like Slim's Comfort Zone, not cool/Bohemian like mine—just happy and pure and wholesome. Frank and I chatted there on the patio for a good fifteen minutes before Benny finally came a-waddling home from work, sporting a beaming, ear-to-ear grin that could only mean one thing —

"Done good, huh?" I said to him, as he came to the table.

"Nope. Piss poor!" he chuckled.

"Well, what'd'ya expect? When you gonna get that dredge of yours fixed?" Frank barked, with an edge to his voice.

Benny shrugged off his brother's criticism, "Might never. Kind of enjoy the peace and quiet of doing it by hand."

Frank handed Benny his lunchtime beer as he introduced us, "Benny, this here's Robert Johnson. He lives up the other side of Giant Gap near —"

"Oh, Rattlesnake Cutthroat Johnson—the writer fellow who lives in the tipi!" Benny interrupted, with flattering enthusiasm.

I was startled, "How'd you know?"

"Oh, some weekend warriors floated through here in kayaks a couple months back and told us about you. At least I think it was them."

Though they are indeed twins, Benny is obviously the younger of the two. This difference is not so evident in appearance (though they are not identical twins) as in the way the two relate to one another; the way Benny whines when Frank bosses him around, as if their rapport was cast when they were four. But don't get me wrong, despite their nit-picking the two get along better than most siblings. They must, how else could they stand to live together for fifty-six years? Another difference between the two has to do with, what we might call *gravity*. That is, whereas Frank has his mental feet planted firmly on the ground, Benny's disposition is more that of a wispy cloud, held aloft the jaded Earth by ethereal thermals—seemingly *in the world but not of it*, or, more bluntly, *flaky*. Such a character gives one the impression that Benny traipses that fine line between open-mindedness and lunacy. But who knows? Perhaps when the veil of this world is blown away like a fog by the winds of truth, and those of us who thought we had a firm grasp of reality suddenly find ourselves clinging desperately to the last fading wisps of this dream, well, suffice it to say, Benny's day may come.

"I've been meaning to hike up to your place to tell you about the ghost I met down here this spring."

"Ah, who the hell you trying to kid, Benny?" Frank scoffed.

"About seeing a ghost?" I asked.

Frank shook his head, "About hikin' up through the Gap. He'd make it about as far as the first waterfall."

Benny ignored his brother's skepticism, "I figured you might be interested in that kind of stuff."

"A ghost, huh? Was he a friendly ghost?" I quipped.

"Come to think of it, this one was kind of cocky," he said, in all seriousness. "I was right down there on the sandbar, right where I've been digging all this summer. It was about eleven in the morning and I was bent over my sluice box. All of a sudden, I hear this deep voice say, *I am the prince of the river.*" Benny paused to laugh. "Now, I knew it wasn't Frank 'cause he was about twelve feet underwater at the time. So, I look up to see who it was. That's when this ghost-guy has the nerve to say, *Don't bother to look. You cannot see me. My robes are too bright for your eyes.* But the fact was I *could* see him, and his robes *weren't* all that bright. In fact, they were kind of dingy. And when I told him as much, it kind of shut him up. Then I asked him his name. And he says, *I am Cayton, prince of the river.*"

"Cayton. Are you sure he didn't say, *Satan?*" I asked.

"No, he said, Cayton—*George* Cayton, in fact."

"George Cayton," I repeated.

"Does it ring a bell?"

I thought hard, "Nope, not a one."

ROBERT P. JOHNSON

I glanced over to Frank to check his reaction to Benny's story. When his eyes swung and met mine he quickly averted them to his beer can, which he then hastily inverted above him. Something about Frank's reaction gave me the feeling he didn't want me to think he believed Benny' tale, even though he probably did.

I turned back to Benny, "What else did Mr. Cayton have to say?"

"That was about it. After that he just turned away and walked off down the sandbar, becoming fainter and fainter with each step until he finally just faded away."

"Well, I'll be damn."

Soon our conversation sank towards less interesting topics with seemingly no bottom in sight. The problem was obvious; the Hutchinson boys were starved for company. There was little doubt in my mind they could carry on this aimless chatter for a month or more before experiencing the utter boredom I was feeling after just a half hour. Contributing to my itchy feet were the six upstream miles lying between me and my cot, and only half a day of sunlight left with which to stitch them. I decided to bid the boys adieu.

"Well, nice meeting you both, Frank… Benny," I said, standing some-what abruptly and shaking their hands.

"You leavin' so soon, Rattlesnake?" Benny whined, frowning.

"Got to: took me nearly five hours to get here. Oh, I almost forgot. Do you guys like trout?" I asked, raising the heavy stringer.

"Love 'em! *Ah*—beauties!" Frank beamed, taking the fish and mar-veling over them closely. "Watch 'em all day long while I'm dredging. Just never take the time to fish 'em out."

Benny's reaction, however, was somewhat less than his brother's glee. This I perceived as a sudden pallor wiped across his face, making him look like he was about to puke.

Frank noticed Benny's reaction and explained it with a half shrug, "Benny can't stomach fish or any kind of animal. But *I* love 'em. I'll cook 'em up tonight!"

"Well, there ya go," I said, edging away from the patio. "Sorry, Benny."

Benny nodded and managed a thin grin.

"Feel free to visit anytime!" Frank shouted.

"I will and likewise."

"You bet'cha. And thanks for the fish!"

"¡*De nada!*"

And, with that, I left.

*

I made it back to the upstream end of Giant Gap just as the sky was turning that pale shade of a fine lager beer, that shade which envelops both dawn and dusk alike in its timeless tipsy. There I ran into Slim, who was just picking up his things after an afternoon of *sniping*—cleaning out small fissures in the bedrock with a crevice pick (or even a screwdriver) then quickly panning it down.

"Any luck?" I asked him.

"Yeah, lookie here," he said, pulling a small glass vial from his shirt pocket and handing it to me. On close inspection the vial contained about a dozen small nuggets, most of which I recognized from similar encounters with Slim. Nevertheless, I couldn't think of a reason for calling him on the lie.

"You better let me invest this for you, Slim," I teased, slipping the vial into my own pocket.

"Oh, that's quite alright, Rattlesnake. I don't mind being poor," he countered, grinning as he gently snatched the vial from my hand.

Slim and I forded a shallow part of the river then hooked up with the river trail on the north bank. The trail here parts with the river to short-cut through a forested stretch. After a mile of this, the waning dusk and the thick forest joined forces to severely limit our vision. Fortunately, this was Slim's daily commute.

"I could walk this trail blindfolded!" he boasted.

"Sure you could," I said, in less than complete sincerity.

As we hiked on, I found it necessary only for me to keep my eyes on Slim's gun belt and the twenty or so copper-tipped .45 caliber hollow-points riding therein; kind of a hikers' autopilot. Suddenly, Slim stopped in his tracks.

"What's the matter?" I asked.

"*Sssssh!*" he whispered. "Look up ahead there."

ROBERT P. JOHNSON

Dilating my eyes as best I could, I followed his point up the dark trail. There, some fifty yards ahead of us, a couple—man and woman—were clearly trying to keep ahead of us. In the quiet of our pausing we could hear the woman huffing and puffing and the man urging her on, "C'mon, hun—they're closin' in!" But even with us stopped, his efforts seemed futile. For, even at a distance of fifty yards, and in the dark, she looked to be a good hundred pounds overweight.

"She's one healthy gal," I whispered to Slim.

"Yeah, they'd move quicker if he just rolled her along," Slim posited back.

Slim and I resumed our progress, trying our best to maintain the distance between us and the terrified couple. As this proved impossible Slim suggested that we just catch up with them and introduce ourselves—"Let's get it over with so they don't have to worry all night about us being a couple of backwoods cannibals."

I nodded, "Sounds like the prudent thing to do."

As we proceeded to close the gap on them, the couple tried to muster an even more hasty flight. It was kind of pathetic. I thought about shouting something reassuring like, *Hey, we won't eat ya!* But figured it might only cause them to amend their original hypothesis to *backwoods cannibals with a penchant for lying.* Finally the couple succumbed to fatigue. Pulling up beside a stout tree, they turned and faced us.

"The fellow has a rifle," Slim whispered out the back of his mouth, as we moved nonchalantly closer.

And indeed he did. And a *cocked* rifle at that; cocked but aimed at the ground... for now. I found myself, for the very first time, glad that Slim had his Colt .45 pistol riding on his hip. I also found myself quite glad that the rifle appeared to be a single-shot .22 and that Slim was between it and me. I mentally practiced the scenario: *Bang!*—Slim catches the first slug in the chest. I draw his pistol from its holster before he drops. *Bang! Bang!*—I win. Twelve nuggets of gold and whatever beer and Snickers Bars the couple had packed down. The victor's deserved spoils.

"Howdy," Slim called out as we came within ten feet.

No reply—there was still hope of gunplay.

But Slim persisted: "Name's Slim. And this here's Rattlesnake."

"Howdy," I decided to say, fighting back an urge to growl at them.

"Howdy," the man finally said. "My name is Steve, and this here is my fiancée," he added, alluding to the plump woman trying to hide behind the tree but still spilling out both sides.

"And, howdy to you, miss," Slim said.

Despite Slim's politeness, the woman didn't mutter so much as a peep.

"*Steve?*" Slim repeated. "You wouldn't happen to be Steve *Wallenda*, would you?"

Genuine shock registered in Steve's face. He hesitated—a bit too long—then admitted, "Yeah, that's me. How'd you guess?"

Slim grinned wide. "Your equipment manager was down here a few months back. Said we could expect you."

Only then did I realize whose presence we were in; Steve Wallenda, tightrope walker extraordinair and *The Last of the Flying Wallendas*.

*

JOURNAL INTERRUPTUS:

The Flying Wallendas were daredevildom's premier family highwire act. In a league of their own for nearly forty years, they teetered over the free world from the early 1920's until tragedy befell them in 1962. It happened in Detroit while performing their famous "Pyramid Act"— sans net as usual. In all, seven of them fell. Two were killed, another paralyzed. Only one survivor of the original act performed again. That was Steve's uncle, Karl Wallenda, whose life was later claimed by gravity while walking a wire strung between two hotels in Puerto Rico in 1978. He was seventy-three years old. Days after this tragedy, Steve began promoting himself as "The Last of the Flying Wallendas." This opportunistic proclamation drew the ire of Gunter Wallenda, Steve's father, who promptly made public the fact that Steve had never been part of the family's act. The senior Wallenda even went so far as to label Steve, "the black sheep of the family." But Steve managed to promote himself faster and louder than his father could lobby against him and thus launched a flourishing career that has brought him fame and modest fortune the world round. Hence it is that Steve remains "The Last of the Flying Wallendas."

*

"You both are welcome to stay at my camp," Slim offered Steve, now that tensions between Steve and fiancée and us "backwoods cannibals" had warmed almost to the point of trust.

"Well, thank you just the same, Slim. But we're already settled into a spot up the draw here a piece," Steve said, pointing towards The Outlaws' Camp.

I noticed then that the .22 rifle Steve was toting was The California Goldminer's. *Had Steve stolen it? Perhaps after first killing California? Or were they staying with him as guests?* These were questions I decided I needed to know, though maybe not right then and there.

"What'cha plannin' on doin' while you're down here," Slim was asking Steve, "a little goldmining and fishing?"

"Yeah, well, maybe. I own some property down here—up the river trail here about a mile, right where some yo-yo's got a tipi pitched. (I gulped on cue.) After we get married we're gonna move down here permanently, build us a cabin... maybe a few cabins. Hell, we got eight kids between my three and her five. It'll be good to keep 'em all out of that bullshit of growin' up in a city... Teach them how to fish and hunt... raise us some rabbits, maybe." Steve then turned to his fiancée and gave her a reassuring hug, "Yeah, we'll raise us some rabbits... We're gonna be happy here, real happy!"

To all this Slim and I just smiled and nodded, both sensing the quiet desperation in Steve's words. By the way Steve spoke so hopefully of the future—as if dreaming aloud—I got the feeling something was terribly amiss in his life. And by the way he shuddered each time he glanced up to the ridge—*to all that bullshit*—I got another queer feeling that he must be running from something—kind of like the rest of us.

We parted companies on amicable terms; Slim and I heading east on the river trail, Steve and fiancée taking the spur trail leading up to The Outlaws' Camp. And even though the little lady hadn't uttered so much as a peep, and even though they may have killed The California Goldminer and taken his gun, and even though Steve had called me a yo-yo, I found I liked them well enough—*well enough* to wish them a lifetime of happiness and prosperity, but not quite well enough that I hoped to see their dreams of a Promised Land, of rabbits and cabins and eight screaming kids, come true.

Our last mile was through pitch-black forest. Here Slim proved his boast of being able to walk the trail blindfolded while managing to keep his wisecracks about the "yo-yo" living in the tipi to a scant few dozen. When we arrived at the tipi I gave Slim two of the remaining four trout. He thanked me then set out upon the last leg of his workday commute, another mile up the river trail to The Comfort Zone. After he had left I began gathering pine needles and twigs from around my campsite—by memory, since by then it was far too dark to see. As I struck a match to my pile of kindling I recalled something that Steve Wallenda had said; that his family had fallen while performing their famous "Pyramid Act."

JOURNAL ENTRY; 9 MAY 1884:

Dear Journal,

Something kind of troublin' happened this afternoon while The Professor and I was working the claim. Three Maidu braves come wanderin' into the valley like it was nobody's business. First we've seen down here this year. They was on the south bank, over on the Chinese side directly across from our claim. When I spotted them I nudged The Professor and said, *Lookie there!* Then he and me just kind of set down our shovels and watched as they walked up along that long, terraced wall (that I call, China Wall) holdin' up the Chinese miners' camp. At the time the camp was deserted. That's 'cause most of the fifty or so Chinamen were up there on the backside of Snakehead doin' their hydraulic mining. They only left three Chinamen down to watch over their camp today and they was down at the river, workin' the sandbar not forty feet from The Professor and me. Once these Chinamen looked up from their sluice box and see these braves starin' down on them, they got all nervous. We could hear 'em chatterin' away. 'Course, even though we couldn't make hide nor hair of what they was sayin', it was obvious they weren't feelin' all too comfortable about the situation!

ROBERT P. JOHNSON

Next thing that happened, the three braves decide they're gonna introduce themselves to the three Chinamen—paleface style. So they climbed down right to the river's edge there and do it, shakin' hands and noddin' and grinnin' and all. The Professor said it seemed to him the Injuns probably ain't never seen Chinamen before. As I was tellin' The Professor that it seemed like that to me too, one of the Maidu braves all of a sudden pushes one of the Chinamen into the surgin' river! The Professor and I couldn't believe our eyes! The Injuns got quite a kick outta this. They was laughin' so hard they had to hold their bellies. The remaining two Chinamen run off down the riverbank to try to save their compadre, but their side's hard goin'. So The Professor and I jumped up and run down our side too. 'Cause ours is flatter we got to the Chinaman first. I swum out into the first calm pool below the rapids and towed him over to his side. The Professor swum over too. But the Chinaman ain't breathin' and so, with the other two Chinamen crowded around, The Professor pronounced him dead.

Tonight at our campfire The Professor told me that the braves must've been conductin' an Injun sink-or-swim test, kind of like the Salem witch trials. Tryin' to learn what?, I asked him. But he could only shrug, "Maybe just tryin' to learn if Chinamen sink or swim."

*

The preceding was my paraphrasal of a friend's paraphrasal of an actual journal entry of a white prospector who lived down in this same valley just over a hundred years ago.

JOURNAL ENTRY; 9 AUGUST 1984:

My "Injun alarmclock" went off bright and early this morning; two tall glasses of water just before bed. Works every time. Next thing I knew I was breaststroking across the river, parting a fog of gnats and mosquitoes with my bowsprit face. Arriving on the south bank I paused at one of my favorite breakfast haunts and munched down about a dozen handfuls of blackberries. With my fingers sufficiently slashed, my tongue stained sufficiently purple, and my belly sufficiently sated, I pressed onward. My early rising was necessary if I wanted to catch The Marijuana Grower's "Sex Tour '84". Which I did. You can starve to death from curiosity. Don't let anyone tell you otherwise.

From the blackberry patch I climbed sixty feet up the riverbank and onto the terraced China Wall of the aforementioned, century-since abandoned Chinese Miners' Camp. Passing through the half-mile long camp I kept an eye out for artifacts left behind by the Chinese miners' (rumored abrupt) pullout. The California Goldminer had assured me I could expect to find treasures from the Ming Dynasty "just lyin' around, intact and *dis*perturbed!" Yet the only thing remotely "disperturbed" I stumbled upon that could qualify as a relic was, in fact, a very *un*-disperturbed (i.e., shattered and rusted) wok. And the only thing remotely "intact" was a rather tack*less* rattlesnake; which, because it was temporarily blind from molting, was striking wildly at anything warm-blooded. This included me though, even on its third try, it missed by a good four feet.

My tour of the Chinese Camp ended at its southern boundary. From there I climbed a steep ravine, up and over the hand-stacked boulders of mine tailings, some the size of V.W. beetles. The ravine was cut by a spunky creek and adorned with exotic poplar trees, leaves spinning like shiny fish lures despite there being no perceivable breeze whatsoever. After gaining approximately 600' of elevation up the backside of Snakehead Point the pitch of the creek levels as the ravine yields to a small hollow. At the opposite end of the hollow is the creek's source, a clear and bubbly spring. It was there, bent over the spring and filling a five-gallon tank, that I spotted The Marijuana Grower. Since he had his back to me I was able to sneak within ten feet of him. Once positioned there I bellowed the loudest Injun whoop I could muster, just to see if I could get him to jump out of his skin. Almost. Before I finished my whoop, he bolted upright and joined in with a whopping whoop of his own. When both of us had thoroughly deflated our lunges, we turned to one another and, with calm nonchalance, politely shook hands.

"Good morning, Robert."

"Good morning, Robert."

"And good morning, Bud," I added, now shaking the paw of The Marijuana Grower's dog who had rushed over to check out all the excitement.

"Are you ready to embark upon Le Tour de Sex, '84?" The Marijuana Grower asked as he strapped the five-gallon tank onto an old Boy Scout "Yucca" pack frame and slung it all onto his back.

"Ready and willing."

"Well, let's not keep the girls waiting!"

He turned and Bud and I followed. In a matter of steps we were climbing a trail that perfectly reflected the personality of its engineer; a no-nonsense, straight as an arrow, sixty percent grade, ankle-deep in dust, briar-strewn, not-much-of-a-trail trail.

"Did you blaze this trail yourself?" I asked The Marijuana Grower.

"You're a god-damn psychic, aren't ya, 'Snake!"

After a hundred yards, to my disbelief, the trail bent skyward into an even steeper climb. Billygoat Bud had prepared for this leg by amassing a full head of steam, which he selflessly threw at the slope. As the pitch of the trail became something resembling the face of Half Dome, Bud became something resembling a popular messiah nailed (albeit backwards) to a cross. The subsequent landslide of dirt and pebbles forced The Marijuana Grower and I to stand back, take cover, and watch the hound go at it.

"I think I figured out Bud's other bloodline," I said.

"Tree squirrel?"

"Lizard."

Once Bud had conquered the eighty-yard, eighty-percent slope it was our turn. To permit the ascent, The Marijuana Grower had tied a long rope to a broad oak at the top of the trail some months ago. With overhand knots tied every couple of feet, the rope looked like a string of rosary beads, dangling all the way down the trail.

"I'm growing tired of this part," The Marijuana Grower sighed as he stooped to pick up the rope from where it lay beside his buried-in-dust feet.

"Hey," I said, stopping him just as he was about to pull his weight against the bottom-most knot.

He turned. "What?"

"Let me carry the water pack."

And though he looked at me like I was crazy, I didn't have to ask twice. Moving quickly (before I could change my mind) he unstrapped the tank-pack from his back and helped me strap it to mine. Soon I was following him, hand over hand, up the long rope, the heavy pack sloshing from my shoulders. After some minutes of this a rhythm arose from the tank's *to and fro* sloshings, giving rise to a similar *to and fro* sloshing of mathematics within my brain: 5 gallons times 7.8 lbs. per, equaling 39 lbs. per trip, times 7 trips per day, times 210 days per growing season, equaling 57,330 pounds, divided by 2,000... *28.5 tons of water!* That's what his back can expect to haul up and down these parched hills until harvest.

By now it was probably no later than ten o'clock in the morning, yet the temperature had already broken 90ºF and was still rising like a soufflé. The unblemished sky was a suicidal blue. The sun loomed overhead like an electric oven element set on broil. The morning's swelter rode heavily across our shoulders like a dead and bloating cowboy strapped across a horse's saddle. The air, as sucked into our wheezing lungs, was as dry as a desert tortoise's sense of humor. Morale was only about as high as the dust kicked up by our dragging hooves; too weary to settle back to the earth, too bored to wander off. *And hope?*—hope lay rotting in its own diaper... like a stinky metaphor.

The flagging heat, of course, was one of the two reasons why the Tour de Sex and the plants' watering has to be conducted as early as possible each morning. The other was to complete the chores before the marijuana-seeking planes and helicopters took to the skies. So far this morning The Marijuana Grower has made five such tank-toting trips. He figures eighteen would be optimal to suffice his plants' needs, yet rare is it that he can muster the energy for even nine. Once he did twelve. Today looks like six.

We are now about half way up the rope. Wearily, he pauses and turns to face me, asking, "What?"

Confused, I ask back, "Huh?"

He licks his parched lips with a dry tongue, then turns forward again—too enervated to bother to explain that he thought I had said something.

Maybe I did.

The matter is dropped.

ROBERT P. JOHNSON

Thoughts become binary…
Energy evaporates…
Communication yields…
Under the searing Sierran sun.

*

As we all know, there are two types of people: those who grow marijuana and those who don't. Of those who grow it there are also two
types; those who do it as a hobby, like some basement wine maker, and
those who do it professionally—driven by the ubiquitous yearn for
profit. Of those who do it professionally there are also two types; those
who use their heads (i.e., employing every technology available in
order to keep their crop healthy and hidden—irrigation, indoor lighting, hydroponics, etc.) and those who, unfortunately, haven't a head to
use. And here is where personality differentiation is no longer possible,
for here psychology meets its indivisible quark, it's lowest life form pos-
sessing too small a brain to divide further. For, of *those who haven't a head
to use,* there is but one type—the *guerrilla* pot grower.

Amongst all marijuana cultivators the guerrilla pot grower is regarded as scum; the proverbial tennis shoe of the tuxedo. Compared to them
he is lunacy. Amidst them he is pariah. Unlike them he is primitive.
Technology for the guerrilla rarely means more than a rusted-through
bucket and a broken-handled shovel. Mental tools of his trade can similarly be numbered on the fingers of a sawmill worker: one, a blunt
head with which he breaks the soil; two, blind ambition, his oxen and
yoke. A character sketch of the guerrilla pot grower might read something like this:
    Sex: invariably male.
    Age: forgets.
    Family: none.
    Assets: lots of energy.
    Employment: *Hah!*—you're dreaming.
    Identifiable scars: broken heart.
    Motto: "When ya ain't gots nothin' ya gots nothin' to lose".
    Scotch: Ten-High Whiskey.

Nudged from the couch (invariably that of a welcome-worn friend) by the double-edged sword of poverty and boredom, the would-be guerrilla pot grower one day announces in glorious soliloquy: "Behold, ye of so little faith, this tatterdemalion before thine eyes. Lavish him, whilst ye still may, with succor and such, before he takest leave of your society to toil for half an annus mirabilis in that most peculiar of pastimes—*work*. From whence he shall returneth a wealthy man, crammed with kind remembrance for those who treated him well!"

Manic now, on the wines of his endeavor, the would-be guerrilla pot grower promptly liquidates everything he owns and hastily reinvests all into the capital goods of the trade: topo maps, bonemeal, fertilizers, seeds, snakebite kit, army surplus clothing, all 119 Louis L'Amour novels, and one *mean as hell* dog. Stuffing all this into his primer pink and gray, uninsured, and no doubt unregistered automobile, he points the latter's hissing radiator towards a geographically suitable (i.e., remote) spot on the map. With one headlight burned out and the domelight stuck on, the guerrilla's iron camel plows forth 'neath the cover of night—bumpers and hubcaps falling off like gorged ticks, the sparks and clamor of the dragging muffler completing the inconspicuous passage. Far beyond the pavement's end does he push his vehicle on towards Middle-o-nowhere Land, not stopping until his car high-centers itself upon some saw-toothed ridge—forever stuck. He is now half way.

Sometime the next week or month the guerrilla pot grower may reach, by foot, his destination. And in a few weeks more his crop may at last be stretching its dormant genes towards the sun. He is now alone; alone to tame the poison oak and briar, alone to fend off both deer and mice, alone to leap from rattlers and to run from bears, alone to shoo away the curious, cower from cops, and hide like an opossum in the weeds with every passing aircraft, alone to itch his scratches, scratch his scabs, twist his ticks and those of his dog, to piss on his wounds, pack mud on his bee stings, bury his shit, hide his tracks, and never quite master the preparation of acorns. In short; he is alone to go where no agriculturist has gone before. Such depravity could make an ascetic monk cringe. And of all from this lowest sub-species of man, the lowliest, most Magilla Guerrilla-est of them all was but a few weary steps

Robert P. Johnson

ahead of me—here, on our ascent up the backside of Snakehead Point. Wearily again, he pauses and turns to me, "What'd you say?"

"Huh?"

He drags a dry tongue across parched lips, then turns forward again.

*

When we finally reached the oak at the top of Snakehead I dropped the rope and sighed with relief. My arms felt as taut as chewed-out bubble gum. He then led us from this southeastern edge of the flat knoll across to its western edge. En route we passed the oak log pyramid we had built almost two moons ago.

"Ah! I see you've weather-proofed the pyramid," I said as we approached the structure, now hidden beneath a tight skin of black plastic.

"Yep, did it so I could move into it on a permanent basis."

"Well?—any paranormal occurrence since then?"

"Just one. Bud chased a skunk into it the other night and woke me up. Before I could chase the blasted varmint back out again it cut loose right under my cot. I haven't slept in it since."

Arriving at Snakehead's western rim we were presented a formidable view of the downriver end of the valley. Three miles away the craggy cliffs of Giant Gap looked like the jaws of a pair of pliers, barely cracked open. Beyond the Gap, the hazy blue foothills melted into the muddy brown skies laying over the Excremento (a.k.a. "Sacramento") Valley. Some degrees north of due west the Marysville Bluffs poked through the layer of brown like the spine fins of a stegosaurus. And a little south of that, the faint blue outlines of Mount Diablo and prominent ridges of the Pacific Coast Range were just visible.

"Try not to drag your feet," The Marijuana Grower said as he began to lead us down Snakehead's western slope.

"Why's that?" I had to ask, assuming he couldn't be worried about wearing an obvious path to his plants at this point since it was already about as inconspicuous as the Ho Chi Min Trail.

"I don't want to wear an obvious path to my plants," he nevertheless replied.

"I see," I said, picking up my feet and biting my lip.

As we continued towards the first plant The Marijuana Grower explained the birds and the bees of marijuana cultivation and the importance of the sex tour: "You see, Rattlesnake, just as caviar is reaped from the female sturgeon, so too are the prized marijuana buds reaped from the female plant. Although the intoxicant THC is found in both male and female pot plants, it is far more prevalent within the female and, within the female, it is most prevalent within the *bud.*"

Bud, who had been plodding along just ahead of us, suddenly stopped and faced us, his ears perked. He thought he had heard his name.

"Why is the THC most prevalent in the bud?" I asked.

The Marijuana Grower continued: "That's because the THC is contained within the sticky resin that the bud oozes in order to catch airborne pollen from the male plant. These buds will continue to grow and grow and grow and secrete more and more resin until pollination occurs. Once this happens, the female plant stops growing buds and secreting resin in order to devote its energies towards seed production, at which time the plant's potency diminishes rapidly. Therefore, allowing pollination to occur is like pouring water into your beer, which is a silly thing to do if your goal is to get drunk. This is why it's so important to uproot the male plants before their anthers have a chance to develop and release pollen."

The Marijuana Grower wrapped up his horticulture lesson just as we came within view of the first plant. Its lush, neon green shade made it stand out amongst the parched native flora like an eight-foot tall transvestite. I was shocked to see he had taken no precaution to conceal the plant.

"Are all your plants so... obvious?" I asked.

Judging by his reaction, I sensed I had stumbled into a touchy subject. For The Marijuana Grower didn't just reply, he *exploded:*

"*Yes*—they're all this obvious! *Yes*—they cause me endless angst! *Yes*—I naïvely thought the pyramid would protect me from ever getting busted when I first cleared out each plant's little private field! *Yes*—I'm well aware of what a dumbshit I was. *No*—I didn't need you to bring it to my attention. *Yes*—I'd rather not dwell on it further!" When he finally stopped his face was beet-red, his lips frothy, his eyes bulging, his chest heaving.

"I was just wondering, that's all."

Like a Dr. Jekyll/Mr. Hyde character, he was able to slip back into a tranquil complacency. By then he was lovingly stroking the first plant's bushy limbs. He then politely introduced me to the plant, as if he were the suave pimp of some classy escort service and she was my date, "Rattlesnake, this is Sugaree," then, she to me, "Sugaree, this is Rattlesnake."

Pulling one limb towards us he closely inspected a prominent, white-haired bud. "Sugaree here was the first of my crop to sex—about a month ago." He then buried his face into the plant's genitalia and inhaled deeply through his nose, "*Ahhhhh!* Smell her, Rattlesnake."

I gently lifted a budding limb to my nose then drew in the fragrant aroma as slowly as I could, tasting it as one would a rose. "Smells like..." I racked my brain to recall the familiar scent, "like a grape popsicle!"

The Marijuana Grower guffawed as he inspected the leaves for signs of thirst. Kneeling beside the plant, he scratched the soil until, at a depth of about an inch, moisture was apparent. "I just watered her yesterday. She's fine for the next couple of days."

Leaving Sugaree, we traversed the slope for some thirty yards until reaching the obvious clearing of the next plant. This one was in definite need of water. The Marijuana Grower unstrapped the tank from my shoulders and began to pour half of the five gallons into its dry reservoir.

"This is Terrapin. Even though she hasn't sexed yet I'd bet my socks she's female."

"How can you tell?"

"See how stout and bushy she is? If she were a male she'd be over six feet by now instead of barely four," The Marijuana Grower said, swinging the tank onto his back and leading us on towards the next plant.

"So, how many plants do you have?"

"Twenty-seven."

"Twenty-seven?" I repeated incredulously.

"You sound surprised, 'Snake. You didn't think I had that many?"

"Well, no. I kind of figured you had *more*—a lot more. Like around four hundred."

"*Four hundred!* Jesus Criminy, whoever gave you that idea?"

"Well —"

"*Slim!* It was Slim wasn't it?"

"Well, yeah but —"

"Fuckin' shit. That ol' miner can't keep his lips closed to save his life! Damn, I even gave him two bushy plants just so it would be in his best interest to keep mum about my crop!"

"Don't blame it all on him. He never said how many you were growing."

"So, how'd you come up with four hundred?"

"Well, isn't that just kind of the pot growers' magic number; four hundred plants—the million dollar harvest?"

"As a matter of fact, it is. And that's exactly how many I started with."

"And now you're down to twenty-seven? That's quite an attrition rate."

The Marijuana Grower exploded again, "That's another topic we needn't dwell upon! My only hope now is that the feds step up their pot busts."

"Why would you hope that?"

"C'mon, Snake. Econ 101—supply and demand. Right now bud is selling at $1,600 per pound. With any luck another month of significant busts will drive the going rate over $2,500!"

We came to another plant, the biggest yet.

"Now meet *China*," The Marijuana Grower announced proudly.

"Let me guess; China *Doll*?"

"Good try; China *Cat*. China Doll is further up the hill."

"I can't help but notice that all your plants seem to be named after Grateful Dead songs. Is there a reason for this?"

"There's probably a reason for everything. But ours is not to ask —"

The Marijuana Grower stopped suddenly, as if the plug had been pulled out on his voice. He was turning a queasy shade of pale as he fondled China Cat's wide limbs. He sighed aloud, hope hissing from his lungs as if through an open chest wound.

"I've never known you not to complete a profound thought. What's wrong?" I asked. "Or is that also something else we needn't dwell upon?"

ROBERT P. JOHNSON

"My girl—my little girl," he muttered sadly, shaking his head in shock and denial. Grabbing hold of his emotions, he similarly grabbed hold of the plant's hefty trunk and, with both hands, yanked it from the Earth. Knocking the soil from its roots he lamented further, "Well, there goes a cool grand."

"So, Terrapin here sexed-out male on you?"

The Marijuana Grower nodded. "See here?" he asked, pointing to numerous tiny pods barely visible in the armpits of many of the plant's limbs, "These are anthers, kind of a male plant's version of a mammalian's testicles."

He pulled a pair of 35-gallon plastic garbage bags from his hip pocket. "For the corpse," he said, as he whipped one open. He folded and stuffed the oversized plant into the one bag and tied a taut knot over it. He then shook open the second bag and stuffed the first inside of it, tying another knot there. He explained the need for the extraordinary precaution: "Botany students often do an experiment to show how it takes just one male anther to pollinate every female plant from that species for miles around. That's why I've got to keep these males tucked away in air-tight bags. Can't even burn them. Amazing stuff, pollen."

With the bagged bag containing Terrapin stuffed into the pack we continued with the Tour de Sex. By mid morning I had been introduced, by name, to all twenty-seven of his plants: Shakedown, Dark Star, Stranger, Jade, Bertha, etc. The results of the tour revealed: twelve definite females, two males (promptly uprooted), and thirteen prepubescents of, as yet, indeterminable gender.

JOURNAL ENTRY; 13 AUGUST 1984; MONDAY:

Time is biodegradable, which is why I must make an effort to re-cap the past few sleepless nights and delirious days before they decompose back into eternity. Let me see if I can:

Friday night was the full moon. The Marijuana Grower was to rendezvous with some friends up top (out on the interstate highway) at five Saturday morning, to catch a ride down to the coast in order to attend a wedding. Since the highway is a good three-hour hike from here, his punctual rendezvous wasn't so much a matter of *getting* up early but of *staying* up late. To this end I abetted his cause by quaffing strong coffee and playing chess with him until we both agreed it was two in the morning and time for him to start his hike.

"Hey, 'Snake, d'ya mind lookin' after Bud?"

"Not at all. When can we expect you back?"

"You mean, how long have you got to rip off my plants?"

"Gotta live up to my middle name."

The Marijuana Grower chuckled, "Three, four, maybe seven days max!"

"No problem."

He then turned and hiked off, up the moon-drenched ridge trail.

The rest of that night I couldn't sleep. I had drunk too much coffee. And so I stayed up, playing solitaire and tossing the stick for Bud until the full moon vaulted the sky like a chip shot and Saturday's dawn belched in my face.

*

Come late Saturday morning an unmarked helicopter began whizzing up and down and in and out of the canyon. Relentlessly. Its modus operandi was to hover over each camp for a good ten minutes then move slowly on to the next, thoroughly scouring the canyon. By the time it made its final pass it had park-hovered above my tipi three times. On the last occasion it hovered within ground effect (twice the length of its rotors), thereby blowing dust and pages of my piece-o-shit novel every which way while I sat—fairly pissed off—at my clackle-clacker. It was 1984 alright, and Thoreau had been introduced to his Big Brother.

The copter's presence was no big surprise, many have been buzzing the river lately in preparation for the annual marijuana busts. In fact, the only thing unusual about this one was the fact of its being unmarked. For, up until now our visiting whirlybirds have been limited to four easily distinguishable species of readily identifiable plumage: the drab olive-green Army copter, the California Highway Patrol's black and white, the green and gold Placer County Sheriff's, and the Tang-orange of the Search and Rescue's; and each with purposes as obvious as their markings. But this unmarked one: what could it want?

*

On Sunday the same unmarked helicopter returned with its same modus operandi; up and down the river, hover here, hover there, never landing, popping in and out of the canyon like bread from a toaster. But Sunday had a silver lining and it came out late in the afternoon, for that's when my good buddy Jae—a roommate from college and at Tahoe— tumbled down the ridge trail to pay me a visit. I first heard him as he sloshed across the creek.

"Jae!" I shouted with glee, thinking at the same time to ask why he wasn't using the stepping stones I had so carefully placed across the shallow creek. Until I saw that he was! Seems the combined weight of his 160 pounds along with that of his pack's 100 pounds proved heavy enough that his every step drove my every stepping stone down through the creek's boggy floor—never to be seen again.

"Nice stepping stones, Bob," he smirked, beneath streams of sweat.

"Thanks," I replied, "And to what good fortune do I owe this visit?"

Jae held up one finger as if to say, *Wait a minute,* swung his pack from his shoulders, sighed, wheezed, pulled us each a can of Meister Brau beer from the pack—*Ssppfftt! Ssppfftt!*—guzzled nine-tenths of his, wiped the sweat from his brow, then elaborated, "You owe it to Sunday newspaper's horoscope."

"Why, what did it say?"

"Beware Tuesday!"

"That was it? No explanation?"

Jae shook his head, "That was it. So, I figured I'd come down here and hide out with you until Tuesday blew over."

"But you don't believe in astrology."

"I also don't believe in tempting fate."

"Carrying this heavy of a pack down the trail was tempting fate," I said, weighing the pack in my arms. "Let's see what you've got in here," I said as I began pulling the contents from Jae's pack: "An extra heavy duty doormat for the tipi, a six-pack of beer, two 3/4-pound bars of bittersweet chocolate, a two-pound brick of Monterey jack cheese, another six-pack of beer, a large rump roast, spaghetti noodles, tomatoes, fresh garlic, bay leaves, oregano, a bottle of burgundy, French bread, yet another six-pack of beer, avocados, pure maple syrup, your binoculars, fishing pole and clothes… Is that it? And this is suppose to last clear through Tuesday?"

"I think there's another six-pack down towards the bottom," Jae said, popping open another Meister Brau. *Ssppfftt!*

As I dug for the missing six-pack I found a rolled up sack of something. "What's this?"

"Fertilizer. For your vegetable garden. Vid said it wasn't doing so well."

I unrolled what had been the fifty-pound sack of lawn and garden fertilizer and peered down to its gray pellets in the very bottom. There wasn't much in there—a pound, maybe two.

Jae explained, "Found that in the garage. Figured it would suffice your needs."

*

Despite the pile of spaghetti fixin's Jae had packed in, we had trout for dinner—for his sake. By nightfall we were as sated as campers could be. Leaning against the sofa log with the fire crackling before us, we nibbled at the chocolate bars, sipped burgundy, and sang the *What-are-we-gonna-do-with-our-lives? Blues.* For optical entertainment we took turns gazing, awestruck, through Jae's binoculars at the nigh-full moon as it lifted into the night like some greasy, pocked and bloated white rhino.

*

Come Monday morning (that's today) dawn caught me brushing my teeth at the spring. Again I hadn't slept. This time I think it was the chocolate. But Jae slept fine, as evidenced by the snores rumbling from the tipi. While still brushing I was yanked about by the sounds of heavy rustling in the nearby bushes. *Bears!*—I quickly deduced as I frantically searched for a pot to beat. Finding a huge skillet, I grabbed its handle with both hands and spun about to meet my foe. But too late, the "bears" had already broken from the brush and were upon me!

"Oh," I said, a wee bit embarrassed by the fact that my *bears* proved not to be bears at all, but mere humans—humans of the Steve Wallenda and fiancee ilk. I set down the skillet to address them with more civility. "Wow, you guys gave me a scare! Why didn't you use the trail instead of the bushes? It's easier," I asked through a mouthful of toothpaste froth.

No reply.

I spat and tried again, "Good morning, Steve."

Again, no reply.

Here was a curious thing; Steve Wallenda was now within handshake of me and yet appeared completely ignorant of my presence. I turned towards the fiancée to try to communicate with her, "Good morning, miss." But here was another curious thing, for not only was the fiancée still faithful to her vow of silence, but she had now, apparently, sworn off walking as well. At least that was the impression I was given by the fact that she was literally crawling, *on hands and knees,* through my camp!

I decided to press the matter. Grabbing Steve's right hand and shaking it vigorously, I barked into his face, "Good morning, Mr. Wallenda!"

This penetrated, but just barely. In response, he calmly turned towards me, smiled politely and replied, "Hi."

"So, enjoying a brisk morning stroll?" I asked, trying to spark some conversation.

"No, just taking a walk," he muttered.

"I see; a *walk,* not a *stroll.*"

He nodded. "Just checking out my property."

I swallowed hard, then wisely decide to play dumb about this private property issue, "Oh, is your property near here?"

"Near enough that you happen to be standing on it."

I tittered nervously. "Oh, er... well—" I began, until he fortunately cut me off.

"This your tipi?"

"Er, yeah," I admitted timidly.

"Nice," Steve replied with genuine admiration of the tipi and nothing that even hinted of anger.

Just then the first ray of daybreak fell off Snakehead Point and lit Steve's thin, but curly blonde locks. As he turned towards it and squinted into the sun, I thought to ask him the question I ask most everyone who stumbles into the canyon. "Say, Steve, what do you know about the pyramid?"

Bingo! At the word pyramid, Steve's cheek twitched like a fish's snagged by a hook. Slowly, his twitch fell into a pouting grin but he said nothing.

I gently kneaded the issue, "Do you think it really exists?"

"Of course it exists!" he scoffed.

"How big do you reckon it is?"

"Big enough. Why do you want to know?"

"Oh, I don't know. I guess it's just human nature to be curious about such things. Why are you so reluctant to tell me?"

"Because *humans* are forever abusing its power!" he shouted, in a burst of anger. After a melancholic pause and near tears, he elaborated, "It's big—not quite as big as the Cheops in the Giza complex but, still, one of the biggest. And like all the others, its capstone was removed."

"Capstone? What capstone?" I asked.

"Ever look at the pyramid on the back of the dollar bill—the ascending capstone there? Our founding fathers knew exactly what was going on."

"But doesn't Cheops have a capstone?"

"Sure, a *stone* one. But not its original *crystal* capstone."

"I see," I said, trying not to roll my eyes. "And what supposedly happened to these crystal ones?"

"They came back and took them away."

"*They?* Who might *they* be?"

Steve grinned wily, "Why, *they* who saw that man was beginning to use the pyramids for self-serving and destructive purposes."

His cryptic reply nudged my questioning into a different tack. "So, where do you think our pyramid is hidden?"

"You really want to know?" he asked, staring daggers at my eyes.

I nodded.

He continued to stare at me. And I continued to hold his stare. It was a stare-down; an event I had mastered in fourth-grade. After a good minute of this he finally melted into a pleased grin, nodding in approval of my mettle. He then turned ninety degrees and, pointing up to the aforementioned Temple of the Moon, said, "There she be."

"You're certain?"

He nodded, "I'm certain."

By this time Steve's fiancée had crawled up to his side and was climbing up his pants like a ladder, using his support to pull herself upright. It worked.

"Good morning," I said, again, to her.

But, again, she yanked her eyes away, uttering not a peep.

"Well, we'll be off now," Steve announced, as he and his honey began to shuffle, hand-in-hand, away. "I've got to check on my mines. I guess you've heard they're all booby-trapped. They were that way when I bought 'em."

I knew the mines Steve was talking about, all three of them. And I knew as well that not a one was booby-trapped. But Steve must have had his reasons for wanting me to think that they were, as I had my own for wanting him to think I believed him. "Alrighty. Thanks for the warning. Bye!"

By now they were slowly sloshing through the creek, with Steve helping his fiancée along lovingly. As expected, neither returned my farewell. I was already *out of sight, out of mind.*

Jae emerged from the tipi just as the curious two-some disappeared around the first bend of the river trail. He rubbed his eyes and stretched, then asked, "Why the early wake up call?"

"What do you mean?"

"You were talking to me—what about?"

"Oh, no—not to *you.*"

Scratching his head, Jae looked about the camp peopled by only he and me, "If not to me, who *were* you talking to?"

"To The Last of the Flying Wallendas—a tightrope walker guy and his fiancée. Well, just to him really; she doesn't talk."

Though I had barely started I decided to stop right there. Jae already had his head cocked to one side and was giving me that *I'm-worried-about-you-Bob* frown, and I knew that to convince him otherwise would have taken an awful lot of prefacing about the legend of the pyramid (to a born skeptic, no less) and how everyone in the valley had come to hear of it. And, frankly, I had no energy for that. So, I took the only option available to me: I lied, "To Bud. I was calling for The Marijuana

Grower's dog. I'm supposed to be looking after him but I haven't seen him all morning."

"Well, relax; he's in the tipi. He slept in there with me."

*

For breakfast: Rattlesnake's cornmeal flapjacks with fresh blackberries.

"These flapjacks taste like trout," Jae whined.

"Do not."

"Do too. Didn't you wash the skillet after supper?"

"Didn't you?" I snapped back.

After breakfast we forded the river to do some goldmining. After running just ten buckets of gravel through the sluice (though Jae swears it was more like twenty) a flat, kidney bean-shaped and sized nugget began shining like the sun from the bottom of the box. Elated at the twenty dollar find, we called it a day and went fishing.

JOURNAL ENTRY; 14 AUGUST, 1984; TUESDAY:

Ah, wilderness!—the whimper of pines swayed by a single puff of wind, the clicking of a grasshopper taking flight from here to there, the gentle purr of dragonflies swimming through the balm, the listless hiss of the river, the throbbing *whop-whop-whop* of a lone helicopter... Yes, it was back again today.

Today was "Beware Tuesday!", as portended by Jae's horoscope. But as Tuesday tumbled slowly towards dusk it was beginning to seem the foreboding would pass as harmlessly as a bout of hiccups. Jae was much relieved by this and, to celebrate, he decided to throw a festive barbecue, the star of which would be the plump rump roast he had packed in. To this end we invited every occupant of the canyon, which meant we invited Slim. We would certainly have invited The Marijuana Grower and The California Goldminer, but the former was still down on the coast and the latter—with another ounce of binge gold in his pouch—had an urgent appointment to keep with a cheap jug of vino in some gutter up top.

ROBERT P. JOHNSON

*

The sun was sitting atop the western ridge like Humpty Dumpty. Jae was carefully filleting the roast into thick steaks. Bud was parked at Jae's feet giving him the best behavior drool. I was stirring the pot of kidney beans that had been simmering since breakfast. All was ready. All were sipping beers. We were now only awaiting Slim's arrival before tossing the steaks on the grill. And then *it* happened—the prophesied *it!* This had been the scene of things here at the tipi in the moments before Beware Tuesday ripped into our serenity like a sawmill blade broke loose.

The *whop-whop-whop!* of the unmarked helicopter tore back into the canyon through its western end and, in a matter of seconds, was again orbiting our camp like a pesky yellow jacket.

"Think they smelled the meat?"

As above, so below. As the copter spun and barked from above, so Bud spun and barked down below—so wildly, in fact, that he nearly screwed himself into the ground. Once the helicopter crew had given us a good look-over, they began to settle down for a touchy landing on the sandbar of my claim directly across river from my camp. Grabbing Jae's binoculars I peered into the cockpit as it slowly sank below eye-level. Therein, stuffed like sardines behind the windshield, were the unmistakable green uniforms and bronze badges of two Placer County Deputies. With them were two men in plain clothes. One was flying the contraption. The other looked like some big, old, red-bearded hippy fellow. The hippy fellow also had a pair of binoculars, through which he was watching me watching him, or vice versa.

I waved.

He didn't.

The helicopter touched down on the sandbar, tarrying there only long enough to deposit the tall hippy fellow and a short but infinitely stout deputy. As these two crouched low to avoid the blurry whirl of rotor blades, the copter's engine revved again to pull it back into its orbit above the tipi. With this accomplished, the two forded the thigh-deep river and pointed their square shoulders for my camp. As they emerged on our side we could see that the deputy was carrying a no-nonsense assault rifle with enough ammunition draped over his broad shoulders to take on the Russkies by himself. The hippy fellow, on the other hand, was dressed like your uncle, the one without a job: worn tennies, torn blue jeans, a soiled Coors T-shirt, and a long, ZZ Top-esque beard. Yes, and he just might have passed for a *genuine* hippy if not for the .44 magnum pistol tucked in his shoulder harness.

"What are you thinking, Jae?" I whispered as we watched the law-men climb towards us up the twenty-foot embankment.

"I'm not thinking. I'm shaking!" Jae whispered back.

Soon the hippy fellow (clearly the man in charge) and his sidekick deputy had scaled the terrace wall and were standing in camp. Between Bud's frenzied barks and the din raised by the low-flying helicopter, it was no simple task to hear oneself think, even loud thoughts. The hippy fellow directed the deputy to park over near my fire pit to provide cover as the former approached Jae and me. The hippy then sauntered to within five feet of us and paused, staring down at us like we were scum. Pulling out his wallet, he quickly flipped it open and shut again. But it was for long enough, for both Jae and I saw the brief flash of badge—Federal Bureau of Investigation. An F.B.I. hippy. From another pocket of his wallet he pulled a card and began reading it aloud:

"You have the right to remain silent and are not required to answer any questions. Anything you say may be used against you in court. You have the right to consult an attorney before you answer any questions and an attorney may be present during the questioning. If you have no funds the public defender will represent you at no cost before and during questioning."

The F.B.I. Hippy tucked the card back into his wallet and the wallet back into his pants. "Do you understand these rights as read to you?"

Jae and I nodded.

"I need a verbal yes or no."

"Yes," Jae answered obsequiously.

"No," I replied, "Are we under arrest?"

I too was hoping for a verbal yes or no, but all he granted was a solemn glower that might have said, *No, pal, you're up shit creek!*

For the next fifteen minutes the deputy kept stoic guard as The F.B.I. Hippy questioned Jae and me. Though the reason for their visit was

ROBERT P. JOHNSON

never disclosed, I assumed they were here to make a pot bust. Despite the propinquity of the Marijuana Grower's pot farm, I found the interrogation exciting, even humorous, but only because I clung to some naive notion that good always triumphs and innocence ultimately shines through. Heck no, I wasn't going to remain silent! What fun would that be? After all, this was a game—a ping pong game of slams and dinkers and cagey spin shots.

"So, do you fellows live down here?" The F.B.I. Hippy asked.

"Just me. He's only visiting," I replied, pointing to Jae.

"Just you. And how long have you been living here?"

"Since el cinco de Mayo of this year."

"Since el cinco de Mayo, I see," he repeated, his words reeking stinky with suspicion. From just two questions I could tell he was the type of cop who liked to repeat everything that sounded incriminating. And the fact of my moving down here in May—in the fat of pot planting season—must have sounded *plenty* incriminating.

"So, what do you do for a living?" he asked me.

"Nothing."

"Nothing? How do you pay the bills?"

"I have no bills."

"You have no bills. What about food?"

"I grow my own."

"I see, you grow your own."

"Sir, the truth is, I'm just here trying to spend a year in the wilderness."

"A year in the wilderness."

"Yeah, as kind of an experiment."

"Kind of an experiment."

"Yeah, like Thoreau."

"I see, like Thoreau."

"Polly want a cracker?"

His non-reply rang the bell sounding the end of the first round of interrogation. The F.B.I. Hippy, knowing he had won it, twisted his lip into a surly grin and sauntered back to his corner. After a short and hushed conference with his deputy he began a slow and methodical meander through my camp, poking his nose into most everything big enough. Soon he came to my writing table. The page sticking out of the typewriter caught his eye. He walked around to the other side of the table to read it. Unfortunately this was the same side of the same table upon which lay the filleted rump roast; the same rump roast which Bud had taken upon himself to defend, apparently to the death if need be. Bud erupted in a ferocious burst of growls and jaw snappings, surprising us all, especially The F.B.I. Hippy. The lawman jumped back, quickly bringing his hand to the butt of his .44.

"Better tie up your dog!" he warned.

As I moved towards the livid hound, I made the simple slip of shouting his name, "Bud, shut up!"

The F.B.I. Hippy's ears perked. "What's the dog's name?"

"Bud," I repeated, without thinking, as I slipped a rope over Bud's head.

"Bud: as in *marijuana* bud?"

"No-o-o! As in *buddy*—you know, man's best friend!"

"I see, Buddy—man's best friend," The F.B.I. Hippy smirked.

Things were not going particularly well for the good guys—the good guys being Jae, me and Bud in case you too forgot, dear Journal. The F.B.I. Hippy had tallied the matter of Bud's name as another victory for his team and had wandered off towards my garden in search of the next morsel of incriminating evidence. I took this opportunity to glance over to Jae in hopes that our eyes would meet in that cheery spark of humor that can sap the threat out of any predicament. But my hopes were dashed, for in Jae's eyes there was no cheery spark of humor to be found. Quite to the contrary, his eyes seemed glazed-over—like those of an Aborigine staring horrorstruck into the Dreamtime—as visions of prison danced in his head. And I knew at once why; for it was, after all, *Beware Tuesday!*

Jae's catalepsy proved instantaneously contagious. A chill shot up my spine. My Adam's apple dropped into my heart, my heart into my stomach, and my stomach into my diaper, as horrid scenarios swam across my mind's eye: a few short bursts from the assault rifle, the hollow pops of the .44 echoing through the canyon, a pair of bullet-riddled human corpses and that of a hound being kicked into a bottomless mine shaft by a shiny boot, a pair of one-paragraph articles deep within a newspaper, "Calcutta: twenty-two die in bus crash with elephant. Sierra Nevada: two more deaths linked to pot wars." Not a pretty sight. I shook the vision from my head.

Jae was whispering to me, "Bob, do you see what he sees?"

I turned to see what Jae was talking about: over at my vegetable garden The F.B.I. Hippy had found the sack of fertilizer Jae had packed in—the *huge*, fifty-pound sack for my *tiny*, hundred-square-foot garden. And the inconsistency hadn't escaped him. Glancing towards us, to be certain he had our attention, The F.B.I. Hippy tapped the sack ever so gently with the toe of his tennis shoe to see how full it was. The all but empty sack all but collapsed.

Jae gulped.

I perspired.

The F.B.I. Hippy smirked—another round won. He then wandered back to his corner to confer again with the deputy. Similarly, Jae and I whispered amongst ourselves:

"So, Folsom or Soledad?"

"Looks bad, don't it?"

"It's a good thing for The Marijuana Grower he's not around."

"Yeah, but a very bad thing for us!"

"Think they spotted his pot?"

"I don't see how they could've missed it—his plants are in plain sight!"

"They're gonna think you're the one growing it."

I nodded solemnly.

The F.B.I. Hippy concluded his conference with the deputy and strolled back our way. By the cool glint in his eye I sensed that a new round of interrogation was about to begin. Singling me out, he came within three feet of me and stopped, still as death. From there he just stared at me. After half a minute of this he took another step forward. It was obvious that he was trying to intimidate me. What might not have been so apparent is that he was being quite successful, for I could feel myself ardently wanting to take a step back to reestablish the space between us. But, outwardly anyway, I stood my ground.

Finally, "That's some fancy horticulture you've got growin' up yonder," he said, with a nod of his head which implied *up yonder* meant The

Comfort Zone. This was fast food for thought: had they only spotted Slim's two plants and not The Marijuana Grower's twenty-seven, or was he bluffing? It was a tough call. I decided to play it as would our role model President Reagan—i.e., dumb.

"I'm sorry, sir, but all my horticulture is confined to what you see right here," I said, pointing down to my vegetable garden.

"And you know nothing of the two, *a-hem*, 'tomato' plants growin' great guns not a mile upstream from your tipi here?"

I shook my head and shrugged, "Sorry."

At this point The F.B.I. Hippy shoved aside any hint of civility. Taking yet another step into my face, he began to snarl, "Have it your way, smartass! I'm gonna call the guys in the helicopter down to watch over you jerk-offs while the deputy and I take a little stroll upstream to see what exactly it is you've got growing up there out behind that little black plastic hot house (Slim's cabin) of yours!"

The F.B.I. Hippy then waved to the hovering copter as if he was calling for his horse. In a matter of seconds the sleek machine settled again to the sandbar and cut its engine. In the matter of a few more seconds the short pilot, dressed in civvies, and the tall, pushing-sixty uniformed deputy were standing at the river's edge, exhibiting obvious reluctance about getting wet. They glanced both upstream and down, as if a river was something you could walk around. Deducing that it wasn't, the pilot bit the bullet and began to ford across, leaving the deputy behind.

I whispered to Jae, "Hey, I know that deputy!"

"Is that good or bad?"

"It's good!"

I then shouted down to the stymied deputy, "What's wrong, Paul?"

The F.B.I. Hippy yanked about. "You know him?" he asked, frowning.

"You bet, Paul and I go way back. We were the only lawmen for the same little gold town up top."

"You were a deputy?"

"Naw, I was the lifeguard. Same sort of thing; enforcing pointless rules."

It was true: for seven years Paul and I both drew Placer County paychecks. There's an unexplainable camaraderie in that. I could feel

Jae sigh with relief. He knew we weren't going to jail.

"Is that you, Bob?" Paul shouted up from the river.

"Sure is!"

"Have you got any spare tennis shoes you could toss down? I've made this mistake before—these boots of mine are slicker than fish guts on a doorknob on wet river rock."

"Sure, I got some right here."

With that I kicked off the tennies I was wearing and tossed them, one at a time, across the river. Thinking this was a game of fetch, Bud nearly pulled the tipi (to which he was tied) off the terrace but, fortunately, couldn't.

Soon Paul and the Pilot joined us atop the terrace. Paul and I shook hands.

"Ho ya doin', Bob. How's your book comin' along?" Paul asked politely, much to The F.B.I. Hippy's chagrin.

"Well, slow—writing is kinda like shittin' through a straw, in my experience. By the way, this is my buddy Jae, he works for the forest service," I said, turning towards Jae.

"Pleased to meet you, Jae. This here's our pilot, Ted—best in the west. Ted, Bob and Jae," Paul said, as the four of us shook hands across one another like some tangled game of four square. This gentlemanly bonding was causing The F.B.I. Hippy to vent steam from his ears. So, he decided to cut it short.

"Paul, d'ya think you could watch over your, *a-hem*, good buddies here while the deputy and I go check out their hot house up yonder?" he asked, with plenty of underlying spite and sarcasm.

"Sure thing," Paul replied, ignoring the slight.

At that The F.B.I. Hippy shook his head, then nodded to the deputy to follow him. As they headed off up the river trail I thought it best to warn them about Slim.

"Oh, guys? That black plastic structure up there is a cabin, not a hot house. Belongs to a miner—good old guy. He kind of appreciates it when people announce their presence before tromping into his camp."

"Is he armed?"

I hesitated; if Slim really had done time (as he purported, but I doubted due to his propensity for stretching the truth) I might be setting him up for an ex-felon in possession of firearms charge. Then again, it seemed potentially more disastrous sending these guys stumbling into Slim's camp unprepared. I decided to downplay Slim's weaponry.

"Well, yeah—he's got a little pea shooter he packs for rattlesnakes."

"A .22?"

"Yeah."

"Rifle or pistol?"

"Rifle. Single-shot."

"And what about his sidearm?" The F.B.I. Hippy asked.

How'd he know Slim had a pistol? Had they had spotted Slim's holster from the air or was this another cagey bluff?

The F.B.I. Hippy sensed my hesitation, "A .38?"

I shrugged, affirming his guess.

At this disclosure the rifle-toting deputy went kind of pale in the face. Seems he didn't like the thought of taking a risk so far away from a bandaid. In as macho a composure as he could muster, he tried to discourage The F.B.I. Hippy, "Ah, let's let the old geezer be."

The F.B.I. Hippy spun about and glared at the deputy, "For all we know he could be making up this story about the miner!"

The deputy frowned and nodded. And with that the two of them continued towards The Comfort Zone.

"So, Paul, how are the pot busts going this season?" I asked as we watched The F.B.I. Hippy and deputy disappear up the river trail.

"Pot busts? I don't make pot busts, I'm too old for that!"

"Isn't that why you guys been buzzing the canyon for the past four days?"

"Hell no. Is that what the F.B.I. fellow told you?"

"Maybe not explicitly, but he sure didn't mind leaving that impression."

"Then what *are* you guys doing down here?—you know, if not for pot," Jae asked.

"Well, this is gonna sound kind of hair-brained, but fact is, we're lookin' for a tightrope walker. Fellow that goes by the name of —"

"Steve Wallenda," I interjected.

Paul's face lit up like the lights on top of a patrol car, "Yeah! You seen him down here?"

Here I was faced with yet another dilemma: sure I had seen Steve, but should I tell Paul? I mean, how many guys could I rat on in one day? Basically, it was a question of to whom I felt most patriotic, the United States government or this tiny niche of hobbits and felons? To which fork of the American River did I owe my allegiance?

As I pondered my dilemma, Paul went on, "Curly blonde-haired fellow, stands about five-seven or eight..." And as Paul went on, I pondered further:

But maybe Steve Wallenda was the real threat here. For his mere presence jeopardized the life, liberty and pursuit of happiness of many. Slim, for one, was probably staring down the long, blue barrel of the law at this very moment—because of Steve. The California Goldminer could get booted from the canyon for squatting on public land or even jailed for harboring a fugitive (if that's what Steve proves to be)—because of Steve. And then, of course, there was The Marijuana Grower who, if caught, could conceivably face life in prison for his "fancy" horticulture—again, because of Steve. And then there were the innocent to consider—Bud, Jae and me. Even our well being was at risk—because of Steve.

Paul must have sensed my hesitance. "Don't worry, you wouldn't be ratting on him. He's not wanted for anything," he assured me. "We just want to make sure he's alright."

"What makes you think he's not?" Jae asked.

"Well, his fiancee called us Saturday morning claiming Steve had been killed in a mining accident down here—in some explosion involving a booby-trapped mine. Prior to that she claims Steve gave her two sealed letters to mail in the event of his death, one to his manager, the other to some reporter."

"What did the letters say?"

"They were identical. All they said was, 'If you have to read this you can assume I am no longer amongst the living. Sincerely, Steve Wallenda.'"

"That mining accident, when did it supposedly take place?" I asked Paul.

Paul shrugged, "Friday, maybe as late as Saturday morning."

"And today's Tuesday," I muttered, trying to recall the days between.

"Well, that doesn't make any sense, because I spoke with him just yesterday morning," I told Paul.

"With who? With Steve Wallenda? You saw him Monday morning?"

"That's right. Right here in camp. He and his fiancee. Right at sun up."

Paul socked one of his fists into the palm of the other in a Batman and Robin like gesture of triumph, "Great, you just shot his story full of holes, blew it out of the water and sunk it!"

"Could the letters have been some sort of publicity hoax?" Jae asked.

Paul shrugged, "Could be. Celebrities are junkies for that kind of shit."

"Maybe he's got some big highwire act coming up he needs hyped," the Helicopter Pilot added.

We all nodded, satisfied not so much that we had solved the mystery, but that we had at least taken speculation as far as possible. And with that done, our conversation drifted to more civilian matters; like whether or not the Pilot's snakeskin boots had been ruined by the river, or whether or not his girlfriend was going to forgive him for missing their dinner date.

It wasn't long thereafter that Slim appeared, strolling towards us along the river trail, with his wrists handcuffed behind him. But gone was the gunbelt and the .38 which once rode his hip. Gone too were his signatory warning shots; the shots I suddenly now missed even before I had the chance to stop hating them. And gone too was that crooked little smile of his—gone for good. The deputy followed closely behind Slim, with the muzzle of his assault rifle pointed at Slim's vertebra. In his free hand the deputy carried Slim's two, uprooted, six-foot and bushy pot plants. And following at some distance behind the deputy was The F.B.I. Hippy, caboosing the procession and carrying nothing but the cigar he smoked and a satisfied grin.

Slim walked right up to me, stopped, and began to stare me down, his black and beady eyes as emotionless as a beetle's. I returned his stare with the same unblinking stoicism. I had had a lot of practice with stare-downs the past few days and was getting pretty darn good at it—too good.

"How'd they know about my guns?" Slim asked, accusingly.

Suddenly the awkward chill of silence swept into camp and parked itself there for what seemed like an ice age. I was frozen by it, unable to answer.

"Alright, let's blow this pow wow before it gets any darker," Paul finally interjected, trying to break the ice, trying to melt it.

With farewells said and their villain in hand, the posse climbed back down the terraced embankment, forded the river, and squeezed back into the helicopter. Soon the copter's engine was whining like a banshee. As it lifted slowly from the sandbar I could see Slim through a side window; watching me watching him, or vice versa.

I waved.

He didn't.

"I think Slim's mad at me," I said to Jae.

"Naw!" Jae scoffed facetiously, "Whatever gave you that idea?"

Standing almost exactly where we had stood for the past hour, Jae and I watched the helicopter shrink to a black speck against the crimson dusk. Soon even its *whop-whop-whops* faded, painlessly usurped by the hoots of an owl.

"I need a beer."

"Me too."

"Ssppfftt! Ssppfftt!"

JOURNAL ENTRY; 16 AUGUST 1984:

The sun floated in the midday sky like a won ton suspended in a bowl of bird's nest soup. Well, sort of. Nevertheless, that was when Slim meandered back down the ridge trail after his two-night stint in the Placer County jail. At the time Jae, The Marijuana Grower (who had returned a few hours before from his week-long vacation) and I were playing three-handed cribbage beneath the three-trunked cedar. Bud growled. I looked up. There was Slim, sloshing through the creek and into my camp.

"Slim! How was the pokey?" I asked.

Slim shot me a brief glower that might have said, *Your days are numbered, Rattlesnake!* and thereafter spoke only to Jae and The Marijuana Grower, ignoring me altogether.

"Not bad," Slim chuckled, with perjured insouciance, "French toast for breakfast, a plain bologna sandwich for lunch, meatloaf for dinner, French toast again this morning. Heck, then Paul even gave me a lift in his patrol car all the way from Auburn right up to the trailhead!" Slim concluded with a hearty laugh, as he sat at the table with us.

"Not bad at all! Three hots and a cot."

"No cot—slept on cold concrete. *And* they confiscated my guns."

"Oh well, at least you got a free helicopter ride out of it."

"Yeah, that was the best part. The first time in twelve goddamn summers I didn't have to hike this son of a bitch canyon!"

"So, what did they stick you with?"

Slim began counting the charges on his fingers, "Possession of wacky tobaccy, cultivation of wacky tobaccy, two counts of an ex-con in the possession of firearms, two counts of unregistered firearms, somethin' else 'bout firearms I don't recall, vagrancy, squatting on public lands, picking my nose with the wrong hand—you name it!"

"Geez, why didn't they just hang you?"

"Said I wasn't worth the waste of rope."

"Yeah, they probably figured it's cheaper for the taxpayers just to let you crawl back here," I theorized.

"Not to mention more cruel and unusual—making you suffer your own cooking, that is," The Marijuana Grower added.

As the above chatter was taking place Jae slipped off to the spring. From the bottom of the first pool he pulled up the thrice-baggied leftovers from the fateful barbecue. He then poured the mess onto a plate, rearranged the steak and beans into a tasteful display, then presented it to Slim complete with a can of beer.

"Welcome home, Slim!"

Slim tore into the steak like a hungry Ididerod sled dog on a thirty-second lunch break.

As Slim gnawed and guzzled his way to nirvana, the other three of us continued with our cribbage game. As we dealt and shuffled and counted points—*fifteen-two, fifteen four, and a run makes seven...*—I could feel Slim's beady eyes bang bitter glances at me. I didn't dare to look up. I knew why he was bitter: I had betrayed him, at least that's what he believed. *Fifteen-four, fifteen-six...* Of course, it could be argued that *he* was responsible for what happened, not I. That he should have known it was a dumb risk with his record to possess those guns or to grow pot. *... and a double run is fourteen...* But the fact of the matter was, Slim didn't see it that way. He blamed me. He was the blameful type. *... and the right Jack make fifteen.* He could probably find a reason to blame Mother Teresa for something. Remind me, dear Journal, not to turn my back to Slim ever again.

Journal Entry; 22 August 1984:

The Second Coming occurred the day before yesterday, and it was worse than I had expected.

There I was: rolling aside huge boulders with the six-foot pry bar I found at the bottom of God's Pool last week, chopping away at dead roots with the ax I unearthed last month, filling five-gallon buckets with the handleless shovel on loan to me from The Marijuana Grower, and pouring the buckets of gravel through the sluice box I'm leasing from Slim. Yes, there I was; minding my own business, working my claim, four feet into the Earth and getting richer by the hour—about $1.75 richer. That was the scene of things around here when the firmament between Heaven and Earth finally ruptured, parting just wide enough for Gabriel's horn to poke through like a hernia.

"BAAAAAAAAAAAB!" it blew.

Its rumble shook the sandbar, leading me to think the large rock I was digging beneath was rolling to crush me. I leapt from the excavation hole. But heard the crazy sound again:

"BAAAAAAAAAAAAAAAAAAAB!"

Definitely not a shifting boulder. I swung my eyes up towards the canyon's distant northeastern ridge to see if a freight train hadn't jumped the tracks. But, as near as I could tell, there wasn't any sign of derailment: no train lying on its backside, clawing at the sky like a tipped centipede, no clouds of dust, no toxic chemicals spilling down the canyon wall. I remained dumbfounded. Then it blew again:

"BAAAAAAAAAAAAAAAAAAAAAAAAB!"

Yes, surely it must be the end of the world, Judgment Day, thy kingdom come! I dropped to my knees and began spitting out *Hail*

Marries as a boxer might his teeth. But even before I could finish up the first Rosary, it sounded again:

"BAAAAAAAAAAAAAAAAAAAAAAAAAAAAAAAAAAAAB!"

And then it struck me: this wasn't the end of the world after all. This was something far worse. This was a small chorus of men shouting my name—*Bob!*—from across the river. Yes, this was something far far worse than the Apocalypse. This was the Second Coming—The Second Coming of The Bros.

Still kneeling and planted there in my digs, I forced myself to lift my eyes towards the northern river bank, to see if my frightening premonition was true. *Alas!*—it was. For there they stood—six of them this visit—bent over and mooning me; Vid, Blaze, Mac, Mitch, Wayner, and Larry. And behind them I could see that my tipi had been artistically draped with toilet paper, yards of the stuff lifting in the limp noontime breeze. They had t.p.-ed my tipi. How clever.

Raising myself from my position of submissive devotion, I dove into the river, climbed out and up the opposite bank, scaled the terraced wall, and strode into my camp with the intent of reclaiming it and sending the yuppie scum packing for home. But there I was met with a hardy embrace not unlike that of a rugby scrum, that rapidly devolved into a dog pile (me on the bottom) full of noogies and shoulder punches and that sort of thing. Bonding. Shortly thereafter, a frosty gin and tonic sat in my hand, complete with ice and a twist of lime. I congratulated The Bros on the t.p.-job but, true to form, they denied the crime with faces straight as church pews.

"We didn't do it, Bob."

*

Early Thursday morning.

After a late evening of liars' dice and hardy partying, The Bros were still passed-out when The Marijuana Grower swung through camp on his way out of the canyon. I was up and picking blackberries in the meadow when he found me.

"Rattlesnake, think you can look after Bud for me again?" he asked.

"Think it's a good idea?—to leave the canyon, that is. I mean, every time you do something bad seems to happen."

"One time!" he scoffed. "This time I have no choice; have to pick up my food stamps. Bud and I can only eat so many ticks."

"I'll be glad to watch after him. But I gotta warn ya, with six guys tossing his stick it might just break him of the habit. It might ruin his career."

The Marijuana Grower shook his head sadly, "Well, that's a risk I've just gotta take," then patted me on the shoulder, "I'll be back tonight," then began up the ridge trail.

An hour later The Bros and I were sipping bloody marys and playing a pre-breakfast round of liars' dice:

"Three sixes! To you, Wayner."

"Four sixes! Mac, hit me on with another refill."

"Haven't you had enough?"

"Maybe you're right. Hit me on with a beer."

"Five twos."

"Oh yeah? Five sixes!"....

And then it began:

"Hey, do you guys hear something?"

"Yeah, I hear you."

"No, shut up and listen!"

We did, and sure enough there it was: the faint drone of a single-propped airplane, straight over head. Craning our necks skyward and shading our eyes against the morning sun, we could now see it: a tiny Cessna circling at about the elevation of the surrounding ridgetops.

"Is this unusual, Bob?" Blaze asked, in reference to the circling plane.

"Not really, but *that* is!" I said, pointing up to the small cylindrical object which had just then been dropped from the plane.

"What is it?" one of us asked. But no one could answer.

Immediately into its freefall the cylindrical object began to unfurl into a long, white streamer, slowly reaching a total length of nearly a hundred feet. By then its rate of descent had slowed to almost nothing, so that it seemed to hang motionless from the sky. With the plane's next pass another cylinder was jettisoned. And with the next yet another, and another and another and another and so on with each successive fly-over. After a couple minutes the sky was draped with no less than seven of these streamers at various lengths of unfurl, hanging in the sky, equidistant from one another, like strings of a harp. A soft breeze out of the west caused all the streamers to follow the first in a listless migration towards Snakehead Point.

"What do you think, Bob?"

"I think you should call Larry up on those five sixes."

"I was referring to the streamers."

"Oh, I try not to dwell on mind-boggling things."

"Blaze, what do you think it is?"

"I think it's beautiful!"

"Hey, maybe it's that artist guy."

"Yeah, what's his name?—Christo!"

"Yeah, it's probably him doing another one of his—well, whatever he does."

"I have another theory."

"Yeah, what's that, Mac?"

"I think it's C.A.M.P. marking The Marijuana Grower's orchard."

"Hmmm, that certainly stands to reason."

"Yeah, they probably have a ground crew moving into the canyon as we speak."

"Shit, I'd hate to be in The Marijuana Grower's boots !"

"You're not alone, ranger!"

"Hell, forget about *his* boots, I'd hate to be in Bob's!"

"Vid's got a point, Bob. Whoever storms into the canyon is gonna think the pot belongs to you!"

"So, what's new?"

"Hey, look now!"

That last command was in reference to the latest and final object to come tumbling from the door of the circling plane. This one was much larger than the streamer canisters. As near as we could figure, from the 1,600 feet between us and the plane, it might be a television set. As the object fell closer we could make out what appeared to be a collapsed parachute trailing behind it, trying to open but failing miserably. Curiously, we found ourselves rooting for the parachute, if only to save the t.v., but to no avail. Down and down and down it fell, faster and faster and faster—plummeting like a school bus full of fat kids. As with the streamers before it, the box crashed down somewhere on the steep slopes of Snakehead Point. After that, the tiny airplane orbited just once more, dipped its wings a couple of times, pointed itself west, then sputtered back into the horizon from where it had come.

"Any additional theories before we close the floor?"

"Homing device!"

"I concur. The box has got to be some sort of radio beacon that's going to lead a C.A.M.P. ground team right to the spot; i.e., the pot."

"But do you think the homing device survived the crash?"

"Sure, they've got transmitters designed to smash headlong into Mars and survive!"

"C.A.M.P. does?"

As the speculation continued I grew ever more anxious about the threat these markers posed to The Marijuana Grower. I felt he was now too close of a friend to let down. Something had to be done.

"Who wants to come with me?" I asked The Bros, scattered about in various positions of repose. They looked puzzled by the question.

"Come with you where?"

"Up Snakehead Point."

"What for? To harvest all his pot?"

I shook my head, "To find the transmitter."

"To destroy it?"

"No, to move it—a couple miles downriver maybe. Just to lead the ground team on a wild goose chase until The Marijuana Grower has a chance to destroy any evidence associating him with the plants."

"Geez, Bob, that sounds illegal."

I shrugged, "Who wants to come along?"

To my surprise, only Vid and Mac showed any desire to comb Snakehead's poison oak, tick and rattler-infested slopes in the 108° heat for the homing beacon. The others seemed perfectly content to stay near their cool drinks, in the cool shade of the three-trunked cedar, beside the cool river. After donning boots and long pants (for bushwhacking) the three of us set out at a hasty pace. We forded the river at the Mercury Pool Crossing, then regrouped there on the south bank, at the base of Snakehead, to plan our search.

"Vid, you head straight for the top of Snakehead up this trail."

"Okay dokey."

"Mac, you bushwhack to the left here a hundred or so yards and head up the east slope."

"Okay dokey."

"Me: I'll head to the right here and comb the west slope. We'll meet up on the top. Okay dokey?"

"Okay dokey!"

Over the course of the next hour and a half the three of us scoured what we could of the mountain's uninviting terrain, independently scaling several times straight up its steep fall lines, then winding our ways back down like the strips of a barbershop pole. On my third trip to the top I took a deserved rest. The oaken pyramid The Marijuana Grower and I had built was handy, so I sat on it. Across the knoll I could see Mac surmounting the southern rim. He spotted me and dragged himself over, climbed up one of the pyramid's corner beams and sat himself beside me on the truncated platform.

"Find anything?" he asked, panting as sweat streamed down his blood-flushed face.

"No. You?"

Rather than speaking, he simply pulled a large wad of toilet paper out of his day pack.

"What's with the toilet paper?"

"That's not the right question."

"What's the right question?"

"The right question is, What was all this toilet paper doing hanging in the trees?"

"The streamers! The aforementioned cylinders dropped from the plane were actually just rolls of toilet paper?" I asked, incredulously.

Mac nodded. "Vid found one. I found two."

"Where's Vid now?"

Mac shook his head and tried to swallow a mouthful of dust. "Don't know. Last I saw he was headed back down the north face."

Right then Mac and I heard a faint but in-unison shout emanating from somewhere beyond Snakehead's western rim. After exchanging a puzzled shrug, we climbed from the pyramid and jogged to the rim. From there a small gap in the firs and oaks allowed us to see all the way down to my camp. There, in front of the itty bitty tipi, the remaining Bros stood in a tight five-some with their hands cupped at their mouths.

"I count five of 'em. Vid must be down there."

Right then another faint shout filtered up to us. This one we could just understand, "We found it!"

Mac and I turned to one another, "They found it!"

By the time we tumbled back down Snakehead, re-forded the river, and scrambled back into camp, The Bros had the rectangular box torn open and had already rifled through its contents.

"You dumbfucks, that's destroying government property!" I fumed.

"Relax, Bob, it's not a homing beacon after all."

"No? Then what is it?"

"Check it out," Vid said, as he tossed the box to me.

The Bros were already snickering amongst themselves as Mac and I peered into the box. And for good reason, for in it we found a very curious assortment of items, which I listed as Mac pulled them from the box:

"One pint of Haagen Daz Vanilla Swiss Almond ice cream, another of Chocolate Chocolate-chip, another of Rum Raisin, and still another of Coffee, a dozen Havana cigars, and, what's this, condoms?!"

"Three dozen condoms, to be precise!" Blaze added, proving he had already bothered to count them.

"I don't mean to pry, but what are the condoms for?" Mac asked the gang.

"As near a we can figure, they must be for this!" Mitch's voice called from directly behind us.

Mac and I spun about to see what he was talking about. And there our eyes were met with the most curious sight of all; one of those life-size, inflatable sex dolls, complete with plastic hair and more gaping orifices than a block of Swiss cheese.

"Her name is Lolita," Larry announced, "At least that's what her tag says."

"She was stuffed in the box with the ice cream and cigars?"

"No, she was the parachute we thought we saw!" Vid added.

"I'm getting to think maybe C.A.M.P. wasn't behind this after all," Mac deduced, "Any clue as to who dropped it?"

Wayner stepped up to Mac and me and presented us with a simple card. Opening the card, we read the eight-word greeting scribbled therein which explained everything, 'To The Bros, with love—signed, Kathy and Mindy.' (Alex's and Wayne's wives.)

*

That evening—while the steaks The Bros had packed down now swung in our stomachs like corpses in hammocks, and yet another round of Liars' Dice had begun without anyone's willful consent, and the crickets and twinkling stars were doing their thing—The Marijuana Grower managed to slither back into the canyon and hide in the brush near the spring at the edge of my camp without any of us noticing. This wasn't as a remarkable feat as it might sound: an elephant could have done the same considering our level of intoxication at the time, coupled with our fervid involvement in the dice game; the seven of us tightly huddled about the table enveloped in the tiny sphere of kerosene lamp light, dice cups slamming down, the Liars' lie going around one direction, the liter of Jack going around the other.

Crouched there in the shrubs, The Marijuana Grower tried to get my attention with a faint: *"Psssst!"* But I, nor anyone else, nor even Bud, heard him that first time. So, he tried again, *"Psssssst!"*

"Hey, who *pssst!*-ed?"

"Must've been Vid."

"Vid, did you *pssst!*?"

"No, but I'm gonna *pssst!* in your dice cup if you don't hurry up and make a call!"

"Alright already. Two aces."

The Marijuana Grower tried again, *"Psssssst!"*

"There it is again!"

"You're hallucinating."

"Bullshit, it's comin' from the bushes!"

"Sure enough, sounds like someone is very surreptitiously trying to get everyones attention."

"Hey, who goes there?" I finally called out.

"It's me!" The Marijuana Grower whispered back loudly.

"Oh, big help—*it's you*. That like narrows it down to every English-speaking male," I tossed over my shoulder to the voice in the bushes.

"Fuckin' scumbags!" he muttered in retort.

I turned to The Bros, "It's The Marijuana Grower," then back to him, "What's your problem? Why don't you come out and join us?"

He gave no reply. Only his eyes, wide and wild as they reflected the lantern's light, gave any hint to what was buzzing between his ears.

"What's he doin'?"

"I dunno."

"Looks like he's checking us out."

"Why?"

"I dunno!"

"Damn, Bob, you've got some fuckin' psycho neighbors down here!"

I shouted to him again, "Hey, bonehead, what's spookin' you?"

Finally, he peeped a hesitant reply, "Where's the Mod Squad?"

"The who?"

"C.A.M.P.—the narcs, the feds, the fuzz, the bacon, the mounties, the *Man*!" he answered with waning patience.

We scratched our numbed skulls and shrugged, "We give up. Where are they?"

"The cops haven't stormed the canyon yet?"

"Not to the best of our knowledge."

"They must be waiting until morning," he mused. And with that he finally emerged from the bushes to join us.

Larry offered the whiskey bottle to The Marijuana Grower, "Here, calm those nerves!"

He shook his head, "No thanks. I've got to keep my wits about me. In fact, I'm gonna have to harvest my crop tonight. Harvest it and somehow get it out of the canyon."

"Tonight?!"

He nodded, "State of emergency."

"Pardon me for asking, but why the haste?" I asked him.

The Marijuana Grower shook his head with disbelief. "Didn't you guys see that spotter plane this morning, dropping markers all over my hill? Jesus frickin' Christ, I had a perfect view! I was up near the top of the ridge trail at the time, having myself one massive coronary after another each time it circled and dropped another streamer. I imagine by first light tomorrow there'll be a hundred or more C.A.M.P. cops raiding the canyon!"

As The Marijuana Grower elaborated, a titter began working its way around the table as we realized his error.

"None of you saw that? Not even when it dropped that homing device beacon thing?" he asked incredulously.

By now our titters had swelled to raucous laughter. But The Marijuana Grower went on:

"That's about when I decided it was foolish for me to stick around for another minute. So, I promptly hiked out to the interstate, scribbled myself a crude N.Y. on a scrap of cardboard, and then tried to hitch a ride east. But did I get a fuckin' ride? No, I did not get a fuckin' ride—not all fuckin' day! This, however, may prove to be a blessing in disguise. 'Cause, by standing there all fuckin' day, I happened to notice that no law enforcement vehicles of any sort got off at our exit, from which I then deduced they must be holding the bust off until morning. That's when I decided it would behoove me to scramble back down here and try to harvest, albeit prematurely, what I could tonight in order to cut my losses."

By this time, we all were so crippled with laughter that each clutched his aching belly as if run through by a jagged lance.

"Yeah, go ahead and laugh! I outta be a comedian, right?" The Marijuana Grower barked angrily. "Well, you won't be laughing tomorrow, shit-fer-brains. 'Cause, though my buds and I will be long gone, there'll still be plenty of pot up there and nobody left to bust but you. Hell, Slim's so pissed off about losing his guns, that I bet he's up at the Comfort Zone right now practicing turning state's evidence on you, Rattlesnake!"

By the time The Marijuana Grower finished his tirade, the seven of us were well into the weeping stage of our gut-retching guffaw.

The Marijuana Grower shook his head with suppressed rage, muttered, "You guys are assholes!" then began to stomp away. "C'mon, Bud—wouldn't want *you* to get shot."

"Wait!" I managed to shout, as I lay there on the ground, nearly spent from the laughter. He turned and listened—at first impatiently, then

Robert P. Johnson

with riveted silence—as we recounted the whole sad tale of the tiny airplane's visit.

"Toilet paper, ice cream, rubbers, inflatable sex mannequin?!" he muttered incredulously.

"That's right," I affirmed.

"And who did this?"

"Alex and Wayne's wives. Blaze's brother-in-law flew the plane."

At this point The Marijuana Grower shuffled a few steps away from the table. Then, staring off into the starry darkness, he began shaking his fist at the western horizon, shouting "You fuckheads!" after the long-gone plane.

With that seemingly behind him, he shuffled back to the table and plopped himself on the bench. He turned to me, "Wimmin, eh?"

I nodded.

He shook his head and began to chuckle. "Gawd! Kind of restores my faith in *wimininity*. Know what I mean?"

We nodded as we re-stoked our dice game. *Four sixes... Six twos...* Larry handed The Marijuana Grower the bottle of whiskey which, this time, he gladly took. Mitch stuffed a long cigar into his mouth and Vid lit it. *Six sixes... Seven threes... Seven sixes....*

After a deep sip and a becalming puff, The Marijuana Grower suddenly leapt from the table to once again shake his fist at the western horizon and shout, "Yo-o-o-u fuckheads!"

Eight sixes... Eight?—bullshit!... Then call me up... Alright, let's see them!... Read 'em and weep... Five, six, seven, fuckin' eight—fuckin' shit!...

Strolling back to the table he took another heartly pull on, first the whiskey, then the cigar. Then, sighing contentedly, he shook his head and muttered almost beneath his breath, "Wimmin—*sheesh!*" Lastly, without so much as an *adieu*, he took fair Lolita under arm and carried her off into the honeymoon night.

*

Friday.

Presently, I'm lying atop the flat boulder in the middle of Mercury Pool, nursing a hangover. Upstream from here the river is a half-mile long washboard of shallow rapids. But here it runs deep again; white turns to blue, the hissing bubbles go quiet, trout hover in space. Squinting skyward I see it's the noon hour of another hot one.

I feel pregnant. That is, I feel there's something within me unborn or unrealized. Certainly, in the wake of The Bros' departure, I feel the same sense of envy and low self-esteem I always feel when my vague aspirations are juxtaposed with their decent-paying jobs, fledgling families, and practical goals. I wonder what the fuck I'm doing out here on this wilderness endeavor. In a fit of desperation, I feel a need to jump back on the treadmill; to become a working class hero. But it feels too late for that—for me. And then I feel suicidal. But soon even that passes, leaving me to feel... well, pregnant again. *Pregnant with what?* A book? No, too self-indulgent. Mainstream, middle-class success? No, too mundane. Rather, I feel pregnant with a challenge. *Yes!* I feel life is challenging me to confront every insecurity, the very insecurities we normally try to patch with material palliatives—chic clothing, fancy cars, big houses. We know these things don't fix our lives, and yet we hunger for them nevertheless. We know that our material desires have brought us to the brink of planetary suicide and yet we keep grabbing for another slice of the pie. *This* is what I feel challenged to do; to *not* grab for a slice! I feel challenged to accept myself as I am—flat broke and unsuccessful.

A wayward electron bridges a synapse, temporarily connecting my memory with the rest of my brain. I recall The Bros. Not quite gone an hour, they must still be on that hot hike out of here: back to their jobs and wives and socially condoned futures, back to the eddies and cataracts of that other *fork* of the American River. And with summer on the wane, whatever glimpse I can catch might be the last I see of them for a long long time. I turn on my side and gaze up the northern canyon slopes towards the switchbacking scratches of the ridge trail; trying to discern The Bros' huffing backpacks from the rust-colored rocks and green manzanita bushes, trying to discern motion from inertia. But I cannot, for the entire canyon is in motion in this searing heat; wobbling to the universal jello.

ROBERT P. JOHNSON

Moon When the Plums Turn Scarlet

"What is history
But a fable agreed upon?"
—NAPOLEON BONAPARTE

Operation Weatherproof.

The threat of rain hung like a ham from the black sky all the day long. This posed a potential inconvenience insofar as tipis aren't all that waterproof and insofar as this belt of the Sierra received 110 inches of rainfall last year. 110 inches, of course, is higher-than-average precipitation, but even half that could have dire effects upon my serenity and dry clothing were I to do nothing about it.

And so I began gathering twigs of about pencil-diameters, which I then snapped into "twiglettes" of four-inch lengths, which I then stuck beneath the cord holding up the tipi's inner canvas where the cord wraps around each pole. The theory here—a Sioux theory—hypothesizes that the rain captured on the fly by the protruding pole tips will then trickle unstymied down the poles' undersides and right out the bottom of the tipi again. To this end the twiglettes—two per pole—raise the cord off each pole, thus providing an underpass of sorts for the rain water to trickle beneath. This, of course, is the famous "trickle-down theory", of which you may have heard mention. As to its effectiveness, we will just have to wait and see.

Well, suffice it to say, not minutes after I had finished my weatherproofing task, the clouds unzipped, raining pumas and wolves into the summer-parched earth. As the continent drank its fill and began its muddy metamorphose, I rescued my clackle-clacker and bedroll and sundry provisions, dragging all into the sheltering tipi.

That was an hour ago and here, now, upon my dry bedroll, I lie still; listening to the downpour beating against the canvas, watching the rain trickling down the poles' undersides and out again. So far so good.

It's dark by now, pitch-black, in fact, but every now and again a flash of lightning lights the tipi's canvas like a flashbulb. After each blast of photons the seared images of silhouetted poles and canvas-seams linger on my eyes' rods and cones, leaving in their wake visual scars of purple and green. I'm trying to crawl my way into sleep but each new flash sets my eyes to tumbling within their sockets like slot machine plumbs. Just as someone else might try to count imaginary sheep in order to bore himself to sleep, I try to detect a pattern to the lightning's *cracks* and *bams!*

Is there a pattern? Yes, but just one, and it never repeats itself.

JOURNAL ENTRY; 9 SEPTEMBER 1984:

The heat's on! We're talkin' forest fires, forest fires touched off by nightly lightning storms and prodded by hot and windy afternoons. For the past two days, perhaps three now, smoke has filled the canyon, obscuring the ridges. As of this entry, it's thick enough to hang a coat on. To the north C-131 borate bombers have been flying in pulses since dawn. They pass directly overhead, bank hard, then drop into their stoops and disappear behind the ridge. Being the children of nature that they are, Slim and The California Goldminer took the fire as a sign; a sign that they should conduct a leisurely evacuation from the canyon, cash in their gold, and rent a good drunk.

What do I hope? I hope the winds change and the fire gets away from the fire crews. I hope it comes racing through the canyon. I hope it licks at my bare feet in the middle of the night as I drag the tipi down onto the sandbar, forcing me to dive into the river along with a thousand bears and rattlesnakes. That might quench my current boredom. That might justify my being here.

And the heat's on for another reason as well. This time we're talkin' *federal* heat. This time we're talkin the *Man!* All this week the aforementioned sundry arms of Big Brother—the Placer County Sheriff, California Highway Patrol, Search and Rescue, C.A.M.P., and Army— have been buzzing the canyon, thumbing their noses at my Waldenesque wilderness. Of the lot, the Army's drab olive Hueys seem the most frequent guests, especially one painted with a bright red cross on every available facet (this, I am told, just being a ruse to keep pot growers from taking pot shots at them).

As now seems to be the rule when the threat of a pot bust appears close at hand, The Marijuana Grower is on vacation. It's been a week now. The luck of the Irish. As a result of the mass exodus from the canyon, Bud and I hunker here alone, bearing the tension of the daily helicopter fly-overs as we pull trout from the receding pools of the lazy, late summer river. Ironically, or maybe not, the thought of a pot bust scares me much more than a silly little wildfire, especially since I'm the only one around at which the Man can point a finger, at which the Man can throw the book.

By noon today the smoke had cleared as the formerly brown sky bloomed blue again and the threat of fire passed us by. In celebration Bud and I decided to hike out of the canyon, to replenish supplies for both the stomach and the soul. Prior to our departure, I dipped a bandanna into the spring and tied it around my head to stave off the sun's wrath for the first few minutes of the hike. Then, much to Bud's chagrin and confusion, I forced him to stand in the spring as I splashed the cold water over him until he was thoroughly soaked. That done, we commenced the climb.

A wise man put the Alta General Store where he did: on a hill suitable for bump-starting just about anything with a motor. Jobs are scarce in this neck of the Sierra, so it follows that scarce too are cars with good batteries, plugs and starters. This is why when you pull up to the store here, you'll probably notice that most every car is pointed downhill, towards the railroad tracks. No accident there. I suspect the store's proprietor hasn't a clue that the hill and his store's position on it, is perhaps the single largest factor to his successful enterprise.

The only other imaginable factor contributing to the store's success is the relatively wide cookie selection, occupying a full quarter of the establishment's shelf space. As I stood there, comparing the distinguishing attributes of Chips Ahoy! to those of Fig Newtons, my eldest brother (who had spotted the Cranbrook parked, grill pointing downhill, just outside) entered the store and hurriedly sidled up to me.

"Robert, I got something to tell you," he said, followed by an unnerving tilt of his head that beckoned me to follow him outside. Which I did, just as soon as I had squared with the proprietor a fair exchange for the Fig Newtons and a six-pack of Buckhorn.

Upon exiting the store, my brother promptly directed my attention to the headlines of the local paper, *The Auburn Journal*, just visible behind

Robert P. Johnson

the newspaper box's scratched and yellowing plastic window: "Placer County Declares War on Pot Growers," it read.

"D'ya got a quarter?" I asked my brother.

With a frown he produced one.

"I'll pay ya back," I assured him, as I popped the quarter into the slot and pulled out a paper. I skimmed the article then, unimpressed, turned back to my brother and posited the most profound question I could conjure under the circumstances: "So?"

"So, the word down at the Monte Vista (the local bar) the other night was that there's gonna be a bust in the canyon!" he warned.

"But I'm not growing pot," I tried, yet again and futilely, to assure him.

"Well, the sheriff thinks you are."

"Who told you that?"

"The same person who told me I better warn you—you specifically!"

"But I'm not the only one living down there!" I protested.

My brother soon grew weary of my pleas of innocence. "Listen," he said summarily, "the sheriff knows there's pot down there, he thinks you're the one growing it, and there's gonna be a bust. I have nothing else to say." And with that he walked back to his truck and drove off.

I tore the article from the paper and stuffed it into my shirt pocket, reasonably certain the *real* Marijuana Grower might be interested in it. With that accomplished, Bud and I hopped back into the Cranbrook—yes—bump-started it, and headed back towards the canyon.

It was just after dusk when the Cranbrook's balding retreads again began to claw their way back up the ridge road. And not too far into the windy journey did the backside of The Marijuana Grower appear from around a turn. Bud, hanging three-quarters the way out his window, barked joyously.

"Howdy, Shitferbrains," The Marijuana Grower said, patting Bud's head as we pulled to a stop beside him. "Howdy, Rattlesnake," he added, climbing into the Cranbrook's front seat.

"Welcome back," I said.

"Thanks. Guess what."

"What?"

"I had the ultimate hitchhiker's experience last night."

"You got laid."

"I got laid."

"Gee, that's great."

"No, it was more than great: it was perfect!"

"Gee, that's great."

"She picked me up just outside of Vallejo, just after sundown yesterday. 'I never pick up men hitchhikers,' she says. 'That's what every woman who has ever given me a ride says," I tell her. To which she replies, 'That's what every man I pick up tells me.' And the rest is lovers' history," he concluded with a sigh.

"So, did you guys do it in the car?" I had to ask.

"Nope. In a motel room in Truckee."

"Jesus, you rode up and over Donner Summit with her, forty miles past your exit!" I said, incredulously.

"Well, you've gotta understand, Rattlesnake, by the time she started talking about the affair her husband was having with her best friend, I had a fair inkling where things were going. Not to mention the fact that, being a hundred pounds or more overweight for most of my life, I haven't enjoyed the civilized company of a woman in a long time."

"Still, riding on an inkling past your exit on a sub-freezing night; that's a pretty ballsy move!"

"Thanks," he said, beaming.

"An irrefutable act of Providence, I'd have to conclude."

"I'd have to concur."

As I watched him there, floating in the lingering bliss from the night past, I remembered the rather *un*-Providential newspaper clipping folded in my pocket—the one prognosticating the big pot bust. But, as urgent as the news was, something about his peaceful countenance, back-lighted by the perfect dusk and silhouetted oaks passing beyond his passenger window, prevented me.

Pulling up to the trailhead, we decided it was too dark to begin the hike back into the canyon. We would have to kill a good two hours until the anticipated full moon had a chance to rise over the eastern ridge and ascend high enough to spill its light onto the ridge trail. To pass the time, I drove us on out along a seldom-used logging road to a rather secret vista point located on the far west end of the ridge.

Named, rather unimaginatively, "Lovers Leap"—like most every other cliff in America—this particular one rises an impressively sheer 1,900' above the North Fork of the American River. From its jutting lip-like rock, the queasy spectator is presented with perhaps the best view of the Sierra north of Yosemite's Glacier Point and south of Mt. Lassen. Unfortunately, the cliff also provides an excellent view of Snakehead Point and The Marijuana Grower's crop, which was the first concern he had when he peered down from it.

I tried to keep his mind off of the subject of his crop's relatively high visibility with a lighthearted anecdote. "A friend of mine from Oakland used to come up and stay with us at our family cabin. And even though this guy—his name was Tom—even though he had pretty long hair, my dad always liked him 'cause he was so goddamn funny. Well, once—I think we were in about the seventh grade—that particular attribute of his came in pretty handy when he dropped my dad's binocular case off this very cliff. He and I were laying on this rock just like you and I are now. And what was so weird about it was that I distinctly remember him checking the neck strap before leaning out over the ledge. Nevertheless, as soon as we peered over, there went the binocular case from his neck. He even made a futile last grasp at the strap that I thought was going to take him over the edge with it, but to no avail— the case was gone." I glanced over to The Marijuana Grower, unnaturally quiet as he lay beside me staring down towards his crop.

"You didn't hear a word I said, did you?" I asked him. Confirming my suspicion, he answered with an apparent non sequitur:

"Does the sheriff know about this place?"

I gazed down towards Snakehead Point, glowing softly now in the moonlight. "I suspect so."

At the tipi we were met by Slim. He had heard our Injun whoops; if not from Lovers' Leap, then certainly from the halfway cedar on our hike back into the canyon. He had taken the liberty of lighting my lantern, which enabled us to notice his rather anxious grimace as we trudged into my camp.

"Why the pout, Slim?" The Marijuana Grower asked as we threw off our packs.

"Bad news," Slim began. "They just busted two fellas up in Emigrant Gap with 400 plants. And just next door over in Nevada County, the sheriff gave a judge an airplane ride to show him how easy it is to spot pot from the air. The judge ended up spotting a $1.4 million operation all by his self, and promptly overruled that law about aerial spotting not being probable cause or something like that." Slim paused to spit, then squinted his fatherly, been-to-prison eye straight at The Marijuana Grower, saying finally, "The heat's on. I just come to warn ya." And with that, Slim promptly rose from the table and sauntered away into the darkness, back towards his camp.

The Marijuana Grower silently watched him go, even long after he had disappeared.

"Hey," I said quietly, as I pulled the newspaper clipping I had been keeping from him from my pocket. "I hate to kick a pot grower when he's down, but I think you should know what you're up against."

He took the clipping and began to read it: "Placer County Sheriff Declares War on Pot Growers...." I started a campfire as he read on in silence. When he had finished he muttered a sullen profanity, wadded the clipping in a ball and tossed it into the fire.

"It gets worse than that," I decided to tell him.

"Yeah? How's that?"

"Well, when I was up top, in town today, I bumped into one of my brothers who warned me that someone very close to the sheriff had warned him that a bust down here in Green Valley was, quote, *eminent*."

"So, the sheriff knows."

"I suspect so."

After a minute of silent staring into the fire, The Marijuana Grower lifted his head to gaze up at Snakehead Point. He seemed enervated by the mere thought of returning. Standing, he bade me adieu.

"Adieu, Rattlesnake. I've got to go home and do some serious thinking." That said, he swung his pack containing his wedding clothes over a shoulder and sloshed off through the creek. Before he had completely stepped from the lantern's light he turned to call for his dog.

"C'mon, Bud; that is, if you'll still have me."

Parked there beneath my table, Bud seemed hesitant about leaving my camp. He looked up to me with his big brown eyes begging to stay.

"Go on," I told him, quietly enough so The Marijuana Grower would not hear. And with that, off he moped in the direction of his master.

"Keep me posted," I shouted after them.

"Yeah, yeah," The Marijuana Grower muttered as he slipped off into the darkness.

In another minute, all was quiet as I sat alone there at my table. Pulling out a deck of cards, I shuffled and dealt a hand of solitaire. Before flipping the first card I blew out the lantern, to play by the light of the full moon. I won the game. I always win at solitaire. I must not know how to play.

Moon of the Changing Season

Many men eat,
But Fu Manchu.
— ANONYMOUS

The river is getting pretty cold. It's all because of the cold nights and occasionally rainy days. The sunny days, hot as they still may be, don't seem to be of much help. Because of this recent cold turn, the miners have all been whining about it being about time to pull out of the canyon for the winter. Seems the icy water sliding past their skinny legs is giving them a bad case of the shivers, which in turn is causing their knees to knock together, which in turn is scaring away the fish for miles around, which is just one of the reasons I hope their pull-out date is soon. The main reason, however, remains my yearning to experience, at long last, some of the genuine solitude I had come here seeking nearly five months ago.

The Marijuana Grower has been whining a lot lately as well, but not so much about the cold river as the increasingly rainy days. It seems all the recent moisture is causing the buds on his pot plants to mildew, which, according to him, is a terrible thing. And even though the last storm broke yesterday and another hot, high pressure system is sitting on us like a fat hen, he's threatened to prematurely harvest his crop at the first next hint of rain. Personally, what with the sheriff breathing down his neck, I think he's just looking for an excuse to pull out early.

Ironically, of all of us here in the canyon—all, what, four of us—I'm the only one *not* whining about the weather. I love the mist-bound and dreary days; the hint of threat contained therein. And although I miss the swimming, I certainly don't mind the added challenge the rising river has given to the trout fishing. After all, survival—bona fide wilderness survival—is supposed to be *nip and tuck, touch and go, hand to mouth;* and, frankly, during the summer, it was too damn easy. Bring on the rains! Bring on the snows!

The California Goldminer tumbled back into the canyon this afternoon; a can of Buckhorn beer in one hand, another in a rear pants pocket, and a bottle of Ten-High whiskey in his other hand. I was surprised to see him: having not seen him this past fortnight or so, I had assumed he had already made his pull out. But, no such luck.

"Hey ya, Grattler!" he said, slurring his intended *Rattler.*

"Hey ya, California," I said back. "We all thought you had pulled out."

"Pulled out? What for?" he said, profoundly puzzled.

"Well, 'cause of the recent cold snap."

"Cold snap? What month is it?"

I could have told him any month and he would've believed me. Hell, I could have well *made up* a month—*Augtober, Julyuary*—but what victory would that have been? I decided to change the subject.

"Hey, where's your backpack?"

"My backpack?" he muttered, his brow contorting as he tried himself to remember. He turned back towards the trail, mentally retracing his steps, when suddenly it came to him. "Oh, yeah, I left it up at the fork in the trail—back up a couple hundred yards or so."

"Why?"

"Why?" he muttered, challenged by yet another perplexing conundrum.

"Because you wanted—" I said, trying to bump start his brain.

"Oh, yeah: 'cause I wanted to invite you and Slim and the Pothead and whoever down to the Outlaw Camp for supper!" he answered, proud that he remembered.

"Supper? Great, I'm starving. What's on the menu?"

"Squirrel"

"Squirrel, huh? Well, squirrel's good; at least, that's what I've heard. Did you shoot them yourself?"

"Oh, yeah!" he snickered.

"How many: four, five?"

"Nope, just one."

"Just one? Must be one hefty squirrel if you think it'll feed us all."

"Actually, he's just an itty-bitty feller, as squirrels go. Doubt if he's even a year old." He was snickering again, which was making me suspicious.

"What kind of squirrel?"

"Whadda'ya mean, what kinda squirrel?—a *squirrel* squirrel, dammit! What's it to ya?" he shouted, getting a bit edgy.

"Well, I was just wondering if it was a ground squirrel or a gray squirrel. I've heard ground squirrels can carry bubonic fleas."

ROBERT P. JOHNSON

"What's wrong with fleas? Fleas is good eatin'. Hell, cooked right, I could eat fifty or sixty of 'em! What, you too good for fleas, Rattlesnake?"

Growing weary of his taunting, I walked out to the edge of my terrace to shout up Snakehead Point for The Marijuana Grower. I gave him an Injun whoop first, followed by a cupped-hands shout: "Hey, Shit-fer-brains, dinner at Outlaw Camp. Today's special: squirrel!"

We listened to my words echo up a side ravine then yield to the river's incessant drone.

"Think he heard you?" The California Goldminer asked.

"If he's up there, he heard me. And if he heard me, he'll be down," I assured him. "C'mon, let's head up to the Comfort Zone and fetch Slim."

We might have made it from Slim's camp, The Comfort Zone, back down to The California Goldminer's Outlaw Camp (some three miles downriver) before sundown had not The California Goldminer uncorked his bottle of Ten-High whiskey en route. As a result, Slim and he were fairly drunk before half the trek was over. And, as a result of that, our progress slowed considerably. It deserves mention that this was purely the fault of The California Goldminer and not Slim, for Slim it seems possesses the uncanny ability—a quasi internal gyroscopic device, if you will—which allows him to stay upright and walking at a fast clip regardless of his level of intoxication. And, suffice it to say, The California Goldminer does not.

Approximately a mile shy of our destination, the three of us arrived at a ravine through which bustles one of the more active tributary creeks in all the valley. The erosion caused by the creek is such that the ravine is, in parts, forty feet or more feet deep and very narrow. In order to cross it, the trail crimps itself into a half dozen or so muddy switchbacks to sink into the ravine, then again as many to climb back out the opposite bank.

Slim and I haplessly descended into the ravine and were in the process of crossing the creek when, from somewhere seemingly overhead, we heard The California Goldminer shout out: "Hey, greenhorns, wanna see ol' California pull a rabbit outta his hat?"

Slim and I looked all about for 'Ol' California'—up the ravine, down the ravine, back up the switchbacks, etc.—but nowhere was he to be found.

"Where are you?" I shouted.

"If I pissed you'd know!" he shouted back, from a direction we now discovered to be *straight* overhead.

Slim and I stopped dead in our tracks to tilt our disbelieving eyes skyward. And there, some thirty feet overhead and teetering on a spray-soaked log—as slippery as fish guts on a doorknob and as rotten as a used car salesman's heart—was none other than the hero of this journal entry; Ol' California. The log, it seems, had lost its balance sometime during the F.D. Roosevelt years and fallen in such a manner as to span the two banks of the ravine, thus creating a natural bridge, albeit some twenty degrees off level and, as aforementioned, damn slick.

"Holy shit!" Slim muttered, gazing up at the spectacle of the teetering drunk performing his death-defying feat, atop a slimy log, some three stories above a creekbed of unforgiving boulders. "What the hell you think you're doin', dumbfuck?"

"Hey, hey—lookit me go!" he shouted back, the amazed spectator of his own foolhardiness. "Shit, the Last of the Flyin' Wallendas ain't got nothin' on ol' California!" he added as he took another step forward, paused to spin an arm about wildly for balance, spun an unintentional pirouette, stumbled a couple steps backwards, slipped until he found himself riding the log like a bareback horse, shimmied forward a few shimmies, clambered back to his feet again and shouted vaingloriously, "Take the net away!"

"Get off there, California!" I shouted.

"Yeah, you ain't never gonna make it!" Slim added.

"If you fall, we ain't carrying you out!"

"And if you die we sure as hell ain't burying you!"

If any of our forebodings penetrated his alcohol-moated brain he didn't let on, at least not for the next half minute. "Hey, hey—lookit me, I'm half way across!... again." But then something must have flashed yellow between his ears, for a sudden grimace came to his face that hinted he wanted off that log in a bad way. Assuming the position of a sprinter in the starting blocks, The California Goldminer settled into a fairly stable

ROBERT P. JOHNSON

three-point crouch and then—*bam!*—raced towards the slimy log's far end.

"Think he'll make it?" I asked Slim, as we watched.

Slim pondered the forces working both for and against The California Goldminer, and posited a confident, "Nope."

Like a cartoon character wantonly tossed into an all-too-real world by an unforgiving god, The California Goldminer's scrambling feet propelled him forward at barely a snail's pace. Soon he was three-quarters the way across and, in another few anxious heartbeats, seven-eights, which is where he began to drift off balance.

"Oh oh," Slim muttered, perceiving the goldminer's left-ward listing.

At this point it would have been futile for The California Goldminer to attempt to regain his balance. And perhaps he was aware of this for, to his credit, he stuck with the only force working for him; namely, his momentum towards the log's western end. When it was clear he was off course and the log was of no more help to him, he mustered one last desperate lunge for the ravine's nearly sheer western bank. The effort threw him against a soft clump of pine needles, which held him for a second before letting him slip, feet-first and on his belly, backwards down the steep, muddy wall towards the creekbed below. Instinctually, Slim and I rushed forward, throwing our bodies between the plummeting drunk and the creekbed's jagged rocks.

Seemingly unaware that Slim and I had just put our lives on the line for him, The California Goldminer stood up and immediately began boasting about his feat as he brushed off the pine needles and mud. "Hah, walk in the park. Next time I think I'll throw me in a couple of cartwheels just to make it a tib bit exciting. Hell, Steve Wallenda ain't got nothin' over The California Goldminer!"

Slim and I looked at one another and did about the only thing an audience can do upon witnessing such self-delusion; we rolled our eyes.

By the time I crossed the unofficial property line of The Outlaw camp, I was a good forty yards ahead of Slim and The California Goldminer. From that distance I was only vaguely aware the two were in an argument. As near as I could tell, the debate was over which of them was a *real* goldminer and which was a cheap wannabe. But I couldn't appreciate the seriousness of the brouhaha until The California Goldminer blew past me in a fit of rage, disappeared into his itty-bitty, black plastic hut, then quickly emerged again toting his trusty .22 rifle.

"Where you going with that?" I asked him, as he marched back towards me, en route back to Slim.

"Outta my way, Rattlesnake!" was all he said, cocking his rifle.

As The California Goldminer came at him, Slim unholstered his new .22 calibre six-shooter and aimed it from his hip. At a distance of some twenty yards, the two drunken goldminers squared-off, the muzzle of each firearm pointed resolutely at the other.

"I don't want you packin' your gun into my camp!" The California Goldminer shouted at Slim. "From now on you leave it back at your place!"

"Hell with that: you're always packin' yours up to mine!"

"That's different."

"Why's that different?"

"'Cause I only bring it in case I cross a rattlesnake."

"Me too!"

"Bullshit, I'll bet you dimes to donuts you ain't even got snakeshot loaded in that thing right now, do ya?"

"Well, no. As it so happens, I happen to be loaded up with hollowpoints at the moment. How about you?"

"Well, I happen to have a hollowpoint in here too, but only 'cause I'm temporarily out of snakeshot."

"I smell bullshit!"

"That's 'cause you're standing in it!"

In that I was rather unfortuitously positioned between the two warring titans, I figured it might behoove my own well-being to quell their little spat. "Hey, you two, knock it off!" I shouted, with all the authority I could muster.

"Stay outta this, Rattlesnake!" Slim shouted back, never lifting his squinted eyes off The California Goldminer's.

"Why?" I asked.

"'Cause this is between California and me."

"No, I'm between California and you!" I pointed out.

"Then you best step out of the way."

Heeding Slim's advice, I took a half dozen steps backwards and off

ROBERT P. JOHNSON

the trail. Now that I was out of the direct line of fire I could ponder, with some objectivity, how best to arbitrate the two drunk prospectors' feud.

"Set your gun down against that there tree!" The California Goldminer was yelling at Slim.

"Only if you put yours down first!" Slim yelled back.

"Well, don't hold your breath, 'cause I ain't!"

"Why the hell not?"

"'Cause you ain't got nothin' to worry 'bout, 'cause I ain't gonna shoot ya!"

"Then why're you aimin' at me?"

"'Cause you're aimin' at me!"

"Then set yours down and I'll do the same."

"You first!"

"No, you!"

With the situation's impasse becoming apparent to all, The California Goldminer summoned me to defend his position:

"Hey, Rattler, tell Slim to put his gun down."

I turned towards Slim. "Hey, Slim, put your gun down," I ordered.

"Why?" Slim rather disobediently shouted back.

I relayed the question back to The California Goldminer. "Why?— Slim wants to know."

"Because I say so!" The California Goldminer reiterated.

"Tell him to fuck himself," Slim suggested, rather pointedly.

I might have suggested we sing a chorus of *Give Peace a Chance*, if I thought it would allay the tension between the two friends-cum-enemies. But I really didn't think it would. I opted to try another tact:

"Okay, I've got an idea," I announced.

"We're all ears," Slim grumbled, with a hint of sarcasm.

"All ears with nothin' in between, in Slim's case!" The California Goldminer cut back.

"Now, now, you two: this is how I'm gonna get you out of this mess so we all can go enjoy that measly, flea-ridden squirrel." I had their attention. "Alright, each of you take one big step back."

"Why?" The California Goldminer asked.

"Just do it!"

They did it.

"Now what?" Slim asked, unimpressed.

"Now, take another."

They did.

"Now another..."

They did.

"And another."

After about a dozen such steps away from one another, it was obvious to both that hitting their foe was unlikely.

"Now what?" The California Goldminer shouted.

"Well, now shoot!" I said, quickly adding, "Just kidding," once it was apparent my humorous intent slipped over their heads. "Okay, now, both of you, on the count of three, put your guns down. Ready?"

Neither nodded or said anything, which I took as implicit compliance.

"Alright then: one... two...... three!"

Ever so slowly, Slim holstered his pistol, allowing The California Goldminer to point his rifle skyward and remove his bolt, allowing Slim to remove his gunbelt and set it on a tree stump, allowing The California Goldminer to lean his rifle against a tree.

Rejoicing in the détente, I shouted, "Alrighty now, let's eat!"

It was late, late afternoon by the time we stumbled into camp, with the low sun barely scraping belly against the Sierra's higher ridges. There being no wind, the firs and oaks stood as granite statues of themselves. Why, for the first time in weeks, I couldn't even hear the river's incessant hiss, due to the mile or more that lay between it and the secretive draw wherein hides The California Goldminer's "Outlaw Camp."

"So, where's this squirrel?" I asked, trying to get the meal underway just so we could get it over with, so I could get on my merry way back home.

"Inside. I'll go fetch it," The California Goldminer snickered as he ducked into his itty-bitty, one-roomed, dirt-floored, saggy-roofed-albeit-tightly-walled, stick-framed, 10' by 12', black plastic hut.

"Why'd he snicker?" I quietly asked Slim, as I built a cooking fire.

"I dunno," Slim answered quietly back, before finishing off the last of the Ten-High whiskey and tossing the bottle into the forest.

The California Goldminer emerged from his hut carrying a 25-gallon galvanized tin wash tub. In the tub, and wrapped in a big plastic trash bag, was something big and, judging by his grunts and strained grimace, quite heavy.

"One measly squirrel, comin' right up!" he snickered again, as he set the tub down with an earth-shaking *thud!*

"Must be one trophy squirrel, California," Slim said suspiciously.

"You could say that," The California Goldminer chuckled as he began removing the bag's twist-tie.

The next thing to hit us was the stench of rotting flesh, which took to wing like a flock of flamingoes the moment the bag was opened.

"Phew! What'cha got there, Cal?" I asked, as The California Goldminer peeled away the plastic to reveal a partially-skinned, partially butchered animal carcass.

"Looks like a dog," Slim speculated, not at all put off by the prospect of eating dog meat.

"No!" I winced, "don't tell me you shot a dog!"

"That's alright: dog's good eatin'!" Slim offered.

"It ain't dog!" The California Goldminer insisted, before Slim could make me any more repulsed than I already was.

"Then what the hell is it?"

Right about then, Slim spotted tiny, thimble-sized antlers sprouting from the creature's skull.

"Holy Thimblelina, it's a buck!" he laughed.

"Yep, a two-point Bambi," The California Goldminer averred proudly.

"That's sick!" I said, though they now virtually ignored me.

"How'd ya get him?" Slim asked.

"Well," The California Goldminer began, turning our attention towards a fallen tree lying about fifteen feet from the front (and only) door to his hut, "see that there log?"

"Yep."

"Well, I've been pouring salt water over it for the past several months—"

"Making a salt lick, huh?"

"That's right. And, well, guess it was three, four, five days ago now,

I was snoozin' in my chateau there—middle of the day—when this rustlin' noise from outside come and woke me up. I figured it must've been you, Slim, so I grabbed my rifle."

The California Goldminer then walked over to his hut and opened the door. "Now, see how tight the plastic is stretched over this door? Tight as a drum. When it's stretched that thin you can see right through it."

I decided to check, since he, like every goldminer, is known to stretch the truth. But to my surprise, he wasn't: from the inside of the hut I could see right through the black plastic and out to the salt lick log.

The California Goldminer continued, "So, anyway, just as I was about to burst out of my cabin and give Slim the what-for, I sees Bambi there, right through the door, lickin' at the log!"

My study of the door brought to my attention a tiny hole through the plastic, which I guessed would measure about .22 caliber. Pointing to the hole, I asked, "Did you shoot him through the door?"

"Yep, I did—right through my goddamned livingroom door! One shot—*bam!* Deader than a doornail. Sonuvabuck fell right into the frying pan almost." He then kicked the galvanized tub containing the deer, and said, "Here ya go, Rattler, you're the only one of us sober enough to butcher. Have at it!"

Despite the fact that I had never dressed a deer before, I was glad to accept the chore; partly for the experience, surely, but mostly so I could monitor quality control with my "sober" eye. Using Slim's Buck knife, I began to cut away and toss into the fire the parts of flesh that were obviously rancid. The greatest spoilage seemed to be in the area of the left rib cage. It looked as if this is where the hollowpoint bullet struck then exploded into shrapnel, though The California Goldminer swears he shot it "right 'tween the eyes."

Slim peered over my shoulder, observing the process like a surgical nurse. As I cut away another filet of putrid flesh and tossed it in the fire, he turned towards The California Goldminer and asked, "When did you say you shot this thing?"

The California Goldminer—who had fetched another bottle of Ten High from his hut—sidled up to peer down at the carcass from over my other shoulder. His reply was prefaced by a half minute of stuttering; the kind of stuttering he always does when he's about to lie: "Er, yesterday, wasn't it? Or, maybe—I guess it could've been this mornin'."

"I thought you just hiked in from town," I reminded him.

"That's right."

"Well, we know this thing was down here, sitting in that wash tub and stuffed under your cot the whole time you were gone, right?"

"That's right."

"Well, how long were you up top?—two, three, four days?"

"Jesus, I honestly don't remember."

"So, it could've been a week?" Slim grumbled, snatching the whiskey from The California Goldminer.

The California Goldminer chuckled, "Heck, it could've been a month."

"You stingy sonuvabitch; hoardin' this thing from us, stuffin' your face 'til it got finally too rotten to eat. Why didn't you jerk it out? You know it had to be over a hundred degrees in that piece of shit cabin of yours!"

And that's pretty much how their conversation went, there behind my backside as I continued butchering. I was now dividing the cuts into four piles, differentiated by the perceived quality of the meat. In the Grade-A pile, I placed the portions which I reckoned wouldn't kill us so quickly that we couldn't climb out of the canyon clutching our bellies and screaming for antibiotics. This pile contained, almost exclusively, the backstraps or *filet mignon* cuts—those choice cuts which run down both sides of the spine. In the next-to-the-best pile, I heaped pieces that I thought I might give to Bud in the morning. On the third pile, the stuff I would definitely not eat even if it meant starving, I piled the cuts The California Goldminer smacked his lips and called, "Stew meat." And on the last and largest and most putrid pile, went the cuts destined for cremation; cuts that could choke a maggot. Included onto this pile went the two full forequarters (front legs).

The California Goldminer sucked down the last precious drops from the second pint of whiskey, staggered about there beneath the inverted bottle for a jig, then tossed it into the fire. He belched into Slim's face, point blank. And Slim returned the favor, proving himself to be every bit as drunk as his colleague. Possessed now by the spirit of the spirits, The California Goldminer grabbed one of the deer legs by the hoof and, waving it tauntingly before Slim's face, made the challenge: "I's a gold-miner. Is *you*?"

Slim answered the challenge with bravery the likes of which this canyon had never before witnessed: he bit into the rotten leg like a pit-bull after a mail carrier, ripping off a quarter-pound chunk which he then chewed down without so much as using a hand or taking his smirking grin off The California Goldminer.

After he had masticated and swallowed, Slim grabbed the other leg quarter from the table, waved it tauntingly at The California Goldminer, and returned the challenge: "Hell yeah, I's a goldminer. Is *you*?"

To his credit, the home team challenger bested Slim's effort by biting off a liver-sized chuck of a particularly greenish hue, then chewed it with a sneering eye as wry as a set of socket wrenches.

Before The California Goldminer had quite finished chewing his piece, he stuck the other leg back into Slim's face to commence Round Two. Slim accepted this second challenge with the same prowess as before. With a savage bite and yank of his head, he ripped off another, slightly bigger chunk and, while it still dangled from his teeth, shoved the leg he held back into The California Goldminer's face. The latter responded by quickly gulping down what he hadn't quite chewed from the first round, and quickly threw his incisors towards another. Together now, sneering into one anothers eyes while nearly touching noses, the two super heroes gnawed down their second helpings, each mustering countenances that tried to convince the other he was actual-ly enjoying the experience. And as curdled globs of buck's blood hung like blueberry jelly in the beards of the two, now indisputable, gold-miners, I began to suspect that the solitude for which I had so long ached might be arriving now sooner than expected.

I melted a pound of bacon grease in two large skillets and in these fried the filleted medallions of the backstrap. I simultaneously diced and cooked the "stew meat" as such in a deep, two-gallon pot, throw-ing good money after bad (or, at very least, good *food* after bad) by adding a few carrots and onions to the vile concoction. Once I was con-fident the filets had cooked thoroughly, I fished three out with a fork and distributed one to each of us. It took a bit of juggling before the filets were cool enough to eat (let alone to hold), but soon they were, so

ROBERT P. JOHNSON

soon we did.

At this point I feel compelled to admit that, in spite of all my whining, the venison was as tender and tasty as any meat I had ever experienced. As we ate and ate some more, The California Goldminer began gloating over the irony that we three—so destitute souls—should be enjoying such a sublime feast. Every once in a while, just to underscore the irony, he would spit out a perfectly splendid piece just to give himself the opportunity to complain that the portion hadn't melted in his mouth as it should have, and may have even, God forbid, required actual mastication.

I had probably eaten a half-dozen of the filets, and listened to The California Goldminer's hundredth retelling of his shooting of the Bambi-buck, before I decided I had had my fill. Standing from my place before the campfire, I bade my neighbors goodnight:

"Goodnight, fellas. Thanks for the 'squirrel' dinner."

"You're welcome, Rattler. Come back tomorrow for the stew."

"Thanks just the same," I said, walking off backwards into the night. "Oh, and I surely hope you resolve the small matter of which of you is the real goldminer and which is the worthless scumbag. Remember, your guns are down there on the stump and leaning against the cedar there."

"Thanks for reminding us, Rattlesnake," Slim said unconvincingly.

 I shrugged, "What're neighbors for?"

Turning away from the light of the fire, I began to feel my way back up the river trail and home to my tipi; through the embracing forest and across the ravine, through the howls of the crickets and coyotes, through the warm belches of whiskey and venison, through the pitch blackness of the new moon.

JOURNAL ENTRY; 1 OCTOBER 1984:

The weather has taken quite a turn for the colder these past few nights. These past seven to be precise. It began September 24th; that was the date of our first frost. That was also the date, perhaps not coincidentally, my tomatoes all turned brown and all my leafy green vegetables all wilted. All except the broccoli, that is. Broccoli seems to thrive in this shit.

This cold spell has gotten me quite concerned about the coming winter; my garden's productivity aside. In the middle of the night of the 24th I awoke, here in the tipi, shivering cold. I tried opening the tipi's smoke flaps and starting a fire, but once the fire died I was shivering again. I then donned my thermal underwear, wool socks and cap, but still somehow could not get warm. The next effort involved crawling into the, as yet unused, mummybag I had purchased expressly for the coldest nights of winter. But though the tag assured me that the bag's synthetic loft would keep me toasty-warm down to "-15ºF", I was still shivering. My last-resort step was obvious: after re-stoking the fire, I then stuffed my winter sleepingbag into my lighter weight summer bag, and crawled therein fully clothed. And though this worked just fine, rendering me all warm and snugly, I could not help but feel a wee bit anxious over the fact that this was but the second day of autumn: what would the dark heart of winter have in store?

This cold snap has changed my daily routine. Now, instead of Ben Franklin's *early to bed, early to rise* school of health and wealth and wisdom, I find myself staying up as late as possible—tapping away at my piece-o-shit novel or reading someone else's, by kerosene lantern and campfire light herein the tipi—in an attempt to become more of a late-riser type. And when I finally do awake, I make certain to wait until the sun has risen high enough over the south-eastern ridge to massage its warming balm into the tipi's frostbitten canvas before I poke my head out of the tipi's door—a proper birth—and begin my day.

Today, for the seventh day in a row, I promptly dressed, grabbed my bowsaw, and went off in search of firewood. Some long-dormant instinct tells me to do this: as much out of precaution probably as by the fact that "wood warms you twice."

JOURNAL ENTRY; 10 OCTOBER 1984:

I should have known my old pal Jae would soon be tumbling back into the canyon for a visit. I should have known this because I had just caught a $14\,1/2$" rainbow trout the day before, which nudged me into the lead—by a whopping $1/4$"—in the 'biggest fish' category of our ever-ongoing, ever-nebulous North Fork Trout Derby. Have I mentioned this phenomenon before?—Jae's uncanny ability to pop in from out of the blue just days after I had finally, after weeks or even months of effort, *finally* managed to land a trout a wee bit bigger than the last one he caught, only to have him top my effort by a significantly larger measure during his brief stay? Perhaps I didn't. And perhaps I shouldn't now. Denial is a healthy thing for fishermen. Regardless, because of that aforementioned uncanny ability/timing of his, I wasn't a bit surprised when he showed up at the bottom of the ridge trail today. Nor was I a bit surprised as I stood there on the river bank beside him and watched my derby 'big fish' category lead be eclipsed with one accidental cast.

"I just want to wash off this last grasshopper from my hook, just so it doesn't dry there over the winter," is how he phrased it as he wandered back down to the pool we had just fished clean. I was already out of grasshoppers, and had my hook hooked around one of my rod's eyelets. For the record, he too was out of grasshoppers but for the last soggy remnants of one, still dangling from his otherwise bare hook like a green snot.

I shook my head as he let his line be carried down the feeder rapids. "Waste of time, ol' buddy," I assured him.

"I know but—" he began to say when, suddenly, the tip of his fishing pole bent violently towards the water. "Hey, I think I had a strike!"

"Probably just a snag," my fishing wisdom felt compelled to share.

"Wait—it's still on the line!" he shouted, getting all excited.

"Yep, you're probably snagged between two rocks. Better cut your line."

"This ain't no snag: it's flopping around like mad!"

"A submerged branch then, bending in the current. Go on, cut your line so we can get on with our lives," I offered anew, turning again for the tipi.

But Jae would have none of my selfless advice: he just kept cranking at his spinning reel, slowly but surely.

"See that?—something flashed!" he shouted.

I turned about and strolled back down to the riverbank, peering over his shoulder down into the soda pop fizzes where the rapids poured into the pool. Together we tried to follow his fishing line as it sliced this way and that in the deep, bubbly-blue water. And then, sure enough, somewhere some four or five feet below the surface, flashed the white belly of something big.

"Aw, Jae, you hooked a carp; and probably by the tail. Best just to cut your line and leave it be," I tried again, this time giving him a paternal, *Bob knows best* pat on the shoulder.

"Carps have yellow bellies. This one's is pure white!"

He was right of course. But that was still no reason to give up my biggest fish category lead without a fight.

"Even worse then; it's probably a sucker. Better cut that line before it's too late!"

"I don't think so, Bob, carp and suckers don't have this kind of perseverance."

Again, of course, his reasoning was sound: those aforementioned trash fish tire quickly, whereas this thing was fighting him like the Devil himself.

"Maybe you hooked the Devil, Jae. How much line did you let out?"

Ever so slowly, Jae reeled the fish as close to the bank as the brush growing at the pool's water line allowed, then began hoisting it methodically over the obstructions.

"It ain't a rainbow, that's for sure," he said, as he landed the writhing fish.

"That's for damn sure!" I said, clubbing the fish over the head with a handy stick, then hoisting it to eye level. Indeed, it was a trout: but what type?

"What do you think: German Brown?" he asked.

"Either that or a Cutthroat."

"Yeah, look at that jaw: probably a Cutthroat."

"Either way, it's definitely not a Rainbow, wouldn't you agree?"

"Yep, definitely not a Rainbow."

"Too bad," I said, shaking my head.

"Why is that too bad?"

"Only because Cutthroats can't be included in the North Fork Trout Derby."

"Why the hell not?" he asked, growing a bit testy.

"For the same reason browns and carp and suckers can't; they're not rainbows!" I explained.

ROBERT P. JOHNSON

"So? Who said they had to be rainbows? I thought this was a *trout* derby?!"

"Nope: it's a *rainbow* trout derby."

"What a crock of shit!"

"Yeah, well, sorry, old buddy. But those are the rules."

When our feet had carried us back to the tipi, Jae immediately pulled down the cribbage board from its hang nail on the three-trunk cedar. It wasn't that he had a sudden hankering to play cribbage; rather, we knew the cribbage board to be exactly 14" long, and thus it had become (some months and hundreds of trout before) the North Fork *Rainbow* Trout Derby's official ruler. Laying the cribbage board down flat, and then the cutthroat over it, the fat beast smothered the board—besting all its dimensions. To adequately measure the surplus, Jae evened the fish's tail with one end of the board, and then picked up a playing card, explaining:

"Well, we know that a standard playing card is 2 1/4" wide."

"How do we know that?" I asked, still not yielding.

"Trust me on that one, Bob," he beseeched.

He then slipped the playing card under the cutthroat's protruding head, accommodating all but the last 1/4" or so of the fish's nose.

"There ya go, Bob—16 1/2". You have until May of next year (my proposed pull-out date) to top that," he beamed.

"Careful, Jae, hubris did in the Greeks, ya know."

Jae ignored my warning. "Six and a half months, Bob. Good luck."

Since we had nine fish between us to eat that evening, we decided to invite The Marijuana Grower to dinner. This invitation wasn't exactly planned; rather, it was merely *extended* to him when he happened to stroll into camp just as the meal preparations were getting underway.

"What a stroke of luck you came to visit!" Jae naïvely exclaimed, unaware of just how often The Marijuana Grower just happens to happen through my camp at dinner time.

"Why, what's for dinner?" The Marijuana Grower asked, already poking around in the pots and skillet.

As is often the routine, we began cooking an hour or so before dusk so we wouldn't have to dine in the dark. This timing afforded us the opportunity to lay out on the soft grass terrace, sipping beers and shooting the breeze, as the rice and fish simmered to perfection, and the last few minutes of daylight crept up the westward-facing hills and ridges. It was right then that The Marijuana Grower suddenly contorted as he spotted something in the northeast.

"Look!" he shouted, pointing in that direction.

Jae and I traced his point, pushing our line of sight up a twenty degree incline to the middle of a steep hillside a little over a mile away. The object of his interest was obvious: a pure black rectangle on an otherwise brightly sun-lit hillside.

"What do you suppose it is; a cave?" Jae asked.

"More likely a mine; it looks manmade," The Marijuana Grower replied before directing the next question to me: "Strike you as a bit odd, Rattlesnake?"

"Certainly does!" I averred, equally as amazed at the sight as he.

"I don't get it: there are mines all over this canyon, what's so surprising about there being one up there?" Jae asked, clearly not sharing our amazement.

"Only the fact that Rattlesnake and I have probably gazed up at that very hillside a thousand times over the past six months without, somehow, ever noticing it before!" The Marijuana Grower explained in a huff.

"So, what's the big deal: you obviously over-looked it!" Jae posited.

"Jae, we didn't *over-looked* it," I tried to assure him.

"You must have. What else could explain it?"

"Perhaps just the nature of that particular hill," The Marijuana Grower suggested cryptically.

Jae frowned. "Just the nature of that particular hill: what the hell're you talking about?"

"You haven't told him, Rattlesnake?" The Marijuana Grower asked.

I shook my head.

"Told me what?" Jae asked, waxing impatient.

"Well, Jae, that hill just so happens to be what many people call 'The Temple of the Moon'," I explained.

"Okay, so?"

"Well, so, it also just so happens to be where many people think Eros's Pyramid is buried."

"Oh no, not this pyramid mumbo-jumbo again!" Jae groaned.

To say that Jae did not share the same belief in the pyramid legend as The Marijuana Grower and I is about as gross an understatement one could make. But he was kind: he only laughed and pointed at us and slapped his knee for about five minutes, before he settled down enough to ask: "And let me guess, this mine shaft opening isn't a mine at all, but rather some sort of secret entrance tunnel into the pyramid which has only just today decided to reveal itself?"

"Well, it certainly stands to reason," The Marijuana Grower replied.

Jae erupted in another guffaw before settling enough to ask: "Yeah? Why's that?"

"Because tonight's a full moon," I tried to explain.

"And not just any full moon; the harvest full moon!" The Marijuana Grower added.

"I don't mean to sound skeptical but, what the fuck does the moon have to do with some dime-a-dozen, piece-o-shit hill that some fuzzheads happen to call The Temple of the Moon?"

"I dunno, it just seems so... *logical!*" The Marijuana Grower replied.

Jae shook his head in genuine pity: "You guys have been in the woods too long."

Indeed, Jae had a point. But, then again, so did The Marijuana Grower. For what else could explain our not seeing the entrance tunnel before tonight? One could no more easily not see a sixth finger grow out of one of his hands. And yet, there it was; all black and perfectly rectangular—as plain as day. There seemed just one thing to do:

"So, what should we pack along?" I asked.

"Let's see... We'll certainly need your lantern and flashlight," The Marijuana Grower began, glancing about my camp. "And a pick and a couple of shovels. Those we can grab from my sandbar on the way there."

"You guys aren't thinking about exploring that tunnel entrance thing now, are you?" Jae asked incredulously, as he flipped the fish in their skillet.

"Well, yeah!" The Marijuana Grower and I answered in unison, with just as much incredulity.

"I mean, it's not like an opportunity like this presents itself very often," I added.

"But dinner's ready! Just take a look at these trout," Jae said, shaking the skillet under The Marijuana Grower's nose. "They're at their culinary perfection!"

The Marijuana Grower began to drool. "You know, Jae's got a point: haste makes waste, Rattlesnake. Let us dine now, and explore the pyramid after dinner. We may need the energy."

"But it'll be dark by then!" I argued.

"I doubt that it would matter much whether we explored it at midnight or high noon, given the subterranean nature of caves," he retorted, already lifting one of the medium-sized trout onto his plate.

I pondered his reasoning. "Sound logic. Let's eat."

I baked some cornbread over the fire in my dutch oven. This slathered with honey and the butter Jae had packed down, made the perfect complement to the trout feast. The Marijuana Grower and I split the eight normal-sized trout between us, leaving Jae with the formidable task of consuming his monster cutthroat. Which, he managed to do. What with the crickets' chirpings, the river's hissing, and the fire's snap, crackle, and poppings, there wasn't much silence to fill with idle chit-chat. Thus, when Jae felt the need to speak, we knew it must be important.

"Okay, supposing there is indeed an entrance tunnel up there, and supposing it does indeed lead into a pyramid," Jae began, protecting his skepticism with a barrage of disclaimers, "what do you guys intend to do once you get inside?"

Still chewing our comestibles, The Marijuana Grower and I turned towards one another and rolled our eyes, incredulous at Jae's naiveté.

"Loot it!" we answered in unison, as if it was the obvious course of action.

"So, you're not planning to notify some bona fide experts, say, The National Geographic Society or some University of California archeology department, in order to let them handle the potentially historic excavation?"

ROBERT P. JOHNSON

We shook our heads, "Not until we're done looting it!"

The Marijuana Grower felt obliged to elaborate, "Listen, we're not greedy. Once we've looted it and cleaned our tracks, and pawned the gems and gold ingots and silver effigies and what have you, and chipped into the walls some of our own meaningless hieroglyphics—you know, to give them some thing to scratch their heads about—then, hell yeah, we'll give some bozo professor/archeologist a call and let him take credit for the discovery of the century. Like I said, we're not greedy."

"I see," Jae said sadly. "But aren't you guys worried about the horrible curses and hexes that may be protecting this pyramid?"

"Oh, Jae, this is no time to get superstitious on us!"

We managed to stretch dinner well into the evening, if only to allow the full moon to rise high enough into the sky to assist our ascent up The Temple of the Moon. The first course of fish and cornbread, was followed by another of chocolate and beer, followed ultimately by a three-handed game of cribbage (despite the fact of the board smelling rather fishy). But sometime during the second cribbage game a weather front began edging overhead from out of the southwest. Soon the firmament above the canyon became congested with black-bellied clouds, like bumper-to-bumper blimps pushing homeward through rush hour skies. And, by the time we had finished our third game, the many clouds had merged into one black slab, obscuring any hope of the moonlight assisted ascent.

"I reckon we'll have to postpone the expedition," The Marijuana Grower said, frowning up at the black sky. "For a few days, at least."

"What are you talking about? We just use lanterns and flashlights to get us there!" I argued.

"That ain't the problem," he sighed, sniffing the air.

"What's the problem?" Jae asked.

"It's gonna rain."

Thoroughly puzzled, Jae looked towards me then, after getting only a shrug, turned back towards The Marijuana Grower. "Yeah, so?"

"So, my plants will get soaked. Which normally is a good thing except that, this late in the season, they'll probably never get a chance to dry out again."

"Which means he runs the risk of losing them to mildew unless he can harvest all twenty-seven before it starts," I added.

"Oh. Well, given the choice between twenty-seven measly pot plants and a pyramid stuffed full of priceless treasures, I can understand his decision," Jae added, winning the last dig.

The Marijuana Grower was holding out his palm. "It's drizzling," he sighed, climbing to his feet. "Thanks for dinner." And with that, he turned and headed off up the river trail, bound for the Mercury Pool crossing, then on up Snakehead Point to begin his hasty harvest, befittingly on the advent of the Harvest Moon.

Soon, and long before he reached his camp atop Snakehead Point, the sky's belly ripped open and began pouring rain onto the Sierra Nevada. From inside our dry sleeping bags, tucked safely beyond the rain's molestation, Jae and I imagined The Marijuana Grower's disposition as he hastily uprooted one premature and virtually worthless plant after the next, pushing on until dawn, up and down that muddy hillside, the dim beam of his flashlight wagging out there before him like the wandering eye of a locomotive. We knew it must be hell, and yet, we knew he must be loving it.

JOURNAL ENTRY; 26 OCTOBER 1984:

A wasp crawled into my sleepingbag with me last night. At first I thought it must have been a ladybug, or any one of the myriad other insects which seem to have had no trouble adapting from their previous state of absolute wilderness to the relative civilization of my tipi—box elders, spiders, potato bugs, pine beetles, and such. But it wasn't. This I discovered once I had finally shaken my rather sovereign-willed flashlight enough to coax it out of a few photons. And there, caught as if by a lone spotlight on an otherwise dark stage, was the above-mentioned wasp; seemingly annoyed by the stark light which exposed him as he was trying to bed down between my legs. And that was all my flashlight would show me before it decided to shut down again for good: just that one horrifying glimpse! This left me no choice but to thrash blindly at the wasp, with fists and flashlight, until I felt the satisfying

ROBERT P. JOHNSON

crunch of its shell; the self-mutilation rendering me, at least, un-stung.

All this occurred sometime around 3 a.m. this morning, although, having no clock or watch with me, I'm only guessing. Once I had extracted the wasp's corpse from my sleepingbag, and the adrenaline coursing through my heart was re-absorbed by my sense of well-being, I became aware of the gentle *pat-a-tap-patter* of rain against the tipi's canvas. This caused me to smile because it would likely force another postponement of the exploration of The Temple of the Moon's entrance tunnel and the, *a-hem*, undiscovered pyramid awaiting therein. Yes, for two weeks now, The Marijuana Grower and I have managed to find some excuse for not bushwhacking our way up to that perfectly rectangular "mine entrance" spotted back that dusk on the Harvest Moon. And half the time rain had been our excuse; hence, it stood to reason, rain again would force another postponement.

"Get up, you lazy shithead," came the call to reveille, via The Marijuana Grower.

"But it's dark still!" I protested.

"It'll be light soon."

"But it's raining!"

"It's *drizzling*."

"But why do today what we can put off until tomorrow?—it seems such a compromise of our ethics."

"Because today's my last day in the canyon," he divulged, with some remorse evident in his voice, as he snapped kindling to re-stoke the campfire in order to put on a pot of cowboy coffee.

"Your last day, huh?"

"That's right. Now, drag your ass outta bed, we've got a pyramid to loot!"

It was just getting light as we chewed down the last of our wake-me-up cups of coffee.

"Let's go."

"It's still drizzling."

"Let's go!"

We hiked up the river trail, past The Comfort Zone (vacant since Slim's pull-out some two weeks ago), and on upstream to a long-abandoned, nineteenth century mining camp, tucked up in the far eastern end of the valley. From there we veered north, away from the river, following a dry creekbed which promised to lead us up onto the saddle connecting The Temple of the Moon with the much higher northern ridge. And the plan was a good one, if not for the fact that, after two hundred yards or so, the creekbed hadn't disappeared, leaving us little choice but to then follow deer trails which seemed to be heading in our general direction and then, after the deer trails disappeared, to follow what seemed, at best, to be mice trails. Thus, as with most of our thoroughly humiliating endeavors, The Marijuana Grower and I soon found ourselves crawling on our bellies up the steep, muddy hillside—through manzanita, buckbrush, chinquapin, and poison oak—like a couple of clueless ticks.

"Get your boot out of my ear!"

"Hold on, I need the foothold."

It was probably noon by the time we reached the saddle, meaning we had spent close to five hours clawing our circuitous way to a point that was no more than two *as-the-crow-flies* miles from the tipi. To complete our ascent, we changed to a due-south course, and followed the saddle ridge a half a mile more and up the gentle slope to the very top of The Temple of the Moon. Within a hundred feet of the summit, The Marijuana Grower paused mid-stride. Leading the expedition at the time, I turned back towards him to see why he had stopped. There—looking, but not with his eyes; listening, but not with his ears—he pivoted himself through a patient 360° turn, not unlike one of those slowly rotating radar antennae mounted a top an aircraft carrier.

"What's up?" I shouted back to him.

After some thirty seconds more, he deigned to reply, "Do you feel it?"

"Which; the rain or the cold?" I retorted, facetiously.

"You don't feel it, do you?"

Because there was a hint of disappointment in his voice I decided I would try to feel "it." I paused, tried to clear my mind of distracting thoughts, and then tried my best to open my awareness to anything that might be knocking on the door of my senses.... But nothing seeped through.

"Nope; don't *feel* a thing," I admitted.

ROBERT P. JOHNSON

"Figures."

His reply struck me as uncharacteristically smug.

"Whatever," I muttered, resuming my march for the summit.

He lowered his arms and followed.

At the peak of The Temple of the Moon, an escarpment of rock pushes skyward like a crewcut. The northeast side of the hill slopes gently from the peak for fifty meters before dropping into a near-sheer stoop for the river. The other three sides of the pyramidal-shaped hill are more consistently sloped, their eroded facets maintaining an approximate fifty percent pitch from top to bottom. The Marijuana Grower and I took seats on the rocky peak, from where we were afforded yet another breathtaking view of our river valley. The 1,200 vertical feet down to the river made the sections of rapids between the long, green pools appear motionless. Wisps of wet, heavy clouds seemed to have snagged on the lush firs and madrones carpeting the canyon walls. The noontime sky was black. The air was perfectly still. A motionless twist of smoke rose from the tipi a few hundred feet into the misty sky like a thin, white ribbon. Indeed, so tranquil was the scene that it took the occasional leaf falling through the otherwise utter stillness, to remind us this was not some huge still-life landscape into which we had been painted.

From there upon the summit of The Temple of the Moon, The Marijuana Grower and I could both agree that our next step was to edge our way roughly one-third the way down the hill's west face in order to get into the general vicinity of the tunnel entrance. What we could *not* agree upon, however, was the small matter of which way was, indeed, west. Suffice it to say, a dispute arose which sent us each scurrying off in different directions; he, I'm convinced, down the southern slope; me, he was convinced, down the northern one.

Our daypacks were stuffed full of tools; all the sorts of things upon which thorough excavations depend: two rather undependable flashlights; two shovels, one a rusty square-point, the other the handleless round-point; an ax with a broken, albeit duct-taped handle; two candles; no matches; and, at least one truly useful item, a heavy duty, battery-powered lantern, which may well have come in handy had I not dropped it off a 15' ledge in my descent. After free climbing my way down to the smashed lantern, I found myself trapped on a narrow ledge which, without a rope, was impassable due to the sheer 30' drop beyond it. Compounding my woes was a steamy pile of bear scat; warm enough still to suggest that the bear had been here probably not more than thirty minutes before. In all likelihood, the commotion of our bushwhacking had scared it off. Still, there was an outside chance that it was still around; even a chance that it had taken refuge in the very tunnel entrance for which we were searching. Such were the matters begging for my concern when I heard The Marijuana Grower shout to me:

"Did you find it?" he called out, probably from more than a hundred meters away, through brush and around a bend in the hill's topography.

"You found it?" I shouted back excitedly, having not heard him as well as I thought.

He then sounded an equally excited Injun whoop, meaning, of course, that he thought I had found it, but misleading me into thinking, of course, that *he* had.

I returned the Injun whoop and promptly began bushwhacking a traverse in his general direction. And, of course, he was doing the same. At the approximate halfway point, we met.

"Where is it?"

"Quit kiddin' around: you found it, right?"

"No, I thought you had!"

"Hell no, I thought *you* had!"

"Well, shit on me!"

"Well, shit on us both!"

The Marijuana Grower sighed as he settled into a saddle-shaped root, emanating from a squat oak clinging desperately to the hillside. For lack of another so comfortable a seat, I had to be content with a good boothold, which then allowed me to lean against the rocky slope. By then it was somewhere near 4 p.m., which meant it was also somewhere near dusk, owing to the shortened days of autumn. This as well meant that we had only another thirty minutes of daylight; either to use in efficacious search for the tunnel entrance, or else to squander here on our lazy asses. We chose the latter.

"I don't get it," The Marijuana Grower whined, pointing down the river valley towards my tipi, "everything lines up: the tipi, that dead Douglas Fir, this rock outcropping—the tunnel entrance should be right here!"

I nodded, shaking my head at the same time.

"Are you sure you couldn't have missed it in your search?" he pressed.

"I scoured every square inch," I assured him. "What about you?"

"Ditto."

"Well, how d'ya like that," I sighed.

We sat through the next half hour in somber silence. I suspect it was especially disheartening for The Marijuana Grower since this had been his last realistic hope at discovering—and, of course, looting—Eros's pyramid. For me there was still time; six and more lonely months' worth. But for him it was now or never.

Far into the west we could see the end of the bank of black clouds that had been squeezing rain upon us all this past week. Beyond the clouds a strip of clear, blue sky cleaved to the horizon like a thin peel: apparently a high pressure system was pushing inland from somewhere over the Pacific. In the next minute, the rump of the sun slid down from behind the bank of clouds and into the thin strip of blue skies, anointing the hillside with a few glorious minutes of its direct and golden light.

The cliff—though not perfectly sheer, but steep just the same—extended some seventy-five meters to either side of us. Similarly, it extended some fifteen meters both above and below us, meaning that we were sitting pretty much smack-dab in the middle of its face. As we allowed those last few rays of sunlight to dry our muddy clothes, I happened to glance to our left, some twenty meters, where a large rock shard jutted out from the rest of the cliff like a pointy nose; a nose of about the same dimensions of Cyrano de Bergerac's were he to be carved into Mount Rushmore amongst the presidents.

"Hey, look at that," I said, directing The Marijuana Grower's attention towards the jutting rock, "doesn't it look like a nose?"

Despite his sullen mood, he managed a smile and a nod.

"The way it juts straight from out of the cliff face, you'd never notice it from my camp," I added somewhat mindlessly.

And that was about when it struck us. Our stupid smiles fled our faces, replaced by grimaces prognosticating the end of an obsessive mystery. Hastily, wordlessly, we scrambled our way across the cliff face until we stood just beneath the jutting nose rock, or, more specifically, *in its shadow!*

"Well, Rattlesnake, my dear friend, once again, we've been duped," The Marijuana Grower sighed.

And right he was, for almost from the moment we stood in the jutting rock's shadow, and turned to the west again to check the alignment—the cliff face, the dead Douglas Fir, the tipi—was it obvious that our "perfectly rectangular tunnel entrance" was nothing more than a shadow cast by the rock, made visible only recently by the sun's southward drift towards the autumnal equinox. And with what seemed to be the proverbial last straw laying across our broken backs, the mystery of Eros's pyramid was beginning to clear: there was no pyramid. It was but a myth. A legend. Impossible to prove, but, regrettably, impossible to *disprove* as well.

"Ever wonder what a trout feels like the moment he bites into a fishing lure?" The Marijuana Grower asked, staring from our *faux* pyramid entrance, on out to the crimson, setting sun.

"Not any more," I replied.

By the time we reached Slim's abandoned Comfort Zone, it was quite dark and raining again. Apparently the passing storm still had some spunk in it. I stoked up the hut's rusted-out woodstove while The Marijuana Grower stuffed his entire harvest into two five-gallon plastic buckets. Since the date of his harvest, The Marijuana Grower had requisitioned the black plastic hut for the drying of his pitiful crop. After hanging upside-down from the rafters for nearly two weeks, some of the buds had dried reasonably well. The majority, however, had mildewed their value away. Of the five pounds of total harvest, he had maybe two of high enough quality to sell, meaning his seven months of ulcers, headaches and nigh-heart attacks might net him all of $5,000.

"I might be able to foist some of this crap off, a joint at a time," The Marijuana Grower lamented, as he snapped the lid closed on the bucket containing the mildewed pot, then turned and sat upon it.

I cooked us up some Bisquick bread but, contrary to his nature, The Marijuana Grower didn't eat a bite. He just sat there, staring silently at the fire through the rusted-through holes in the woodstove.

"Are you nervous about hiking out with all that pot?" I asked, exploring his mood.

He shrugged. "Yeah, sure, I guess. I mean, shit, I'll only be trying to hitchhike all the way down to fuckin' Santa Cruz while toting enough fuckin' contraband to land me in fuckin' Folsom Prison for twenty ass-fuckin' years! I guess *nervous* is the appropriate adjective."

"C'mon, what's *really* bugging you?" I asked, half in jest.

To my surprise, he had a sincere answer: "I'm a failure."

"Why, just because you didn't find the pyramid?"

"No—fuck no. The pyramid doesn't have shit to do with it!"

"Why then, 'cause of your meager harvest?"

"No. If I had come down here for the express goal of growing pot, then maybe that would be the reason. But that wasn't why I came," he said, almost snapping with self-hatred.

"Why'd you come?"

He glared at me.

"Sorry: it seemed like the obvious next question," I explained.

He turned back towards the woodstove, and the dozen or so quills of fire light that emanated from it through the smoky darkness.

"I came here, primarily, in order to change. But I didn't. The same fuckin', selfish, idiot, slob/derelict who tumbled into this canyon seven months ago will be climbing out again tonight."

Though I had no idea he had come to the canyon with any such noble intent, I knew exactly how he felt. For I too had dragged myself hither into the wilderness, not to fish, not to write a book, not to solve the mystery of the pyramid, or accomplish any such banal goal, but, rather, to try to perfect myself, to try to forge myself into someone I could bear to look at in the mirror—to try to *change*. And yet, was this possible? Was it prudent? Here he had come, and tried and failed: was it likely that I— now six months into my proposed year-long stay—am just halfway along to a similar failure? Or one even more profound? Clearly I wasn't halfway better: that much was obvious. So, am I too regressing, de-evolving? If so, then perhaps there is something to be gleaned from The Marijuana Grower's failure: perhaps I am going about this amelioration process ass-backwards. Certainly we've heard the Zen masters say it all before: that the final obstacle to enlightenment is the very desire for enlightenment. Perhaps then, I should forget about trying to perfect myself. To make perfect: what the fuck does that mean anyway? Ours is a relative universe, whereas perfection is an absolute—existing only in the imagination, or in Heaven, but surely not here on Earth! So, perhaps then, my remaining six months might be better spent *not* trying to become perfect. That's not to say my new goal should be *im*perfection; but rather that I should try instead just to accept myself as I am—imperfections, foibles, insecurities, and all. If so, if possible, oh, what a treasure that would be; worth more, I dare say, than all the treasures we could have even hoped to have looted from Eros's Pyramid!

The patter of rain against the plastic roof lightened.

"Time to go," The Marijuana Grower said.

In a gesture of goodwill, I donned his backpack, stuffed with everything he owned. It did not weigh much. This I would carry until our trails parted forever at my tipi.

"Thanks," he said. He then handed me two other five-gallon buckets, saying, "Might as well put your arms to use."

"What's in these, more pot?" I asked, weighing the additional buckets.

"Nope. One contains Bud's dogfood. The other some things I thought you could put to use."

"Lolita!" I shuddered fearfully.

"No. Like every other woman in my life, Lolita left me."

"Dragged off by ants?"

He shrugged, "Either that or a gust of wind."

"Oh, well, it's probably for the best. I never thought it would work out between you two. She was just too—"

"Good for me?"

"Quiet."

"Yes," he said, a tear almost forming in his eye. "Anyway, that's not what's in the bucket," he added, as he stood. He then picked up the two buckets of pot and, turning towards the door, said, "Let's hit it."

I closed the door of the woodstove with my foot, then followed The Marijuana Grower and his faithful dog, Bud, past the wet blanket that served as the sad hut's door, and out into the dark drizzle.

"I need to ask a favor of you," The Marijuana Grower began, as we

ROBERT P. JOHNSON

hiked—me in front of him, he carrying a kerosene lantern and his buck-ets of pot—the dark river trail from The Comfort Zone to the tipi.

"Yeah, what?" I asked, expecting the worst.

"I need you to look after Bud here."

"Look after Bud, you say."

"That's right."

"You're not planning on abandoning him on me, are ya?"

"Of course not!" he feigned dramatically. "It'll just be until I can find us a place to live down in Santa Cruz—two, maybe three weeks max."

Up ahead, in the lantern's faint light, I could see Bud, shirking along silently; pretending not to be listening, like a red-headed stepchild who knows he's about to be passed along yet again.

"Two, maybe three weeks," I repeated, expressing doubt with my tone.

"Yeah! Why, don't you believe me?"

"Nothing personal, it's just that this dog Bud of yours—"

"Yes?"

"Well, you're his third master, right?"

"That's right."

"And they've all, including you, been Roberts, right?"

"That's right."

"And each new master had had Bud abandoned on him by his pre-decessor with the same *I'll-come-back-for-him-in-two-maybe-three-weeks line*, right?"

"That's right."

"And my name's Robert as well, right?"

The Marijuana Grower paused in his tracks to build the dramatic ten-sion. Then, mustering all the incredulous, feigned indignation he could muster, asked, "Rattlesnake, you don't really take me for one of those heartless jerk-offs who goes around abandoning their beloved hounds on other jerk-offs, do you?"

"The thought never crossed my mind," I assured him, walking on.

Pulling into my camp, we parked, somewhat out of the drizzle, beneath the small plastic canopy covering my writing table. And there did The Marijuana Grower open his bucket of possessions, and began the benevolent act of bequeathing.

"I hereby bequeath upon you *this*—the remainder of my sustenance!" he stated grandly, handing over a quarter-full, one-pound bag of brown rice.

"Gee, thanks."

"Save your thanks, there's more!" he winked, as he began pulling one item after the next from the bucket. "And *this!*"—his restaurant-stolen bottle of Kikkoman's containing a last few drops of precious soy sauce. "And *this!*"—his opened jar of moldy salmon eggs. "And *this!*"—his fourteen remaining rounds of .22 caliber ammunition, snakeshot, shorts, and hollowpoints. "And *these!*"—his six dead 'D' sized batteries for my 'C' sized, sovereign-willed flashlight. "And *this!*"—his rusty Super Duper lure, missing two of its three hooks. "And, last but certainly not least, *these!*" he said, reaching to the bucket's very bottom and pulling out his deck of tarot cards.

"Your tarot cards? But I don't want you tarot cards. In fact, not to sound unappreciative, but I don't want any of this crap!"

"Aw, you're just being polite," he assured me, as he removed the rubber band (which broke) from around the tarot cards. "And, as a special gesture of my appreciation for your looking after Bud for these next, *a-hem*, two, maybe three weeks, I'm going to read you your fortune!"

"But you already read me my fortune. Remember, back in June?—I selected the 'Hermit' card."

"Sure, but that was for only until your final reading."

"But I don't want another. I came here for solitude: the 'Hermit' suits me just fine!"

Ignoring my protests, he fanned the deck of tarot cards out before me, gently ordering me to, "Pick a card, any card."

With great reluctance, I extended a hand and, eventually, plucked from the deck the most unobtrusive card I could find.

"Turn it over," he said.

I turned the card over, finding there the rather gruesome image of a skeleton hanging from a noose.

"Well, this looks cheery," I facetiously remarked.

"Ah, the 'Death' card."

"And what's it supposed to represent?"

"Well, *death*," he chuckled ruefully.

"Great, that oughta give me something to ponder these dark winter nights."

"Don't worry, Rattlesnake, often these things are more symbolic than literal."

"*Often*, huh?"

"Yeah, as in the death of the *old* you—you know, a rebirth!"

"But I was just getting to like the old me."

"Well then, it could be prognosticating the death of someone close to you: a family member or friend. Or maybe even the death of your dog here."

"*My* dog?"

"The point is, it doesn't have to mean your death."

As much as I appreciated his efforts to put me at ease, I knew he was glad not to be in my shoes; not to be stuck here in this spooky canyon, all winter and all alone. I watched as he tied a lease rope to Bud, then tied its other end to one of my table legs. He then knelt beside the dog and hugged him.

"Take care of him," he muttered, although I couldn't be sure if he was speaking to me or to Bud.

With that, he stood and we hugged. After our embrace, I lifted his backpack up off the ground for him to don. He wiggled into the shoulder straps then clipped the hip belt, announcing, "I've never buckled this belt before: never been skinny enough to." Lastly, he picked up the two sealed, plastic, five-gallon buckets.

"Are you sure you've got the right buckets?" I asked. "I'd hate to send you up the trail with Bud's dogfood and all that good stuff you bequeathed upon me, and me get stuck here with all your pot."

"Believe me, I'd be better off," he said, confident he had the right buckets. He then turned towards the trail, hesitating momentarily.

"It's pretty dark," I pointed out.

"Planned. I don't want to reach the highway much before midnight."

"Want to borrow my lantern?"

"No, thanks. I don't want to draw attention to myself."

He was still hesitant to leave, like his boots were spiked to the earth.

"Alrighty then...." I said, as a psychological nudge.

"Alrighty," he said with a heavy sigh, and at once began away up the trail leading out of the canyon. In ten steps he had disappeared, swallowed by the dark of night.

Bud began whining, tethered by his leash. I knelt beside him and comforted him the best I knew how; by plucking ticks from his coat. After unscrewing some thirty blood-gorged ticks, I imagined The Marijuana Grower must have made it to the Halfway Cedar by then. I stood and, facing the northern ridge, sent up the loudest, longest Injun whoop I could muster.... But there was no reply.

I'm glad The Marijuana Grower abandoned Bud on me. I was hoping he would. I needed the company. The fourth Robert. Robert the Fourth.

I hang the lantern back up above the table and get out my journal to try to record all that has happened today. For that to get done, I clear the table of the pile of crap The Marijuana Grower "bequeathed" upon me. On top of the pile is the 'Death' card. A gust of chilly wind sweeps up the canyon threatening the lantern's flame. It dances a bit, but manages to stay lit.

Amazing; the terror I feel.

Moon of the Falling Leaves

"If a mind snaps in the woods,
Can anyone hear it?"
— MIKE MCINTYRE

Journal Entry; 31 October 1984:

The Moon of the Falling Leaves lived up to its name today when a sudden gust blew through the canyon, spinning like a top. Up in the meadow, in one swirling yank, the gust tore nearly every leaf from every deciduous limb: alder, pear, apple, plum, madrone, dogwood, and oak. In one crimson twister, autumn was harvested.

There seems to be some invisible vortex down here into which everything—the warmth of summer, visitors, my savings, etc.—seems to be draining. Of course, the only one of these I feel I have any control over is the latter. Hence, down to my last $67, I vowed today to begin a daily mining routine; come Hell or high water. That vow got underway when Bud (my dog) and I forded the river and resumed mineral extraction operations at Bob's Big Bar (my claim). The fervor lasted for about three buckets of gravel; right up until a fair-sized nugget flashed up at the top end of the sluice box, and then was promptly flushed by the current out the bottom. I decided to call it a day.

Fording back across the once-again icy, knee-deep river, I decided I should take at least one last bath before it got too cold. But, once submerged in the shockingly cold liquid, I concluded that that date must have come and gone weeks ago.

After dinner and dusk, Bud and I decided to do a little trick-or-treating. Insofar as Halloween had kind of snuck up on us, we probably didn't get as early a start as we should have, especially considering the intermittent nature of my sovereign-willed flashlight. Nevertheless, it was a memorable Halloween, made all the more haunting by the fact of me being the only person in the canyon; and by the thought of the ghosts of those thirty-nine dead Chinese miners up the far side of Snakehead Point, and that also of the Santa Claus-esque Joe Steiner; not to mention the all-too-popular belief of tonight—All Souls' Day—being the night when the veil draped between this and the spirit world is the thinnest and, hence, likely to be the night that I would see a ghost or gremlin or goblin or whathaveyous if I was ever going to see one. It didn't happen, thankfully, but I never stopped thinking that it might.

"Trick or treat!" I shouted, as we stole that last can of Spaghetti-Os

ROBERT P. JOHNSON

from The California Goldminer's long-abandoned Outlaw Camp.

"Trick or treat!" we screamed, as we pilfered a roll of clear visquine from Slim's almost-as-long-abandoned Comfort Zone camp.

"Trick or treat!" we cried, as we plundered a last, overlooked can of Hershey's Cocoa up there in The Marijuana Grower's recently abandoned, oaken pyramid, high atop Snakehead Point.

And "Trick or treat!" we sighed pleasurably, there back at the tipi, after having survived the ordeal of combing through the miles of canyon, all alone and in the dark; and after having mixed the cocoa with hot milk and honey, and had filled our bellies—both Bud's and mine—with the heavenly elixir, and—lying on my cot within the warm and glowing tipi—had belched its balmy vapors up towards the open smokeflaps, to be carried skyward with the fire's smoke and heat, up to the firmament, knocking once before passing through to the spirit world.

JOURNAL ENTRY; 4 NOVEMBER 1984:

Johnson's Break-Up.

I haven't seen anyone in over a week now; my longest stretch of solitude to date. Perhaps unrelated, the winds have been pretty rowdy these past few nights. All night long the tipi gets pelted with pine cones and branches. By morning the ground is littered with debris brought down by the maelstrom. Every now and then I'll hear a tree crash to Earth; a truly wondrous sound so long as it's heard from a distance greater than the height of the falling tree. These winds, however, they're making me suspicious; suspicious that Mother Nature has something up her sleeve. A siege of some sort. She against me; me her lone scapegoat for all the harm which humankind has inflicted upon her. I can't understand her turning on me like this: me of all people! We seemed to be getting along so well last spring. Wimmin—*sheesh!*

Aside from the wind, it rained very hard last night. Poured, in fact; enough so that I had to get up in the middle of the night to close the tipi's smokeflaps. I've never had to do that before. By morning the river was roaring like thunder. I could hear huge boulders being rolled down the riverbed like marbles. When it was light enough, I climbed out of the tipi and into the spitting drizzle. Glancing down at the river I was shocked to see it running at easily four times the volume it had just twenty-four hours ago! What had been clear, almost languid pools, were now indistinguishable segments of one long, raging, muddy torrent, sweeping past like a runaway freight train, dragging with it a whole tree here, a half tree there.

As I stood there on the terrace, gazing down at the raging river, Bud stood beside me, his ever-present stick in his mouth. I snatched the stick away and tossed it out into the middle of the swift current. Normally, of course, he—this greatest of all fetchers—would not have given a second thought to dropping off the terrace, racing down to the river bank, and leaping in after the stick. But today was clearly different. Instead, he just sat back on his haunches and whined a bit as he watched the current drag the stick away, then turned his apologetic eyes up towards me, as if begging for a beating so to be absolved of his sin.

Turning my attention across to my claim, Bob's Big Bar, I was at first confused, then miffed, to discover that it no longer existed. What had, just yesterday, been an all-too familiar work site of strewn boulders and dig holes, was now submerged beneath a fathom or more of silty surge. Indeed, over the course of some ten hours, I had been wiped out; sluice box and buckets, shovels and picks, lock, stock and barrel! I can hear my grandchildren now: "Why, we'd've been fat-rich if'n ol' Grandpappy Rattlesnake hadn't've gone and overslept durin' the flood of '84!" Fuck 'em.

By nine or so this morning I was well into my routine: sitting out beneath the dripping boughs of the three-trunked cedar, the drizzle blowing sideways and thereby circumventing the sole purpose for my piece-o-shit canopy, my fingers numbly pecking away at my clacker-clacker, my piece-o-shit novel seeping slowly from my head like post-nasal drip. In perhaps a vain attempt to shake this miserable weather, I've placed my novel's characters in Palm Springs today ("The sun rose like a welder's torch. By ten it was cutting through the roof of the car. 'Water... *water!!!*' Roy Tann panted. 'Sorry, dear, all we have are bloody marys,' Poly replied, as she steered the Cranbrook's sneering grill towards the Mexican border...."). But it doesn't seem to help: I'm still cold, still wet, still miserable. All of which kind of brings us to the subject of the day; the aforementioned "Johnson's Break-Up."

ROBERT P. JOHNSON

Basically, I worry about only one thing: my sanity. In an effort, hopefully not vain, to fight off the chaos chewing at my mind, I've begun therapy. Well, therapy of sorts: I use the term loosely. My particular therapy involves brief immersions in society. And my psychiatric hospital, as it were, is the lone bar in the tiny goldmining town up top, The Monte Vista Inn; teeming with local color, and hospitably staffed by the blessed trinity of Sierran watering holes: an affable bartender, frosty beer mugs, and a seemingly bottomless tap, even if it is only Miller Lite and Budweiser.

The laughter, the chatter, the cleavage; it's all very therapeutic. But there does seem to be one glaring problem: they all think I'm crazy. Which makes it all the more challenging to hit on the girls. In fact, there's really just one guy up there that will spend any time in actual conversation with me, and I suspect he's more crazy than I am.

"Are you an alien?" he asked me last time we spoke.

"You mean, like, illegal?" I asked, confused.

"No, like, otherworldly."

"Oh.... I can't be certain."

Now, just because *he* happens to be off his rocker, you wouldn't think *I* would have to worry about my sanity. But I do. And I think I know why. It's because in him I see myself: in his crazy notions I see my own; in the same pitying manner with which the rest of the bar patrons treat and/or avoid him, I see them now treat and/or avoid me; in his manic pipe dreams of writing books and movies and stories and.... Well, suffice it to say, I'm worried.

So, dear Journal, what gives? Am I going insane? Is this Johnson's Break-Up? It seems that the biggest problem with solitude is that it provides no basis for determination. Society seems to be the litmus test for sanity, and society I have none. Living by myself out here in the wilderness, all sanity and insanity are contained within me, and me alone.

There's a five-gallon bucket sitting over by the fire pit. In a puddle. About, oh, fifteen feet from the toe of my out-stretched boot. It's one of the buckets The Marijuana Grower bequeathed upon me, and I must glance at it a thousand times a day. It's label is still clear, and informs us it once contained an industrial wax remover manufactured by the

Johnson Wax Company. The label therefore reads—in big, bold, all-too-visible letters—"Johnson's Break-Up."

I hate that bucket. It's but one of chaos's myriad gnashing mouths chewing away at my sanity. I hate tarot cards with skeletons hanging from nooses, for exactly the same reason.

Once again, I find myself pondering whether or not to pull out of the canyon prematurely. Once again, it's a matter of prudence. What would *he*, that prudent man, do?

JOURNAL ENTRY; 7 NOVEMBER 1984:

Lying on my cot, within my mummybag stuffed into my summer bag, clad in long underwear, mittens, wool cap, and two pairs of socks, with only my face exposed, I exhale. My breath rises in a cloud up to the convergence of tipi poles, condenses, freezes, then falls back upon me like a caved-in igloo. It's cold this morning.

As I fight my way out of the sleepingbags, I find that Bud has been sharing the cot with me, down near my knees. Fine: the more the merrier. As he perceives me heading towards the stack of wood I keep within the tipi, he wags his tail. It thumps against the cot like a drumstick. He's cold and stays wound in a tight ball and knows that I'm about to start a fire and is trying to convey that he approves of the idea. The holiday ball-o-dog.

I have another woodpile outside under a tarp. That's my main one: about a cord's worth and growing. But I keep my choicest wood here in the tipi. Cedar splits easily and, being the driest, makes the best kindling. Manzanita burns the hottest. California Bay is aromatic. Fir snaps, crackles and pops, reminding me of something though I can't remember what. Oak's primary attribute is its longevity. And Alder seems to have no redeeming qualities whatsoever, but I feel compelled to keep some in the stack just for variety, or perhaps just to see if I can get a piece of it to ever dry out. I also have a small kindling stack of pitch wood, which burns like highway flares and is therefore great for starting fires. These woods have become my wines, each carefully aged and bottled. I open them with my hatchet, sniff the cork, sip them thoughtfully.

With the fire blazing and the tipi, if not warming then, at least, filling with smoke, Bud and I take a peek out the tipi's doorflap. Much to our surprise, it is snowing. There's already about four or five inches and seems no end in sight. The tree limbs sag beneath the weight of the early winter.

"This better be worth it!" I catch myself muttering.

Moon of the Popping Trees

Duke Senior: "Now, my co-mates and brothers in exile,
Hath not old custom made this life more sweet
Than that of the painted pomp? Are not these woods
More free from peril than the envious court?
Here feel we not the penalty of Adam,
The season's difference, as the icy fang
And churlish chiding of the winter's wind,
Which when it bites and blows upon my body
Even till I shrink with cold, I smile and say,
'This is no flattery: these are counselors
That feelingly persuade me what I am.'
Sweet are the uses of adversity.
Which like the toad, ugly and venomous,
Wears yet a precious jewel in his head;
And this our life, exempt from public haunt,
Finds tongues in trees, books in the running brooks,
Sermons in stones, and good in everything....
Come, shall we go kill us some venison?"
— WILLIAM SHAKESPEARE, *As You Like It*

Journal Entry; 7 December 1984:

"Room 11"; that's what some school kid wrote on page edges of the textbook. "English Composition: High School"; that's what the publisher printed on its cover, so we could judge it. It's not my textbook, though I think I had one just like it. I remember hating it. This particular one I bought at a rummage sale in the goldmining town up top. Ten cents. I'm somewhat embarrassed to admit that I've had the book down here with me for over seven months now and have never so much as opened it. In fact, right now marks the first time I've put it to any practical use. It happens to be propped up against the three-trunked cedar at the moment, some twenty feet away from me, and I'm aiming at it down the sites of the .22 caliber rifle I packed into the canyon last week.

More than just a fitting recompense for all the painful tests the textbook has inflicted upon innocent school children, this is a ballistics test. I'm comparing the various destructive attributes of the three types of .22 caliber bullets I brought along. I currently have a .22 "short" in the chamber. *Bang!* It strikes the upper left-hand corner of the book's cover. I load now a .22 "long", aim and fire. *Bammo!* It hits the upper right corner. I load a .22 "hollowpoint long rifle" bullet, aim, and... fire. *Ka-blammo!* It finds its mark smack-dab in the middle of the cover.

Retrieving the text, I find the bullets' entry holes indistinguishable from one another. It's in turning the book over, however, where the exit wounds make obvious the considerable difference in each bullet-type's capabilities. The "short" emerged rather unceremoniously, leaving a hole only about the size of a dime. The "long" produced a more lethal wound, about twice the circumference of the "short's". But, as one might expect, it was the "hollowpoint long rifle" bullet which inflicted the most damage, leaving a smoking, uneven crater of over two inches across. From this I decided "shorts" would be best for game up to the size of, say, squirrel; "longs" for something up to the size of, say, raccoons, and the "hollowpoint long rifles" for anything bigger. With the ballistics computed, I felt in the mood for a field test.

"C'mon, Buddy. Put on your nose, 'cause we're goin' huntin'!"

Bud couldn't contain his excitement. He zipped all around the terrace pissing on every rock, bush, and tipi he crossed.

Over the last month we had been scaring up a lot of quail about a half mile upriver from the Comfort Zone, so it was in that direction we headed. En route we found the upper valley still patched with the snow that fell a couple weeks ago, though most of this had been washed away by the subsequent rains. Today was another such snow-melting day, with drizzly conditions hovering around 40ºF.

Our meandering brought us as far upriver as the old mining digs near the base of the Temple of the Moon. Along the way Bud had managed to flush several coveys of quail, their stubby, beating wings sounding like helicopter rotors as they took to wing. Unfortunately, Bud's enthusiasm was such that he rarely allowed me within even *sight* of any of the intended prey, thus denying me even a single shot.

It was somewhere up near the upper end of the valley when—after a couple hours of mindlessly following my breath clouds and watching my worn-through tennis shoes sink into the soggy, pine-needled, forest floor—I was suddenly struck with the feeling that I was, at long last, *there*. "There" was the place which had always come to mind in the form of daydreams back, years ago, when I was first considering this wilderness sabbatical. And today was just the sort of day I had always imagined: a wet, gray, late autumn day; neither winter or summer, neither snow-bound or blistering hot; but rather, something smack-dab in the middle. A normal day. An average day. Half the year behind me, and half still lying in wait. The past and future teetering precisely on the fulcrum of the present. And this, in a general sense, was just the sort of activity I had imagined myself doing: meandering around in the obscuring mist, in lackadaisical pursuit of a prey I could hear but barely glimpse. To glimpse the bull, in the hope to one day ride it home.

Besides the oft-mentioned river trail, there's another trail—or, at least, remnants of one—which runs the length of the valley. It too parallels the river's north bank, though it keeps a good quarter mile away from it most of the time. Bud and I chose this rarely-used route for our return trip to the tipi in the hope that what it left to be desired in terms of easy passage it might make up to us in the form of abundant game. But as the bushwhacking miles passed slowly under foot, and the ticks climbed aboard us, two and three thick in places, and n'er a game, big or small, did we encounter, it was becoming ever the more apparent I had made a poor choice.

Eventually, we reached the point where this raggedy trail intersects the ridge trail heading out of the valley; up near the high end of the meadow above my tipi and very close to Joe Steiner's grave. It was late afternoon by then, and the plan was to merely follow the ridge trail the two hundred yards or so, back down through the meadow to the tipi, and call it a day—a fruitless day of hunting. But that is when we stumbled upon a stout doe, grazing on the meadow's snow-matted grass not twenty yards away. Fortunately for all concerned, a southerly breeze carried our scents away, preventing Bud from catching a whiff of the doe and she of us. And, fortunately also, Bud and I were mostly hidden from her by a hedge of wild azaleas, over which only I could see. With images of deerskin boots and jerked venison bouncing on electrons between my ears and salivary glands, I removed the "short" from the rifle's chamber, fumbled in my shirt pocket for a "hollowpoint long rifle", and quietly loaded it. Though the resulting clicks from the rifle's bolt action were too subtle for the doe to hear, Bud caught them. He perked his ears and turned towards me, a befuddled *what gives?* cock to his brow. I leaned over and gently scratched his head, which relaxed him enough that he decided to sit and tend to his testicles.

"Good boy," I whispered.

When I looked back up, the doe was staring in our general, but not exact, direction. Whatever it was she heard or sensed, it obviously did not concern her enough to give her cause to stop chewing the clump of grass—likely her last meal—protruding from her jowls. I lifted the stock of the rifle to my shoulder and slowly drew aim. The three points fell smoothly into line: the rear sight, the muzzle sight and subtle depression on the doe's forehead, right between her eyes.

Bud whimpered, confused no doubt by my focused silence. The doe heard him, stopped chewing, and turned her slender head to the left, the better to listen. Denied the former target, I adjusted my aim to just below her right ear. I then took a deep breath and slowly began to release it as I squeezed the trigger—a hunting tip gleaned from an *Argosy* magazine article I once read while waiting in a dentist's office.

It was at this point I realized the hunt was over. Or, in the inimitable words of B.B. King: "The thrill was gone." Sure, I could finish squeezing the trigger and bring this beautiful mystery to an abrupt end as far as the doe was concerned. But whose victory would that be?—some ballistics engineer at Remington's, or maybe the guy who invented gunpowder's. In either case, not mine; all I had to do was pull the trigger. Compounding my wavering resolve was the fact that I wasn't short on food supplies at the moment, and I really didn't need deerskin boots or anything. Without trying to sound like some sort of tree-hugging environmentalist, it just kind of struck me as, well, needlessly and selfishly cruel to kill the doe. If I was hungry; that would be a different matter.

I lowered the rifle, then tried to point the deer out to Bud. "Get the deer, Bud."

Bud stopped licking at his balls to look up at me.

"Fetch!" I shouted, pretending to toss a stick in the doe's direction.

Hearing this, the doe bounced into instant flight, bounding west towards the thick forest. Bud heard the commotion and himself leapt to his paws and bounded out into the meadow. But by then the doe was gone, leaving only her thick scent swirling in the moist air, like a windcock in a twister, as clue to her escape route. As a result, Bud was duped; running off in the direction the breeze carried her scent rather than the direction her flight had carried her. His pursuit, however misdirected, was nonetheless impressive: off like a shot, springing high every few gallops in order to peek over the tall grass, following a scattered trail of mere molecules with his keen snout—away with the call of the wild.

JOURNAL ENTRY; 22 DECEMBER 1984:

I've been having a recurrent nightmare; not about rattlesnakes, but rather that I'm a homeless street derelict. By day the dream finds me wandering the streets of Oakland wherein I was once accepted. I piss behind buildings, wear soiled clothes, and, at all costs, avoid the glances of strangers. I have a long and tattered coat which I must wear even in the warmth of day for fear of losing it. Off in the distance I see a former schoolmate. I duck behind a wall so not to cross paths with him, fearing I could not endure the contact.

In the dream I seem frantically headed towards some specific place of salvation, though I know not where. Night always manages to fall before I arrive. And the nights are all the same: I find some hedge to crawl beneath, there to spend the better part of the evening flicking ants from my bare ankles until sweet sleep can deliver me to a brighter world. But, instead of sleeping, I awaken—into this world.

The most frightening aspect of the nightmare is that I feel so very sane; that is, every bit as sane as I feel at this very moment. Thinking about it, I imagine every derelict must feel, to himself, sane.

Awakening, I stared up through the tipi's open smokeflaps, through which I could see that, not only was it morning, but also that the sky was a deep, cloudless blue.

"We might see the sun today, Bud. We might just get warm!"

My enthusiasm elicited wags from our holiday ball-o-dog's tail—
thump-thump-thump—against my cot.

I pushed past the stiff, frozen tipi doorflap and out on to the terrace. By then it was probably close to 10 a.m., which meant it would be another hour at least before this shy, winter solstice sun rose above the southern ridge. Turning towards the north, I could see that the edge of day had worked its way only about halfway down into the canyon. So impatient was I, I considered hiking up to meet it, but decided instead to stay down in camp and try my best to enjoy this, the longest morning of the year.

Bud was having trouble pushing through the frozen doorflap, but finally managed. Half asleep still, he dragged himself over to the woodpile to take a leak, then over to the spring to get his morning drink. On this morning however, apparently the coldest so far, the spring's surface was frozen. Hence, Bud's tongue dragged across the surface as if it was cold steel. He stared at it with puzzled frustration, then turned his disappointment towards me, quite certain this was one of my practical jokes.

After breaking the ice for Bud with the heel of my boot, I began running tight little sprints around the tipi, pumping out push-ups, and boxing my puffs of breath, all in an attempt to get warm. But nothin' doin': there was no escape from the cold, no turning up the electric blanket, no just waiting for the car to warm up, no hot shower salvation, no siree; this was the real and bitter thing—Old Man Winter.

Two ducks tried to zip unnoticed down the river, flying low, under radar, for warmer climes. But I caught them. "Slow down!" I shouted after them. Bud likes my sense of humor.

The sun finally rose at about eleven this morning; its low arc resembling a flubbed drive of a golfball, as it skipped across the southern ridge's piney horizon, to set after only a three and a half hour flight. Short, though it was, the day was nonetheless productive. For one thing, I got my laundry done. That involved stirring my few clothes, sans soap, in a galvanized bucket of boiling water over a roaring fire (more a process of sterilization than cleaning) then hanging it all out on a line to either dry or freeze then dry. All my whites are now pink; roughly the shade of my once-red long farmer john underwear.

The second task accomplished was that of my own sterilization.... Perhaps I should rephrase that: I took a bath. To pull this feat off, I carried a boiling bucket of clean water over to an area near the creek which I call my "kitchen," though it's more just a patio area cobbled with flat river stones in order to keep the mud at bay. (This same area I use to wash all my utensils and where I keep and rinse my jars of alfalfa sprouts, one of my primary sources of nutrition.) I then split this bucket of 208° water by pouring it into two plastic five-gallon buckets, diluting each with spring water until the desired temperature of approximately 105° is attained. One bucket I use for washing; scrubbing from my feet up (remember: it's *really* cold!) using a washrag and Dr. Bronner's Spearmint biodegradable liquid soap, saving the shampoo cycle for last. With that accomplished, I move promptly into the rinse cycle; first by dunking my head in the bucket of clean warm water, then by raising that bucket overhead and pouring it over me for the final rinse. And though this final step takes all of five seconds—there in the blinding glare of the raw sunlight and steam, my skin exposed to both the bite of winter and the blessing of stored summer warmth—the experience is nothing short of blissful!

And for the third and last task of the day (more of a reward, some would say) Bud and I went fishing. We decided to try our luck downstream, in a pool I named "December Pool" some months ago, based on

Robert P. Johnson

its unmatched depths and in anticipation of its winter accessibility. But, though the river was running crystal clear, after forty-five minutes with every lure and packaged bait imaginable, not a single bite did we get. Considering this has been the trend since late November (the date of my last fish), I must surmise that trout—at least these trout—go dormant for the winter.

By 3:30 p.m. the sun had already dipped below that cursed southern ridge, thus beginning the year's longest night. To celebrate—or, at least to stave off the suffering of the subsequent temperature plunge—I cooked up a big pot of spaghetti for Bud and me, complete with marsala sauce, parmesan cheese and what broccoli still held its head upright in the garden.

Presently, it is pitch dark outside with the temperature probably at about 20ºF and dropping. We have retreated to the tipi where a roaring fire, at least, gives us reason to believe we are warm. I am at my crude desk/bookshelf, fashioned last month by hatchet and twine and that aforementioned need to work. The kerosene lantern hangs from a tipi pole somewhere above one shoulder. Bud is curled up at my feet. I scratch this entry into you, dear journal, with a knife-sharpened pencil, since the ink pens all seem to have frozen. And I am done with today's entry except for one last thing, a last morsel I would like to jot down just to see if it makes any sense when I reread it, say, ten years from now. This *morsel* is the peculiar mood which has currently swept over me like a drunkenness. It's a mood I shall call *realness* for lack of a better word. The amber light from the lantern glows dimly through this smoky conical world, touching just a few things: Bud's tail, these scratched words on the smooth page, the tin can of pencils and goodfernuthin' pens, the crackling fire, the umber glow of the tipi canvas, the dark convergence of its poles, the pitch-black night and brilliant stars visible through the smokeflaps, my puffs of breath, my butt against this hard seat.... It's difficult to describe other than just to say, it all feels so *real*.

JOURNAL ENTRY; 24 DECEMBER 1984:

Dear Journal, this is my last entry: I'm sick of this.

"Grab your favorite stick, Buddy, we're pullin' out!"

Bud stopped chewing on himself long enough to look up at me from the comfortable little nook he had dug and melted himself in the mud and snow, there beside my table. Yes, he looked up at me, but there was no cheer in his eyes; no cheer, no trust, nor even any real concern that any changes in his life were truly at hand. For this was the third time this week alone I had told him to, *Grab your favorite stick, Buddy, we're pullin' out!* And he simply couldn't believe me anymore. Little did he know that this time, *this time,* I really meant it!

"You'll be sorry, Bud. You'll be the only dog up at Lake Tahoe without a stick!" I tried to warn him, as I packed my dearest belongings into my backpack. But did he heed? No! Did he even listen? Hardly! Quite to the contrary, he had the gall—nay, the *indignity!*—to yawn at my dire forebodings and then wind himself back into his holiday ball-o-dog wad and close his eyes. What Bud couldn't obviously know about this particular pull-out, which made it, in fact, inevitable, was that our savings account was now down to a scant thirty-two dollars. This added to the no-small matter that we were without sluice box, tools, trout, garden, and anything resembling hospitable weather, meant that it was next to impossible for us to survive in the canyon much longer. "You'll be sorry," I muttered, as I closed up the tipi for the winter.

The plan was desperate but simple: I would spend Christmas with my father and stepmother, then head up to Lake Tahoe for the New Years, find a friend's couch to crash on, a job, and, ultimately, a place to live, regroup and plan a new life. Simple. Then, at some point in the spring, I would return for the tipi canvas and my remaining valuables. Anyway, that was the plan.

I swung the pack onto my back. It was the heaviest I've felt it in months. Amongst other crap, I had stuffed into it my unfinished manuscript, leaving me no choice but to carry my clackle-clacker under one arm, while my other toted my rifle, and a sports satchel containing to pairs of swim masks, snorkels and fins.

"Got that stick, Bud?"

This time he had it.

"Alrighty then, let's move 'em out. Hee-yah, rawhide!"

And with that we commenced our pull-out.

Yesterday's storm had laid six inches of snow in the meadow, leaving only a subtle trench-like depression running up its middle as evidence of the trail that lay beneath, up which Bud and I trudged. Prior to our trespass, tracks revealed that a bobcat and her two kits, a deer (probably the doe I didn't shoot), and something I assume to be a raccoon, had already taken the opportunity to mar the otherwise pristine blanket of white. But whereas all their tracks, and even Bud's, who sniffed after them, were meandering and playful, mine were direct and purposeful: for I was in flight. In fact, it wasn't until we were up near Joe Steiner's grave marker that I even bothered to turn around, for a last sentimental glance back down towards the tipi. And there it was: nestled like a pinhead amidst the magnitude of wilderness: the meadow shimmering in the early sun like a sequined carpet running down to its door, the black river its icy blood flow, the towering firs its lifeline to the great spirit grandfathers in the sky, the forest green canyon wall its ever-humble exemplar.

As often happens on a still day in the wilderness, it took movement— in this case, a tiny avalanche of snow slipping down the north side of the tipi, and piling at the base—to remind me I wasn't looking at some vast landscape painting. And that somehow precipitated an intangible sadness to fall over the scene, for suddenly the tipi looked abandoned, past its glory, lifeless. Now, sans occupants, it had no purpose, no *raison d'être*. Now, it was just another ruin.

Misinterpreting my pause for yet another aborted pull-out in the making, Bud began to whine.

"Don't worry, Buddy. We're really doing it this time," I assured him, with a gentle head-scratching.

And with that we turned back towards the northern ridge and resumed our retreat trek. As we marched past Joe Steiner's grave, I sensed the prospector's ghost laughing at us, that disparaging kind of chuckle old-timers reserve for us greenhorns. Free at last of any superstitious repercussions his spirit might inflict upon me, it seemed like a good opportunity, if not my last, to give ol' Joe a piece of my mind: "That's right, Joe; you're the tough guy, I'm the wussie. Yessiree, you sure showed me. So long, sucker!"

Joe said nothing. On we climbed.

We hadn't gotten more than a half mile up the trail and into the switchbacks before I became aware of two grave miscalculations on my part. The first pertained to snow depth and my erroneous assumption that, because the temperatures had stayed well below freezing though-out this last storm, the six-inch snow cover down at the tipi's elevation would be consistent all the way up and over the ridge. Wrong. My second miscalculation, a product of the first, concerned our leisurely, noon-time departure, based upon the assumption that we could make the hike in the standard one to two-hour time frame and would thereby have plenty of daylight. Wrong again, for by just a quarter of the way up the ridge the snow was already a foot deep, with its infamous "Sierra cement" density weighing down the limbs of the brush to the point where often we could not discern the trail (we thought we knew so well!) from the thicket on either side. This reduced the dignity of our ascent to clumsy bushbanging until we reached the manzanita belt.

By the halfway cedar the snow depth was eighteen inches, and even more dense than before due its direct exposure to the late afternoon sun. By this point, Bud was content to follow in my tracks rather than to blaze ahead in his usual fashion. He had also abandoned his stick; adding convincing testimony as to just how difficult the climb had become. Since beginning this endeavor seven and a half months ago, this is the first time in some twenty-five treks, that I was making the hike in long pants, let alone long pants and long underwear. The added resistance and weight was very noticeable, as was the sweat produced when under the sun's glare. But, unfortunately, I needed the extra protection so there wasn't much I could do but grin and bear it.

After three hours of trudging we were three-quarters of the way up and entering the stretch where the steep canyon pitch begins to yield to the ridge's more gradually-sloped shoulder. Nevertheless, each new step proved more exerting than the one before it as the snow depth crept up over my hips. Adding to our woes, the sun blew us a farewell kiss then ducked behind yonder ridge, leaving the surrounding horizons blushed with alpenglow. It was then that a very sobering thought came to me: we weren't going to make the trailhead by dark, if, indeed, we were to make it at all.

A ravine, two hundred yards deep and wide, cuts across the ridge. On the opposite side of the ravine from us, an Amtrak passenger train

ROBERT P. JOHNSON

pushed uphill, towards Reno and parts east. As the cars slipped by, I could clearly see the passengers riding therein; some in t-shirts, some snoozing or reading, some taking advantage of the breathtaking, starboard-side view of the canyon the last bend had unexpectedly presented them, and all unmistakably warm. When the dining car came past, I could see people sitting before steaming mounds of mash potatoes, turkey and gravy, slurping down soup and stuffing hot-buttered rolls into their pallid cheeks. So transfixed was I by the passing feast it felt as if my eyeballs had been sucked from my head; stretching my optical cords clear across the ravine and sticking my drooling pupils to the windows. "That lady left a pea on her plate, Bud!" I said, imagining with incredulity the waste of every precious, *warm* morsel.

Two passengers were enjoying the brisk wind from the open door near the rear of one of the coach cars. One was pointing towards Bud and me. Whether truly at us or just towards the sunset, I cannot know, but it did make me suddenly self-conscious of how, well, *insane* I must look. And that got me worrying; not so much about *dying* but, ironically, about what my friends and family would think when they found my body next spring. Namely, what my curious cargo—typewriter, snorkels, masks and fins, etc.—would lead them to deduce about my mental stability at the time of my demise. Namely, that I had "lost it." Fueled by this fear even more than of freezing, I pushed on.

Four hours into the trek, and just before the last dregs of dusk had drained from the sky, we made the ridgetop. The fact that we made it has to be credited to the unlikely fortune that someone (two people, judging by their boot prints) had apparently tried to hike into the canyon earlier in the day, and had thereby broken trail for us, trampled rut that it was. Whether this was happenstance or bona fide Providence, I can never know. All I do know is that it, quite literally, saved my life. (I learned later these tracks were made by my father and a friend who had tried to hike out to a point from where they could peer, with binoculars, down to my tipi, in order to check on me.)

Upon arriving at the spot on the top of the ridge where the Cranbrook was parked it was instantly obvious that, due to all the snow, there would be no bump-starting the old beast if the six-volt battery couldn't turn it over. But, lo and behold, and half a can of starting fluid later, it did just that; resuscitating the hibernating flathead back to sputtering life. While the engine was warming, and Bud was busily trying to lick-thaw his manhood on the backseat, I shoveled a fifteen-yard path out ahead of the car in the hope that this runway would enable the Cranbrook to achieve the vital momentum needed to plow through the virgin snow the half mile or more down to the main, and likely plowed, ridge road.

Suffice it to say, p=mv. We were probably doing twenty miles per hour (though the speedometer read sixty) by the time we ran out of downhill and hit the flat, with the actual road somewhere far below the tireless clawings of the thin retreads and the parted snow flowing over the 'Brook's sneering grill like the wake before a surface-cruising submarine. Yea, our momentum pushed us for a good mile like that, then beyond and on out to the plowed and paved county road—home free.

And speaking of home, presently—with a warm holiday dinner nestled comfortably in my stomach, a perfect wedge of mass-produced pumpkin pie dolloped with an artificially sweetened non-dairy whipping cream on nice china on the t.v. tray before me, watching Vanna White spin that Wheel of Fortune for her hysterical idolaters, here with my mindlessly engrossed father and stepmother before a gently crackling fire in their cozy livingroom, the greedy hands of the have-nots lovingly held at bay by the ever-protective interests of mass consumerism and their antipersonnel mines, land and sea-based ICBMs, and spy satellites—I wonder: What was Thoreau's problem anyway?

ROBERT P. JOHNSON

Moon of Frost in the Tipi

"Nothing fails quite so thoroughly as bragging."

— ME

JOURNAL ENTRY; 1 JANUARY 1985:

The Cranbrook, Bud, and I made it up to Lake Tahoe. My plan for the New Year was to look for a job and a place for us to live, but after a few inquiries, I found there to be a dearth of both at present. So, I checked my post office box. And therein—along with *seven* W-2 1984 tax forms for the numerous and sundry shit-jobs I held during the first four months of last year—awaited a letter from a friend of mine. We'll call him "Nick" since that's his name and, as far as I know, he's not wanted by the authorities for anything. The letter was sent to inform me he was flying off to Hawaii in a couple days to attend the annual chimney sweeps' convention. He'll be gone a month and, insofar as I was a chimney sweep for the past few years while living up at Tahoe, he wants to know if I would like to run his Santa Cruz-based sweep business while he's away. I check my post Christmas bank account statement: forty-two dollars and four cents. I give Nick a call: "I'll see you in about five hours."

Five hours later The Cranbrook, Bud and I reach the central coastal town of Santa Cruz, California. Nick is out on sweeps so I kill time by driving downtown. We pull into a diagonal parking place. I slip the meter a quarter. In return it grants me a thirty minute deed. For a limited time, I own a parallelogram of real estate. I am a land baron. Life is great.

I slip a collar over Bud's head and attach a leash, perhaps the first he's ever worn. I recall The Marijuana Grower saying now that he used to tie a noose on thin cotton rope and use that as a leash when needed. The original choke collar. I'm spoiling this damn dog. As we walk away from The Cranbrook I happen to notice a small puddle of motor oil on the asphalt beneath its crankcase. Probably just a coincidence; our parking over someone else's oil pool. We drift up the street, purchase a coffee latté from a sidewalk vendor, and press onward into civilization's organized chaos.

Up another block we can hear a band playing. A crowd is gathered, summoned by the strange gravity of music: no, of *spectacle*; for a fistfight would surely gather the same crowd, as might—just maybe—a naked woman. My mind drifts. It's the coffee. I crane my neck over the crowd to find that what I had assumed was a band is actually just one fellow with guitar in hand and a host of other instruments bolted, duct-

208   ROBERT P. JOHNSON

taped, or otherwise fastened to his feet, knees, back and lips. A one-man band. He is a hippie playing hippie music to the little bit of hippie still festering in us all. At once there seems something both sad and transcendental in the event; something pathetically naive in his reverent re-singing the songs of billionaire Beatles, Stones & Dylan Inc., yet something as well, undeniably... *nourishing*. Glancing down at his guitar case, I note that this one-man band is financially better off than I, so I don't feel obliged to tip him.

On down another street, we wander up to a supermarket. Safeway, it claims. Sounds auspicious. I tie Bud to a bubblegum machine out front. He seems scared of it, and growls at the little kids who approach. One little kid drops his nickel and runs off crying. There's potential here. I stumble into some invisible movement detector and the store's doors open graciously. "Welcome!"—a sign says, with a pride and civility all but lost to the sentient beings. Flattered, I heed. I enter.

In short order I find myself pushing a shopping cart. How did it get there?, I wonder. "Thank you!" a placard in the shopping cart tells me, and it means it. "You're welcome!" I tell it right back, and I mean it too. We round a corner, from aisle 8 to aisle 9. There, before me and my cart, an old lady lies cold on the linoleum beside the pantyhose rack. Safeway "Bingo" cards spill from her inert purse. The undetectable stench of death spreads like a bone-chilling fog in all directions, reminding us that our meter is ticking. A paramedic and a cop run towards me. "I didn't do it!" I feel I should tell them, but they don't seem to want to hear. The hard, rubber wheels of the shopping carts begin to roll again, pushing past the old lady. Mine too. We push past with feigned indifference; trying to convince one another that the old lady's demise doesn't bother us, that just because it happened to her doesn't mean it will happen to us, that we are stronger than death and fear it not, that we understand it. But it's all a ruse: it scares the shit out of us.

"I guess it wasn't her year," someone quips, bringing me back to my senses. I'm somewhere down near the end of the aisle, staring into a tall, wire bin filled with plastic, brightly colored beach balls. If there was a dial on me, that old lady turned it: I feel much more aware of my body mass, of the cool air I turn warm, of my heart pumping precious molecules out to my extremities. I feel frighteningly mortal.

There's a long queue in the "express line" but the tabloids are there to solace my troubled soul. Something hideous was born. Something alien was captured. Something scandalous occurred. Something God-like was seen. And therein, lay hope for us all.

It comes my turn to pay. Dog food. Human food. The checker hands me my change. She needn't say "Thank you!" for the cash register already printed it out on my receipt. And with my receipt comes a "Bingo Card," and my chance to win $50,000.

Outside the store, squatting beside Bud and his admirable collection of nickels, I scratch away at my "Bingo Card." The numbers '82' and '31' slowly become legible. Eighty-two and thirty-one?—I don't get it, did I win? A blast of siren announces the departure of the ambulance carrying the old lady. Good thing they blasted that siren. And what of that old lady: did she win? That is; now, here in the moment of her truth, does she know if or not she lived a *prudent* life? Does she have any regrets now as she thrusts fistfuls of "Bingo" cards at St. Peter there at his pearly gates? Or might she have better prepared for this moment?—a moment which, for her, is verily the end of the world, and perhaps even Judgment Day.

I ask Bud these things as I unleash him. If he knows, he ain't talkin'.

Journal Entry; 28 January 1985:

Nick had returned home from the chimneysweep convention in Hawaii yesterday. With him now back at the helm of his business, there remained nothing in Santa Cruz to hold me any longer.

After packing up Bud and my few belongings, I waved good-bye to Nick then backed the Cranbrook from his driveway and out onto the street. "Cowabunga," I shouted, practicing his peoples' vernacular, as I dropped the 'Brook into first.

"Cowabunga, *haolie*," he shouted back, playfully slapping the trunk hood, then kicking the bumper, as I pulled away. I flipped him off. He flipped me off. I tooted the horn. And, in a matter of minutes, Santa Cruz was gone.

Fifty-fifty: that's how Nick and I had agreed to split the revenue

ROBERT P. JOHNSON

brought in this month. His home, truck, and chimney sweeping equipment. My labor. And, after just four weeks, our co-venture proved surprisingly lucrative for us both, even for such a notoriously slow chimney sweep month as January. My cash reserves surpass the five hundred dollar mark and have thereby nudged me, once again, well into the comfort zone. The plan now is to return to Lake Tahoe and find some scrappy, little cabin for Bud and me.

JOURNAL ENTRY; 31 JANUARY 1985:

What with my decision to abort my year-in-the-wilderness and relocate to Lake Tahoe, I didn't expect to be scribbling anything more into this journal. But today was rather significant. So, I felt I should.

To bring you up to date: I have been crashing on a friend's couch the last two nights, while working, minimally, with another friend's chimney sweep business the past two days. Not an ideal situation, but not a bad one for a recent immigrant.

Anyway, early this morning, I had been dispatched to the remote town of Truckee, California to do a sweep. As was often the case when sweeping chimneys in the Sierra, the cabin I was doing today was a vacation home with the owners somewhere far away. Sweeps, as a rule, love this kind of job. For not only does it offer the peace of mind of working beyond the owner's critical glare, but it also affords us certain, shall we say, *liberties*. Thus, after surviving a fall from the steep-roofed A-frame (the twenty inches of fresh snow both caused and broke the fall), I promptly pursued one of those very liberties by rifling through the kitchen cabinets in dogged search for the ubiquitous bag of cookies. After successfully locating such, I settled into the livingroom couch, put my legs up on the coffee table, and began filling out a billing receipt, sack of Mint Milanos at my side.

It was then that I happened to notice the *People* magazine laying in a basket of other magazines, there on the coffee table. And I probably wouldn't have given it a second glance if not for the rather startling fact that a boyhood friend of mine was pictured on the cover; the same friend, in fact, mentioned in this journal some months back as having dropped my father's binocular case off Lovers Leap. The photo was of him and a lithe, blonde mermaid; the apparent stars of some current hit movie called *Splash*. Her name is Darryl Hannah. His is Tom Hanks.

Though I hadn't seen or spoken with Tom since he graduated, a year before me, from high school in Oakland, the shock of reading of his immense good fortune bowled me over with emotions. Sure, I felt a great joy for him, and even a bit of pride in the fact that *one of us*—one of us middle-class kids from the not-so-great part of Oakland—had made it. But the juxtaposition of our lots in life made me also feel, in medical terms, like a loser. After all, he had become a star; veritably, a higher life form.

After finishing the *People* article and the package of cookies, I locked up the cabin, hid the key back beneath the doormat, and made the long drive back to Tahoe City. En route I obsessed about Tom's and my relative situations: about the millions he was probably making compared with the sporadic "Jackson" I was shaking out of chimneys; about the Hollywood players who no doubt fawn and swoon over him compared to the *don't-call-us, we'll-call-you* treatment society reserves for us fringe dwellers; about triple mocha cappuccinos and thrice-boiled cowboy coffee; about Range Rovers with all the bells and whistles, and rusty, $155, oil-dripping, '53 Plymouths. Often I caught myself staring, as if at a stranger, at my reflection in the rearview mirror—soot-faced, dressed ever so smartly in the chimneysweep's requisite tophat and tails, $545 in the bank. How amazing the difference a few random career choices can make in two peoples' otherwise similar lives.

JOURNAL ENTRY; 1 FEBRUARY 1985:

I've decided to return to the tipi in order to finish my year in the wilderness. "Completion is vital!"—those were Mary's words, and they have haunted me ever since my pull-out. So, once again, I vow to heed them.

JOURNAL ENTRY; 1 FEBRUARY 1985, EVENING EDITION:

Being that it was just starting to snow again as the Cranbrook, Bud and I climbed up and over Donner Summit, I wasn't surprised to find it falling fast and furiously when we reached our offramp an hour later.

Pulling off Interstate 80, I parked the 'Brook, threw snow chains onto the rear wheels, then pointed its sneering grill beyond the pavement and up towards the unplowed, unimproved, dirt road servicing Moody Ridge. Despite the valiant automobile's determination and momentum, we made it only as far as the first turn before we ran off the shoulder. We didn't hit anything, fortunately, but we *did* get stuck; stuck enough that I decided *The Prudent Man* would not tempt misfortune again, especially this close to dusk.

After an hour of digging, I was able to drive the Cranbrook, in reverse, back down to the plowed county road where, after negotiating an exhausting seven-point turn around, I continued westwardly—loose chains slapping the wheel wells—another couple miles, down to the tiny, goldmining town of Dutch Flat, and into the parking lot of the infamous Monte Vista Inn.

Being that it was the Monte Vista Inn, the place was virtually dead. Which was fine with me. There was only ol' Doc down at one end of the bar (asleep on his stool, nearest the beernuts, per usual, with another fallen cigarette butt burning yet another char mark in the otherwise finely-polished, not-too-sticky wood counter), and ol' Louie up the other end, squinting at the TV's crappy reception; thinking it must be his eyes rather than the common knowledge that the storm of '82 had knocked the joint's antenna off the top of the pine tree out back.

"S'posed ta snow!" Louie was telling the bartender as I sidled up to the bar.

I ordered a hamburger, fries, and a draft beer, then—exploiting perhaps my last chance at a smooth writing surface and reasonable light—promptly went about filling out my 1984 state and federal tax returns. The bartender set my hamburger and beer off to the side of my paperwork, then un-dimmed the lights a bit for me.

"Thanks," I said.

"Hell, don't mention it; it's taxpayers like you that keep our clientele liquid, if ya know what I mean," the bartender replied.

Filling out a tax form is, for me, like a glance into a mirror. For instance: mine reminded me that just during the month of January of last year I had *five* different employers—just during January! These jobs included everything from pizza cook, to snow shoveler, to janitor, to Squaw Valley chairlift operator (until I was fired for trying to organize a strike), to, yes, even chimneysweep. Funny, I had never thought of myself as one of those who can't hold a job, yet my reflection in the 1040 form proves otherwise. Another thing that was revealed was that, for now the ninth year in a row, I have again "failed" to make over $5,000—the minimal taxable income. I pointed this fact out to the bartender.

"On the house," he said, as he poured me another draft.

The bartender kicked us out somewhere around eleven. It was still snowing, so I ended up sleeping on the backseat of the Cranbrook, there in the parking lot cut out of a pine forest, behind the bar. Bud slept on the front seat. Though the seats were plenty comfortable, it seemed that every time we had just about dozed off, another wet clump of snow would drop from a towering tree bough and slam onto the car's roof or hood. Sixteen meters per second squared. Eventually, sometime around midnight, I suppose, the storm broke, causing the temperature to plummet and the snow clumps to stop falling. Only then were we able to sleep.

ROBERT P. JOHNSON

Moon of the Dark Red Calf

"The world of our sight is like habitation within
a cave, the firelight there to the sunlight here,
the ascent and the view of the upper world is the
rising of the soul into the world of the mind. Put
it so and you will not be far from my own surmise... but God knows if it is true."

— PLATO, *The Republic: Book VII*

Journal Entry; 2 February 1985:

It was a banner morning; the kind of crystal-blue skied, crystalline snow-white morning that get skiers chomping at the bit. After scraping the ice from the Cranbrook's windshield, we drove up to the Alta post office and mailed in my tax forms. I'd be counting on that refund. After that, I set course again towards Moody Ridge to see if the road had been plowed. It had, so we pressed on up to the trailhead. As we drew near to my regular parking spot I shoved the gas pedal to the floor. Once sufficient momentum was achieved I purposely ran the car through the snow berm and off the shoulder of the road. Long-term parking, wilderness style.

With my backpack donned and stuffed with enough provisions to see us through the next four months, Bud and I stood poised to resume my year in the weeds. If there was one thing of which I was certain, it was that I was thoroughly tired of this world of frustrations and fears. I ached for *meaning*. I ached for *confidence*. I ached for *change*: it needn't be transcendental, but I hoped, at very least, it would be profound.

"C'mon, Bud," I said. And with that we stepped over the road birm and onto the buried trailhead, and began to ford our way through the virgin snow back down into the canyon.

Journal Entry; 6 February 1985:

Upon slip-sliding back into the canyon, four days ago now, I was pleased to find the tipi had weathered its month alone. In fact, other than being besieged by wintering box elder beetles, it looked pretty much as it did the day I left it.

But that was then and this is now and today is Babe Ruth's birthday, which means it is also Ronald Reagan's, which means it is also mine. I reckon that to be about the only thing the three of us have in common; the Babe, the Gipper, and, yers truly, Rattlesnake Cutthroat. So much for astrology.

It's no accident that I happen to be spending this, my twenty-eighth birthday, in the wilderness. The fact that Thoreau happened to be twenty-eight when he did his gig at Walden Pond gig is probably only coincidental, for my reason for doing it now is based upon the theory of "septenary cycles" of development as espoused by mystics of yore. The theory went that the human psyche graduates into a higher state of awareness every seven years. In the first stage of development, from birth up until the age seven, we are ostensibly *introduced* to this reality; the theory here being based on the theory that reality is subjective rather than objective. During the second stage of development, our perception ossifies to the point where, by age fourteen, we become firm believers that what we perceive of the world is all there is to reality. Childhood fantasies here become a thing of the past, with celebratory rites given in honor of this transition to puberty. Next, between the twenty-first and twenty-eighth year, the mind is given some respite from the hormone surge, and thus the opportunity to embark upon the study of the *Dialectic*—the art and practice of the logical investigation of the Truth. By stepping back a bit, the mind establishes a critical distance from the world, the better to ponder its nature, source and ultimate realness. It is during this stage then that we first come into the possession of the mental tools required of philosophers. If all goes well, the theory maintains, then by age twenty-eight the successful philosopher should arrive at the conclusion that the universe is illusory by nature; that it is nothing more than a mental construct somehow created by our own mind or minds. Upon arriving at this conclusion, the philosopher may then attempt his or her transcendence from "the cave" up and into the light of the Truth. This, possibly, is "the arduous ascent of the soul into the world of the mind" of which Plato spoke, or the process of being "born again into the spirit" of which Jesus spoke, or the "enlightenment" of which Buddha spoke, or the "awakening of Vishnu" of which Hindus speak, or the "veil removed" of which Mohammed spoke, or the "heaven" of Moses. Thereafter, by age thirty-five if all goes well, the theory suggests that the now enlightened soul must return to the cave, "to come back to a life which is less good" (as Socrates put it) in order "to bring to the world deliverance and its bliss," that being "the task of holiness."

Well, there you have it; my secret reason for coming to the wilderness—transcendence. I never tell people this for fear they will think of me as yet another flake. It's easier just to let them believe I'm here to write a book, mine for gold, or grow pot. That's a sad reflection of our society, methinks.

Moon of the Snowblind

There are more people alive today
than have ever died.

— A TROUBLING FACT

My solitude was temporarily interrupted with the arrival of a newcomer to these parts; a greenhorn, if ever there was one. Seems he tumbled into the canyon with last week's sunny weather and an itch to become a gold-miner. His pseudonym will remain Greenhorn, for legal reasons, and his home, apparently, will be the Comfort Zone. As he explained it: he had bumped into Slim in town uptop. Upon learning Slim was a goldminer, he shared with Slim that he was looking to set up digs down on the American River for awhile. Though there were two reasons for his want-ing to do this, he only offered one; that being, that his young wife and their two toddlers could not legally collect welfare if he lived with them. It was a ruse then that he moved out; a ruse not uncommon in these parts. Not uncommon in America. Feeling sorry for the greenhorn, Slim sold him the Comfort Zone Claim, lock, stock, and barrel. $100 cash paid.

When I met the guy and heard his story, I too felt sorry for him; so sorry, in fact, that I didn't have the heart to tell him that there was no Comfort Zone "claim," just a one, itty-bitty, piece-o-shit, illegitimate, black plastic cabin with a rusted-out woodstove. Slim had duped the newcomer good.

"Ya know, that Comfort Zone Claim is pretty good," I said, putting it gently to the Greenhorn on that, his first, day, "but it's a far cry from being *great*, if ya know what I mean."

"I think so," he muttered, his eyes revealing an intelligence quotient somewhere in the bovine range.

"Tell ya what: d'ya got yourself a sluicebox?"

"Sure do," Greenhorn said with pride, "Brand-spankin' new one. Bought it for $100 from a fella uptop calls himself The California Goldminer. Worth $250, he said. Never used!"

"*Uh-huh*," I said, trying not to roll my eyes too loudly. "Well, tell you what: my claim, that's it right across the river there, " I said, pointing down to Bob's Big Bar, "my claim hasn't ever been mined before. That's because it was formed by a recent landslide, come off that yonder hill there. But all the others, see—especially the Comfort Zone Claim— they've been picked-over for the past hundred years or more. Which means they've been picked clean of all their nuggets. Which means that about all you could hope to pan out of them is *flood* gold."

"Flood gold? What's that?"

"Flour, powder—fine little flecks of gold dragged downriver by the high water each spring. Pain in the ass. You want nuggets," I assured him. "Yeah, nuggets: big, fuckin' nuggets!" he said, getting excited.

"Well, then, tell you what: you bring your sluicebox on down to Bob's Big Bar there tomorrow morning and we'll partner-up."

The Greenhorn eagerly agreed to the proposition, grinning like I had just deeded him the Royal Dutchman Mine. We shook on it. "Fifty-fifty." In reality it was as good of a deal for me as it was for him, seeing how I didn't have a sluicebox and he didn't have a claim.

Anyway, like I said, that was last week; back when the partnership still looked promising. But from that point on things went fairly quickly downhill. The first morning we were hoping to run fifty buckets of gravel through the sluicebox, but he called it a day after just sixteen. The next morning we decided to shoot for a hundred buckets; you know, to catch up. But, after just eight, he wanted to call it quits. Come day three we vowed—"on a stack of pancakes"—to run two hundred buckets. But, of course, ended up running only four before he started whining about his sore back and missing his wife and kids. I was beginning to detect a pattern. Then, come the next morning, he didn't show at all. Nor did he for the next four days after that, which is where in time we find ourselves this fine, sunny, brisk, winter's day.

"Oh well, easy come, easy go," I sighed to myself, admiring my brand-spankin' new sluicebox.

In truth, I don't mind him not holding up his end of our little mining partnership. For one thing, I enjoy the solitude, especially when the alternative is listening to him blather on endlessly, usually about things I know to be utter bullshit.

"Oh, sure, I play chess. In fact, I plan my moves *twenty-five* in advance!" he assured me once.

"Oh yeah? Then how do you explain my checkmating you in just *four* moves?"

"Well, see, the games got to go over twenty-five moves before my game-plan kicks in."

"*Ahhh,* of course."

ROBERT P. JOHNSON

For another thing, with money enough in the bank to see me through until spring, I don't really need to be mining. If I choose to do it, it's purely for recreation: just twenty or so buckets through the sluice to break the monotony of reading, writing, and tossing sticks for Bud. If I strike the motherlode in the process, well, so much the better.

Speaking of striking the motherlode; that's kind of what happened today. I had just run my sixth bucket of gravel through the sluicebox when, there, down in the mesh riffles, it appeared; a nugget, flipping around like a gaffed tuna. Under the clear, swiftly flowing water, it looked to be biggest and brightest nugget I'd ever come by of my own efforts. Upon fishing it out, I found it to be flat and about the shape of a double peanut, though about half the size. And though it weighed probably no more than a pennyweight, its size and jewelry quality made it worth two or three times the mere sixteen dollars one can fetch for an equal weight of gold flour. "Mister Nugget"—that's what I named it. And in honor of its discovery, Bud and I called it a day, and went off to try our luck fishing, or rather, to see if the fish had yet to emerge from their winter dormancy, which, some fruitless hours later we felt confident to conclude that, no, apparently, they had not.

JOURNAL ENTRY; 14 MARCH 1985:

I shaved my head today...

JOURNAL ENTRY; 15 MARCH 1985:

... it seemed like a good idea at the time.

JOURNAL ENTRY; 16 MARCH 1985:

Suffice it to say, my thoughts have been few and far between lately; increasingly so. I imagine this must have to do with my increasingly scant contact with others of my species. It's been over two weeks since the Greenhorn returned to the canyon. We mined for a half a day then he was gone again. Don't even think he spent the night. If not for the contact with him, my daily reading, and my increasingly inconsistent writing, I wonder if my thoughts would eventually cease altogether. Or maybe it's nothing so quantitative; maybe the actual *number* of thoughts remain pretty much the same, but it's just that I'm becoming a bit better at not having to verbalize them. What about that boy raised by wolves?—surely he must have thoughts despite the fact that he had no language with which to verbalize them. What goes on in such a mind? "Bud? What's going on between your ears?" Bud turns towards me, cocking his ears and head in that archetypal pose of bewilderment. Drawing a conclusion, he picks up a stick and drops it at my feet. I know what he wants without having to verbalize it to myself. I toss the stick, *wantonly*, into the rapids. He goes, *excitedly*, after it. Wonder. Confusion. Cruelty. Humor. Joy. Fear. Love. What's going on here?

Well, I must say, this new haircut sure is low-maintenance. I'm getting to really appreciate that aspect of it, especially now that we're moving back into tick season. Maybe I should shave Bud. I guess it bears mentioning that, prior to my completely shaving my head, I first carved out one of those "Mohawk" hairdos. I was pretty proud of it, or at least of what little of it I could see in the broken shard of mirror glass I had requisitioned from the Comfort Zone a few months back. The front half of my Mohawk looked fairly orderly. It was the backside however, which I could not see but could feel was kind of out-of-whack, that caused me shave it off completely a few hours later. As fun as the Mohawk was, I don't think Bud misses it much. For it seems it filled me with the odd compulsion to chase him around the outside of the tipi, wielding a tomahawk and screaming a war cry. At first he seemed to be having fun with it. But then, after about the twentieth lap, he started to get nervous. Finally he ran off, positioning himself a good fifteen yards from me for the better part of the afternoon. Silly dog.

On the weather front: the three feet of snow from last week's storm has been all but melted now by this week's balmy blue skies. It seems a high pressure system has moved into this part of the Sierra Nevada and is content to sit, Mother Goose, atop us until we hatch. Well, fine with me: winter sucks.

This evening I finished reading, for the second time, *Black Elk Speaks* by John G. Neihardt. It's the first book that, as soon as I had finished

ROBERT P. JOHNSON

reading the last page, I turned right back to the first and began anew. It's an extraordinary work not only because Black Elk (1863 - 1930), an Oglala Sioux medicine man, led an obviously unique life, but also because of the boggling similarities between the fate of his people and the similiar threat confronting us, on a global level, today. In particular my fascination was piqued by the perceptions taking place within the Native American zeit-geist during the later half of the 1880s; the years which, culminating in the Massacre at Wounded Knee, proved to be the ultimate demise of the Indian Nation. The author refered to that period as "The Messiah Craze" due to the unprecedented number of messianic visions which occurred to tribes all across the continent. Black Elk was just one of many natives to whom a "great vision" came; a vision of a new world beyond reach of the Wasichus (white man), and into which the Indian Nation would one day flee, leaving this world to "roll up like a carpet and fade away."

I guess what really fascinates me about Black Elk's era is that I sus-pect we today are in the early years of our very own "messiah craze," brought upon by such threats to our survival as nuclear or biological warfare, ozone depletion, pollution, famine, AIDS or other plagues, and, the antecedent of every problem, over-population. As evidence to this, I submit the fact that there are presently over 1,600 religions prac-ticed today, two hundred of which appeared in just the last ten years. In most all of these "cults" there seems to be a conspicuously common theme of dire forebodings in the very near future, afterwhich time a messiah, or some such vehicle of salvation (some seventeen cults sub-scribe to the belief that UFOs will come for them), shall deliver their flock into a Promised Land.

So, what does this say of the human psyche; that seemingly each time we are faced with a threat of annihilation some part of our mind creates these messianic visions of salvation? Is it some evolved trait which serves only to provide us hope, albeit false, when we are truly desper-ate? Or, if the world really *is* subjective, are these visions then somehow real; meaning that Black Elk and his people really did go off into a world beyond the Wasichus, and Christians will likewise be delivered into a Heaven beyond the reach of the "fornicators, murderers, and practitioners of spiritism," and Mormons will each inherit their own planets; and the Buddhists reincarnated again and again? Or could it be that each of these visions of salvation are no less illusory than the images projected on the wall within Plato's cave?—meaning that this world and the envisioned heavens and worlds thereafter shall all come to pass after we have made the arduous ascent into truth.

> "Lift up your eyes to the heavens, and
> look upon the earth beneath: for the
> heavens shall vanish away like smoke,
> and the earth shall wax old like a gar-
> ment, and they that dwell therein shall
> die in like manner: but my salvation
> shall be forever."
>
> — ISAIAH 52:6

JOURNAL ENTRY; 17 MARCH 1985:

If my recollection of the last calendar I glimpsed serves me right, today is St. Patrick's Day. If not, then it isn't. Which I probably didn't need to explain. But, if today is indeed St. Patty's Day, then I have reason to be excited, for usually, and quite inexplicably, something big always seems to happen to me on this otherwise minor holiday. And today would prove no exception.

It happened during breakfast: Bud and I, sitting before the campfire, squinting from the eye-stinging smoke, choking down the cornmeal flapjacks that have become our staple breakfast (forty-five in a row and counting) and quaffing cowboy coffee—you get the picture. Anyway, that's when I happened to glance down between my boots and spot the arrowhead. There it was, floating right on top of the sooty dirt beside my firepit; a brown obsidian, bona fide authentic, nearly perfect, arrowhead. The most startling aspect of this discovery was the fact that, despite nine months and countless hours squandered on this very log, I hadn't noticed it sooner!

So it was that, once again, I felt St. Patrick's Day had come through for me with "something big."

After our leisurely breakfast, Bud and I headed upriver to do some fishing,

ROBERT P. JOHNSON

venturing as far as daylight and the spring run-off would allow. We must have gotten a later start than I thought, for the sun abandoned us long before we even reached Euchre Bar, forcing us to turn back for home with only a half limit of rainbows.

On our return back downstream, we stopped in at the Comfort Zone to see if Greenhorn had made one of his irregular and increasingly infrequent tumbles back into the canyon. He hadn't, so Bud and I pressed on for the tipi. By then it was pitch dark, with the afternoon's drizzle turned now to light rain. If I had anticipated our being gone this long after dark I would have brought along the kerosene lantern or, at very least, my sovereign-willed flashlight. But I hadn't, so, once again, the point was moot, leaving Bud and me to fumble along, guided by his nose and my vague recollection of the trail.

There is only one particularly difficult section in the mile-and-a-half stretch of trail between the Comfort Zone and the tipi; the steep downgrade which follows a cataracting creek back down to the river near the Mercury Pool Crossing. I had slipped twice along this stretch, adding mud to my already wet clothes, but managed the descent sans injury. When I reached flat trail again, I could hear Bud growling at something some thirty yards up ahead. Like the many voices of a cat, dog's have a way of emoting exactly what is on their minds by the particular growl, bark, bay, whine, yelp, or whimper emitted. So it was that the unprecedented ferocity of Bud's growls led me to assume he had encountered something of considerable threat; a bear perhaps, or maybe a mountain lion. Needless to say, I wasn't thrilled by the prospect of a tangle with either, but neither was I thrilled by the prospect of losing my best pal. So, onward I pressed, trying to look as menacing as I could to any nocturnal eyes that might be watching.

It was not until I was standing just behind Bud that I could see what it was he was growling at. And though I could see it, I still couldn't make it out. From the distance of five yards it just looked like a large, black rectangle draped over a subtle mound on the forest floor. As Bud continued to snarl and growl at the enigmatic threat, I managed a slow, reconnaissance circle around it, my eyes straining in the darkness. By all accounts, it seemed to be nothing more than a plastic tarp measuring some ten-feet square which, perhaps, some campers or hunters had tossed over their gear to protect if from the rain. With me arriving back at his side, Bud felt brave enough to end his growling and venture closer in order to give the dark patch a fair sniffing. But as he drew near, the subtle mound began to move. Bud began to growl anew.

"Howdy," I called out to the mound beneath the tarp, in the friendliest voice I could muster. "Don't mind the dog. He's just doesn't know what to make of you: we don't get many visitors down here this time of year."

There was no reply from beneath the tarp.

"Are you okay?"

Again, no reply. Which, in retrospect, made sense: I'd doubt if I'd care to strike up conversation with some rain-soaked, shaved-headed hermit with a pissed-off dog, out in the smack-dab middle of nowhere on a pitch-black night, were I in his or her shoes. Wouldn't be prudent.

Bud again mustered the courage to sniff closer. This time, however, the corner of the tarp nearest to him began to lift slightly. In frightened response, Bud began to back-up his fierce growls with sharp barks and bared teeth.

"Bud, knock it off. Get over here!" I shouted, but to no avail.

About then, the business end of a rifle barrel began to slide slowly into view from beneath the raised corner of the tarp, its blue steel muzzle pointed directly at Bud's face.

"C'mon, Bud," I said, this time trying a calmer tone, "Let's be gettin' home."

I then grabbed Bud by the tail and began to pull him away, all the while speaking as cordially as I could in an attempt to assuage the stranger's fears: "Anyway, my name's Robert, and Bud and I live in the tipi you probably passed on your way into the canyon. Stop on by for breakfast tomorrow, if you care: we make a mean cornmeal flapjack!"

Still, not a peep from beneath the tarp. Still the barrel remained pointed at Bud.

"Well, you sleep tight."

I turned my back slowly on the mysterious stranger as I commenced our retreat, making damn certain to keep my hands where he could see them. For longer than I care to recall, I was deathly aware of my backside; fearful that a bullet might come ripping through it at any moment. But, as luck would have it, each step carried us further out of sight and range, until finally I felt safe again.

Our pounding hearts eventually led us back to the tipi, the sight of which proffered a sense of security, however feeble it may be. Despite there being no moon tonight, the tipi's white canvas glowed nonetheless, causing it stick out of the otherwise pitch-black night like some garishly lighted public phone booth. I felt queasy: if this mysterious stranger cared to hunt us down and riddle us with bullets, he certainly would have no problem finding us.

I sloshed across the creek, somehow missing every steppingstone I knew by rote. I tied Bud outside to the leg of my writing table. Tonight he would be a guard dog: earn his keep.

As I flung open the tipi's doorflap and lifted one foot through the hole, a brilliant flash of lightning exploded off the canvas; close enough that the flash and boom were simultaneous, bright enough that my eyeballs reeled from the glare. I knew at once what it was, but that didn't keep me from imagining it could just as easily have been a gunshot. As the echo of thunder reverberated throughout the canyon, I recalled the last tarot card reading The Marijuana Grower gave to me on a drizzly night much like this: a skeleton hung from a noose—Death.

I turn around to see if I have been followed back to the tipi by the stranger.... It seems not.

I'm inside the tipi now, lying sleepless on my cot. I find myself regretting I hadn't packed my .22 rifle into the canyon with me after my January break. But, what if I had? Would I sneak back up to The Mercury Pool Crossing to shoot the stranger before he had the chance to shoot me? More lightning. The canvas flickers. Thunder rumbles in the distance—Mister McGillicuddy. A pine cone drops from a tree striking, with a dull *pong!*, the bottom of one of my overturned pots by the firepit. Bud growls at it. Good boy, Bud.... Yes, St. Patrick's Day: always something big.

JOURNAL INTERRUPTUS:

I have not been fair with you, dear Journal, at least not when it comes to admitting what really brought me to the wilderness. I've hinted at the reason often enough, with oblique references to the spiritual quests undertaken by Thoreau or Plato or whomever, yet somehow I always managed to keep from divulging my own impetus. What do we call this?—fear of rejection, fear of ridicule, I guess. Anyway, my most recent hint was the statement "something big always seems to happen to me on St. Patrick's Day." And now I feel obligated to explain:

It happened the evening of March 17, 1982—St. Patrick's Day. It was a particularly austere time for me: a year out of college; renting the smallest, coldest, cheapest room available; shoveling snow and chipping ice for a living during the heaviest winter anyone could remember; living in the crack of affluence in wealth-friendly Lake Tahoe. But all was going fairly well. Vital signs were stable.

Anyway, this particular evening found me sitting on the edge of my "bed"—an insulite camping pad which lay on the floor—shivering and reading, with a sleepingbag wrapped around me. At one point, as I was reading down the left page, I became aware of a peculiar yet somehow familiar sensation. It came on slowly; slowly enough that I knew I would be able to finish the paragraph before having to set down the book— before having to set down *everything*. What happened next I can only describe as the temporary but complete vanishing of the entire universe— utter, infinite, silent obliteration. The world as I knew it—all sense of body, earth, air, gravity, planets, stars, matter, desires, fears, thought, light, dark, space and time—simply dissipated like the illusory structures of a dream, and left in its wake only an immense and very personal awareness of my most fundamental being. That was it. That's all that remained of this universe: just one, all-encompassing, overwhelming sense of *Self*.

This Self, I suspect, is the personality we all unknowingly share. Much as the seemingly separate "people" who populate our dreams at night all share the same fundamental, albeit sleeping, essense—"you" or "me"— this Self is the source for all of us on this plane of existence; the boundless and eternal Self in which we are all (to use a tiresome new-age phrase) *one*.

Countless religions use the term *God* as an euphemism when speaking about the Self. And yet the actual experience of it is so far beyond the capacities of our tiny, three-dimensional minds, that the term "God" falls hopelessly short of conveying its true magnitude: during the experience, the concept of God means nothing because it is but one of our creations. To even label the experience belittles it.

Robert P. Johnson

In all, my glimpse of (what I hope was) the Truth, came and went about as quickly as the picture of a television set can be turned on, seen, then turned off again. After probably no more than thirty seconds, the brief clarity I had enjoyed became fogged-over again by worldly matter, then all-too-quickly solidifying around me into the same old world. As the universe reassembled itself, it seemed obvious that nothing in it was innate—not the earth or moon, not hell or purgatory or nirvana or heaven, not reincarnation or auras or chakras or ghosts or karma or any such religious dogma, not life or death, not the devil or God or even the nothingness described as being beyond God. All these were nothing more than the wisps of the dream which clear when one awakens. All these were nothing more than the notions which vanish before the ultimate and absolute Truth.

And so it was, that on that glorious St. Patrick's Day three years ago, I truly believe I was dragged up the arduous ascent and given a brief glimpse of the real world. But, maybe not. Maybe I just suffered a mild stroke or seizure or some inexplicable rush of endorphins or something: who knows? Regrettably, I seem to be the same person today that I was before the experience; just as stupid, just as spiteful, just as neurotic. If anything, maybe I'm just a wee bit more aware of how I *should* behave and what I *should* value, though it hasn't seemed to have had much of an effect.

Which brings us back to why exactly I felt I needed to come to the wilderness: You see, I felt blessed for being given that experience. And yet, in the years since, I've come to feel guilty for lacking the courage to do anything with it. For that reason did I come here: to attempt to have the experience once again but, this time, to have it and to not let it go! I came here in the hopes of unfettering myself—*completely,* this time—of the chains which keep me submerged in this cave-like existence; to free my soul so to make that arduous ascent back up and into the real world, and there to abide for eternity in the glorious light of Truth. Yep, that's why I came hither. But, so far, it hasn't happened. So far, even out here in the weeds, I find myself ever more mired in the vain preoccupations of the world. *C'est la vie.*

JOURNAL ENTRY; 19 MARCH 1985:

I reckon it's true of just about anything, even a crummy job; that there's an unavoidable sadness when it's nearly over. This morning I awoke to such a sadness, possibly for a couple of reasons. The first was for the passing away of my bittersweet foe, winter. For, as miserable as it was, here, now, near its passing, I almost wish it could start all over again. Almost. The second reason for this sadness is for the gradual passing of my wilderness sojourn in general, for now that spring is upon us I realize that my year in the weeds is ten-twelfths over. I could change that, of course. I could stay again through the soft months of summer, or even another year, but I choose not to. There are things here I can live without: deerflies nibbling at my ankles, ticks burying into my armpits, that all-too-invigorating buzz of rattlesnakes, or just having to worry about each new boogeyman who tumbles into the canyon, with a rifle and a mysterious past. Yeah, I can live without that.

Winter or not, it was shaping up to be a warm morning, with the re-assertive sun squeezing the chill out of both ends of the canyon almost as soon as it popped over the horizon. This change of weather brought the grasshoppers out of hiding, which in turn got Bud and me out trying to catch them, which was just what we were doing when a strange voice called out from the river trail, "Howdy."

I turned, grasshopper cupped in one hand, and stared at the fellow approaching me. He approached slowly and empty-handed, squinting in the glaring sunlight like he had just crawled out from under a rock. His eyes were puffy and bagged from lack of sleep. His short, hack-cut, greasy, black hair was covered, convict-style, by a blue bandana. A white t-shirt with the sleeves ripped off, and tight, greasy jeans revealed a solid frame. He was stout; some two inches shorter than me but about three times as wide, about as wide as a locomotive—a Mike Tyson in trashy white. He extended a hand, forearms tattooed and bulging like Popeye's, though I don't recall Popeye's being so tracked with hypodermic needle marks.

I switched the grasshopper I was holding cupped in my right hand to my left and shook his hand. "Howdy," I said back at him.

"I come to take you up on that breakfast offer you made the other night," he said.

"So, that was you under the tarp?"

He nodded, "That was me."

Just as I was cooking up the flapjacks, Greenhorn showed up. If I didn't

ROBERT P. JOHNSON

know him as well as I did, I might have thought it merely a coincidence.

"Hey-ya, Snake," he said, smirking at his timing, "That wouldn't be somethin' cookin' I smell, would it?"

When the stranger turned around and glanced up at Greenhorn, I noticed Greenhorn kind of wince; not like he recognized the new fellow, but just that he knew trouble when he saw it. I introduced the two:

"Greenhorn, this is... er, this is..." I waited for the stranger to offer up a name. But he took another sip of coffee, without doing so. This made Greenhorn wince again. Something told me I should make up a name: "Bob! " I lied, "This here's Bob."

Greenhorn nodded nervously, "Hey, ya, Bob. How's it goin'?"

The stranger took a drag on his cigarette, and just kind of squinted back through his own smoke.

"Bob's gonna be working the claim with us," I told Greenhorn, which elicited a raised brow of surprise from them both.

"That so?" Greenhorn asked, trying to act pleased.

To this the stranger said nothing, which we quickly took to mean, *D'you gotta problem with that?*

JOURNAL ENTRY; 21 MARCH 1985:

Well, the stranger, Greenhorn and I have been mining together now for three days in a row with fair to middlin' success. It's a strange mix of personalities; here at the Acme Mining Co. On my right I've got the ever loquacious Greenhorn, adding hyperbole to fibs faster than he can think them up. On my left, the ever taciturn stranger, who drags himself to my breakfast fire, sweaty and sleepless, as he goes quietly about trying to shake the heroin monkey from his back and veins, cold turkey. And somewhere between the two, me; the would-be writer, the would-be yuppie, the would-be monk. Oh well, at least we're contributing to the economy.

By noon we had run some forty buckets of gravel through the sluicebox, the bottom of which was showing some good color. Greenhorn was getting nervous that we might be losing some of our gold, so we pulled the sluicebox out of the river to clean it. As Greenhorn panned-down our morning haul, the stranger and I rolled up a couple of cigs and smoked them on the sandbar. The sun was high and hot. I removed my worn-through tennis shoes to thaw my feet from the hours of sub-mersion in the icy river. As I did, I glanced over to the stranger who had wandered off to take a piss. While relieving himself, his eye had been caught by a beautiful patch of tiger lilies sprouting from the serpentine rock wall. He was trying to smell them, assuming they must be every bit as fragrant as they were beautiful. And though they are virtually odor-less, he kept trying; seeming to attribute the blame to his own years of self-destruction.

"I think we got ourselves another pennyweight here," Greenhorn shouted from the river's edge, as he stared down into the swirling pan of black sand and metals.

"Which gives us just under three now," I called back to him.

"What's gold fetching these days?" the stranger asked.

"Three-eighty an ounce, last I checked," I said. "Which translates down to about thirty-two dollars for what we've got, once the assayer takes her cut."

"I say we cash in, 'Snake. What d'ya say?"

"You guys've pretty much eaten me outta house and home: I say we ain't got much of a choice there."

"Alright, I'll hike up today," Greenhorn offered, "Who's coming with me?"

"Well, not to sound like a prick," I began, "but being that it is my food you're eating, my claim you're jumping, and my solitude you're invad-ing, I think I'll just stay put and let you guys make the hike."

"Alrighty, the Snake has spoken. How's that by you?" Greenhorn asked the stranger.

The stranger had no immediate response to the question. Instead, he just kind of squinted up toward Moody Ridge and the trail that led back to civilization, courting a grimace which conveyed an unmistakeable hint of dread and apprehension. Nevertheless, after due consideration, he capitulated to the undertaking with the subtlest of nods.

"Fine then," Greenhorn said, "If we leave now, we can hitchhike down to Auburn, cash in the gold, buy supplies, and be back by sundown."

The stranger didn't move.

"If we leave now —" Greenhorn shyly began to repeat.

The stranger stood from the rock upon which he had been sitting

ROBERT P. JOHNSON

and, with no further hesitation, told Greenhorn, "Let's go." And with that, he began fording his way across the river.

Shaking his head and grumbling something to the effect of "scary motherfucker," Greenhorn hurriedly poured the morning's catch of gold and other metals into an empty salmon-egg jar.

"I'll clean it up at my wife's house uptop before we head down to the assay office," he told me, as he stuffed the jar in his shirt pocket.

Halfway across the river, the stranger paused and turned towards me, then called out, "What kind of wine do you like, Rattlesnake?"

"I dunno... red. Maybe a nice Bordeaux?"

"I was thinkin' of getting some Maddog 20/20," he replied.

"That'd be fine," I assured him.

He nodded and resumed his fording of the river.

Greenhorn managed to flash me a shuddering, *I-trust-this-guy-about-as-far-as-I-can-throw-him* look as he hurriedly donned his backpack.

I shrugged for him.

He shook his head, muttered, "Shit," then, against better judgment, followed the stranger's lead across the river.

Vernal Equinox

"There are three words for love in the Greek New Testament. First, there is *eros*. In Platonic philosophy, eros meant the yearning of the soul for the realm of the divine."

—DR. MARTIN LUTHER KING JR.

JOURNAL ENTRY; 22 MARCH 1985:

I'm not sure I mentioned it or not, dear Journal, but I've pushed the writing of my piece-o-shit novel to the back burner, so that I might focus more on you. What with all the pot growing, FBI raids, brushes with death, world-class trout fishing, sex and violence, and now, this mysterious stranger business, I have higher hopes for you than my aforementioned work. To this end I have been trying to locate a speech of Dr. Martin Luther King's I once read wherein he spoke about Eros. And, to that end, I've recently stumbled upon some rather boggling coincidences.

The first coincidence, the lesser of the two, occurred a few weeks back. I had hiked up to the payphone at the general store uptop, and placed a call to a medical expert friend of mine just to ask him how to spell *giardia*.

"G-I-A-R-D-I-A," he replied.

"Well, yes, that makes sense, I guess," I said, more than slightly embarrassed.

He then asked me how the book was coming along.

"How's the book coming along?"

"Well, you know, so-so. I've been trying to find this article on Eros I once read in some magazine some three or four years ago now, but I just can't seem to track it down—"

"What did you say the article was on?"

"Eros; one of like three words the Greeks had for love."

"That's funny: just last night I read an article on Eros in a book I'm reading."

"Oh yeah? What's the book?"

"I've got it right here: it's called, *A Testament of Hope: The Essential Writings of Dr. Martin Luther King Jr.*, edited by James Melvin Washington."

The sheer improbability of the happenstance bowled me over.

"That's the very article I've been trying to track down for months! Holy shit, what are the chances that you would *happen* to be reading the same obscure article?"

"I don't really know," he dryly replied.

"It was a rhetorical question. But I assure you, we're in the one-in-a-million odds bracket here!"

Though he wasn't as convinced as I that *Providence* had played a hand in our little coincidence, he did offer to photocopy the five-page article and mail it up to me.

Well, I received the article last week and promptly read it, the passion and wisdom of which immediately brought tears to my eyes. And yet, it wasn't until I had reread the article just this morning, that I happened to notice the editor's footnote, which listed the source and date of its original publication, and which was the greater of the two "coincidences" surrounding this incident. The source was the liberal Protestant journal, *Christian Century*. And the date that the King article first appeared was the sixth of February, 1957—which happens to be the very day I was born.

*

There are only three moments in the course of a day in the wilderness in which the watch-less recluse can be reasonably certain what time it is: dawn, high-noon, and dusk. And it was at the latter of those that the mysterious stranger fellow finally came a-tumbling back into the canyon, two days late and whistling the rueful tune to *Turn Out the Lights, The Party's Over.*

"Why the rueful tune," I asked him.

"Well, that's a long story, Rattlesnake," he replied, as he splashed water on his face and neck at my spring.

"Where's Greenhorn?"

"Well, now, that's a long story too; kind of one in the same." He squeezed the sweat from his bandanna.

"Where's our supplies?"

"Well, now, that's a short story," he replied, settling now upon the log before my campfire. "We never got 'em."

"So, where's our gold?"

To this he only shrugged and grinned.

"Oh. Well, that about explains everything," I snapped, heading off to wash my dinner pots and pans. Fuck him.

"Rattlesnake, I've got something to tell you."

"Doesn't sound like it."

"C'mon, settle down, it's a good story."

I sat across the fire from him to hear him out.

"No Maddog 20/20 even?"

He shook his head, there was a pause, and then he said, "They nabbed Greenhorn."

"Who's they?"

"The sheriff."

"Oh, yeah?" I said, trying not to reveal too much skepticism. "What, did you guys find yourself a little trouble the other night?"

"Nope, seems like Greenhorn had himself plenty of it coming to him already: two outstanding warrants for his arrest from Colorado."

"No shit?"

"None whatsoever."

"What were they for?"

"Brandishing a deadly weapon—a knife, I was told—and battery."

"Tell me more," I said, beginning to believe him.

"Well, we hiked up, when, Wednesday?"

"That's right."

"And today is—"

"Friday; two days longer than it should've taken."

"Time flies," he smirked.

My patience was wearing. "So, what happened?"

"So, we hike out of the canyon, all the way the hell up to that little town uptop, and all the way across town to his wife's little shithole cabin. By then it was already after five, so we were going to have to spend the night and hitch a ride down to the assay office the next morning. Let me say right here, that he and his wife didn't seem to be getting on so good."

"Yeah, she recently told me that Greenhorn socked their two-year old boy in the eye. She wasn't all too happy about that," I added.

"That could've done it. Then again, that could've just been the tip of the iceberg. Anyway, there we were; Greenhorn and me eating breakfast in their shabby ol' kitchen, when his wife slips past for the door mumbling something about heading down to the post office to pick up the mail. Greenhorn then suggests to her that, it being only eight o'clock, the mail wouldn't be sorted yet. To which she replies that she hadn't checked it yesterday, so she'll just go on down there anyway. This, of course, didn't make a whole lot of sense, so Greenhorn starts yellin' at her, tellin' her that she ought to just kick back for an hour or so, so that the postmaster has a chance to sort today's mail, so she can go down and pick up both yesterday's *and* today's. To which she screams back something to the effect that, Well, I don't see that it much matters seein' how we never get any mail anyway! And, with that, she swoops up one kid in her arm and takes the other by the hand and whisks them out the door."

"*Whisked*, you say."

"Yep, like she was in some kind of hurry to get the hell outta there."

"Then what happened?"

"Well, I bet it wasn't five minutes after that there come a knock at the door. I happened to be sitting at their kitchen table at the time, rolling a joint from a bag of weed I had. Greenhorn answered the door. From across the room and through the doorway I could see three or four Placer County Sheriffs. As they stepped into the house I tossed the bag of weed out the kitchen window, then just raised my hands in surrender. This is it, I told myself; you see, I thought for sure they had come for me. When they spun Greenhorn around and 'cuffed him; well, it surprised the shit outta me! Then they just escorted him out of the house and tucked him in to one of their squad cars. Greenhorn didn't struggle or nothin'."

"So, ol' Greenhorn was a wanted man," I mused. "That explains why he was down here hiding out in the canyon."

"Shit, Rattlesnake, of course that's why he was down here! Ain't that why we're *all* down here?"

"Well, no. But I'm getting the feeling that's why *you're* down here."

The stranger just kind of shook his head, letting his sad, bemused grin begin the story. "Sheee-it, if you only knew." He then commenced to level with me; to spill the beans; to come clean.

It all started rather abruptly the afternoon of March 14, just a little over a week ago. For that was when a SWAT team stormed his girl-friend's house in search of him. He dove for the nearest cover, which happened—quite unimaginatively—to be a pile of dirty laundry. One of the SWAT cops searching for him poked the muzzle of his rifle into the laundry pile, yet did not detect him. Another cop asked the first if he had checked that pile of laundry. To which the first answered, "Yep. He's not there." And, a few minutes later, they were gone.

That very night—that very, drizzly, cool night—a friend of his gave

ROBERT P. JOHNSON

him a ride up Interstate 80 and dropped him off at the trailhead to our fair canyon here. He tumbled in with little more than the clothes he wore, a sheet of black plastic, a .22 caliber rifle, and a sizable "monkey" on his back. As he explained it: "I hadn't eaten, I hadn't slept, and, to top it off, it was the first day in three years that I missed my fix (of heroin). And who should come a-be-boppin' along the trail in the middle of that rainy night, while I'm shivering and sweating and hallucinating?"

"Me?"

"Yeah, you: scared the shit outta me, motherfucker!"

"But you had the gun."

"Yeah, and you're fuckin' lucky I didn't use it! Shit, yeah—last week was stressful enough, then yesterday has to go and happen. There I was; hands stretched to the ceiling, there in Greenhorn's piece-o-shit kitchen, thinkin' to myself, This is it! Then off they fuckin' go and hand-cuff fuckin' Greenhorn and drag him off and leave me—fuckin' *me* of all people—just fuckin' sittin' there with my hands up to the sky! Fuckin' pinch me: I can't fuckin' believe it!"

"I don't mean to pry, but it sounds as if you're wanted pretty big time," I stated, inviting him to tell me as much as he wanted.

He looked me over; trusting me yet allowing himself to imagine the worse. "It might be best for both of us if you didn't know all the details, Rattlesnake. Suffice it to say, they have me classified as armed, psychotic, and very dangerous, and we'll leave it at that."

"Fine," I said, "we'll leave it at that. But, one last question."

"What's that?"

"If Greenhorn's bust went down yesterday morning, where did you spend the rest of yesterday, and last night, and most of today?"

"Well, like I said, Greenhorn and his wife didn't seem to be getting on so good," he hinted, with an adulterous glimmer.

"In spite of all, I still believe that man is basically good," Anne Frank wrote in her diary. I guess I believe that as well. That is, I believe we all behave as we do in the hope of earning the admiration of our peers. Whatever the act is, the intent is love. I behave in the manner by which I hope to win the respect and love of The Bros. The Fugitive (as I feel compelled now to call the stranger) behaves in the manner by which he hopes to win respect within his circle of rascals. Even The Pope's behavior may be dictated more by his peer group's values and expectation than by his devotion to God. Man's behavior, whether we judge it good or evil, is no more complex than this.

The foregoing, anyway, is one of the two reasons why I didn't sneak out of the canyon later that night to go rat on The Fugitive; because he seemed basically good. The other reason wasn't nearly so philosophic: we'll call it self-preservation and leave it at that.

The Fugitive announced that he was dog-tired and headed back to the Comfort Zone. As he was crossing the creek he turned and blurted back, in a surprisingly cheerful tone, "Hey, Rattlesnake, guess what!"

"What?" I felt obliged to ask.

"Today's the first day of spring: I found out uptop."

Like the ring of a public telephone, the news caught me completely by surprise. Spring! But, of course—the blossoms in the meadow, the balmy winds sweeping up the canyon, the swaying firs, the dance of sunlight coming in waves up the water's surface, the deep blue sky, the too-hot sun, the way Bud scratched himself—it should have been obvious. It was spring!

Moon of Grass Appearing

"Indeed, if I were ever to kill myself, it would
not be out of depression so much as *curiosity*."
— TREVOR NOSNHOJ, "Notions of the Absolute"

Journal Entry; 23 March 1985:

The Fugitive spent the day planting marijuana seedlings throughout the north corner of the valley, thus giving new meaning to "The Moon of Grass Appearing." Seeing how Greenhorn was behind bars in Colorado, and Slim hadn't yet returned from his winter migration down to the San Francisco Bay Area, The Fugitive and I could think of no reason why he shouldn't take over the most isolated campsite on this side of the river—the Comfort Zone. And so he did. The fact that he asked me was only a formality; respect for the fact that I was the longest (and only) resident of the canyon. Had I said, No, he would have moved in there anyway. He has a way of getting his way; a vocational skill he no doubt acquired in prison.

Sure, there are good people and there are those who are bad to the bone. But then there are those rare few who possess characters big enough to carry more than their fair share of both virtue and evil. The Fugitive is one of these; the consummate villain who happens to be a better human than most "good" people. And yet, I must remember, I've only observed him in nature, where it's something of a challenge to be an asshole. Were he back in Sacramento, back in his circle of n'er-do-well peers, well, suffice it to say, I might have a different impression of him. But here, now, he's doing alright. In fact, at the moment we're headed upstream a piece for some elementary fishing; trout fishing 101. (He's very much a beginner, so I'm not taking him anyplace challenging. No need to frustrate him.) Anyway, he's up ahead, pausing now to smell the blossoming azaleas:

"God damn, have you smelled these, Rattlesnake?"

"Yeah—reminds me of Hawaii."

"Reminds me of a fuckin' drawer full of panties!" he says, giving Nature his highest compliment.

To see him now makes it hard to believe that, just two weeks ago, he was hiding under a pile of laundry as a SWAT team searched his girlfriend's apartment for him. Or that, prior to his coming to this canyon, he hadn't missed a single day of heroin anytime over the past three years, including even an eighteen-month stint in Folsom. If a judge could see him now, he'd probably commute his sentence.

Later today, just as the sun was punching out, three members of The

Robert P. Johnson

Fugitive's family tumbled down the trail, rolling to a stop at my tipi. The Fugitive had warned me to expect them "any day now." He even gave me fair descriptions, each of which sounded as if he was reading them off a "Wanted" poster: height, weight, race, color hair, color eyes, scars, etc. (And, likewise, he had somehow managed to get to them a fair description of me: "The shaved-headed freak living in the tipi.") If anyone fitting those descriptions hiked in inquiring about him, I was to lead them to The Comfort Zone. All others I would point in the opposite direction. An ingenious plan.

Pops, The Fugitive's father, was the first to wander into my camp. And although I recognized him immediately, both from The Fugitive's description as well as the obvious familial resemblance, I pretended not to; just to play the role of the distrustful accomplice. And likewise, he pretended not to recognize me.

"Howdy," Pops said as he stepped up near my campfire and waited, thumb up his ass, for me to offer him a seat on my fireside sofa-log. But I didn't.

"Howdy," was my only reply.

Racking his brain for conversation, he craned his head skyward and remarked, "Purdy evenin', ain't it?"

I glanced up at the scarlet, turquoise sky, leveled my gaze back at him, and nodded.

Growing impatient with my inhospitable hospitality Pops expelled a weary sigh then announced: "Welp, reckon I'll be movin' on."

"Where're you rushin' off to? Take a load off," I finally offered.

"Why, that's mighty kind of you," he smirked, swinging off his backpack and settling into my sofa-log like it was the most comfortable couch in the county.

"Don't mention it," I smirked back.

His next big task was to remove a considerably oversized jug of cheap burgundy from his considerably undersized, yard-sale backpack. After considerable struggle, he opted to perform a ceasarian extrication: "Can I borrow your knife there?" That done, he unscrewed the jug's cap as I scrounged up a pair of coffee mugs. He topped them off with the bloody swill. We clinked vessels, then drank... then drank some more... then a little more.

"Do much fishin' down here?" he asked.

"Yep."

Assuming the ice had been sufficiently broken, he sidled closer to the point: "Seen a fellow come into this part of the canyon lately?"

"Lot of fellows come in here."

"A young fellow; this one."

"They've all been young fellows, up until you."

"Well, this particular young fellow is pretty husky, but otherwise prob'ly bares a rather striking resemblance to me."

"Now, why would that be?" I asked, playing dumb.

"Just does," he replied, playing dumber. "Seen him?"

I took a long pause. "Well, now, that depends."

"On what?"

"On who wants to know."

"Me—I want to know."

"Yeah, well, who are you?"

Pops licked his lips, well aware of the game of honor amongst thieves we were playing; the loser being he who divulges his identity first.

"Well, now, that depends too," he deflected.

"On what?"

"On if or not you're the Man?" Pops asked delicately. "Ya know, ya gotta tell me if you are!"

"I know. But I ain't. Are you? Ya know, ya gotta tell me if you are."

"'Course, I know that. But I ain't either."

"Good, that makes two of us."

"At least we both know who we ain't."

"I suppose that's progress."

"Here's to progress."

We clinked cups and took another sip of burgundy.

Right about then we began to hear some serious cussing coming down the trail. It belonged to a man and a woman; lovers, it would seem, in the throes of a heated spat.

"Here come the lovebirds," Pops muttered into his cup.

"Who're they?"

"My ex-niece and her ex-husband."

"Ah, dos equis."

"What?"

"I was just wondering how it is that a niece can ever be an ex-niece," I invented.

"Oh, well, she's my ex-wife's niece actually."

"I see."

When the forty-ish pair finally came into view, I was surprised to find the man was carrying the woman piggy-back, and even more surprised to see that this considerable effort on his part still couldn't deter her from berating him as if he were the most worthless piece of shit to hit the planet; even in the presence of me, a perfect stranger!

"He's been carrying her since about halfway up the trail, and the whole time she's been bitching!" Pops muttered to me.

"Quite a gal."

Pops had to shout at them to garner their attention: "Hey, Chrissy, Stoner, shut up a minute. This here's Rattlesnake."

They turned their vitriols off as easily as water from a faucet, at once smearing friendly smiles and extending the most cordial howdy-does.

"Rattlesnake's our contact. He's gonna take us to where Kenny—" Pops tried to put on the brakes.

"I don't think you're supposed to tell Rattlesnake his name, Pops," Stoner told him.

"I know. It slipped!" Pops said, mad at himself.

"Who's name?" Chrissy asked, "Kenny's?"

"Chrissy!" Stoner hissed, pulling a finger to his pursed lips.

"What?"

"Shut up!"

"You shut up!"

Even though I hadn't known The Fugitive's real name until then, I decided to put their minds at ease by making up an alias for him on the spot.

"Now, you three obviously went through some considerable rehearsing to get me to believe his name was Kenny, and it would have worked if only he hadn't already told me his name was Robert." I lied.

"Ah, so you know?" Pops said, thinking his boy had duped me.

"Yep," I assured him.

"Yeah, ol' Bobby always knew who he could trust," Stoner added, winking to Pops.

"Bobby? Who's he, and who's Robert?" Chrissy spewed, chipping away at Stoner and Pops's subtle ruse. "I thought we come here to see Kenny!"

"Shut up, Chrissy," Stoner whispered.

"*You* shut up!"

Stoner tried elbowing her.

"And quit elbowing me!"

As the two continued to hiss at one another, I turned to Pops. "She's good," I said.

"Oh yeah, should've been an actress," Pops sighed, shaking his head.

The first stars were shining down like sunlight through the roof of a bullet-riddled barn as we followed the intermittent beam of my sovereign-willed flashlight towards The Comfort Zone. And though it's a good mile and a half up to there, the time was quickly passed listening to more sweet cooings emanating from our dragging ex-lovebirds:

"Carry me!"

"Carry yourself!"

"I can't help it if my feet blister easy, dammit!"

"Shit, whad'ya 'spect wearin' them prissy boots of yours? Hell, you knew we wasn't goin' to no fashion show!"

"Nobody asked you to come along. You ain't no kin of his!"

"Oh, like you are; ex-cousin fifty times removed!"

"Kin's kin!"

"Yeah, well, no kin is worth shit if she can't carry her own lazy ass!"

"You just watch that filthy mouth of yours, asshole!"

"Fine; helluva lot better than watchin' that filthy trap of yours."

"You take that back!"

"I won't."

"I said, take it back!"

"And, as you might recall, I said I won't!"

"Then you can just turn your sorry ass right around and start carrying me right back out of this here canyon!"

"And you can just screw yourself!"

"Well, I sure as hell ain't gonna screw you ever again; not as long as

I live!"

"Well, at least I won't have to wait long."

Anon, anon, anon....

Soon we arrived at the front trail leading down into the gulch wherein The Comfort Zone is hidden. From there, as planned, I sounded a long, loud Injun whoop; to let The Fugitive know the visit was friendly. If I were to come by way of the seldom-used back route, and call out in any other manner, he would know to expect trouble and would flee accordingly. Before I even finished my whoop, The Fugitive shouted—as merry as I've ever heard him—up from the wooded gulch, "Pops! C'mon down! Ya-hoo!"

The reunion of deadbeat dad with renegade son, torn asunder by the long arm of the law, could have brought tears to the eyes of Idi Amin. First The Fugitive apologized for being such a troublesome son. Then Pops apologized for having run out on the family when the boys needed a father's guidance most. Then Chrissy passed along the rest of the family's love and well-wishes. Then Stoner pulled a half dozen steaks out of his pack and began barbecuing them over a fire of crackling manzanita.

With the steaks polished-off and the wine jug making slow orbits around the campfire, the conversation turned to The Fugitive's brush with the law. I played the proverbial *fly on the wall* so as not to hinder the confidentiality of the discourse in the least. At one point The Fugitive grumbled something to the effect of: "None of this would've happened if only Ricky's little girlfriend hadn't shot off her mouth to that judge/friend of hers. She don't know the wasps' nest she stirred up!"

"And I reckon she never will... now," Stoner said, in a tone that was somehow foreboding despite it being mumbled through a mouthful of cookies.

The Fugitive stared at him for a long time then asked, "Why's that?"

Stoner looked up, shocked to hear The Fugitive ask that. His eye's darted from The Fugitive, over to Chrissy, who looked really scared all of a sudden, across the fire to Pops, who shrugged to him, then back to The Fugitive. Stoner swallowed then spoke: "'Cause she's gone."

"Gone where?" The Fugitive asked, with convincing innocence.

"Where? *No*where; she's *gone* gone."

The Fugitive's face paled like he had crapped his pants.

"Killed?" he asked.

Stoner nodded.

The Fugitive gave it some thought, then asked, "Shot, stabbed, or strangled?"

Stoner shrugged: "No one knows; they ain't found her yet."

"So, she might not be dead, right? I mean, she might've just skipped town," The Fugitive theorized hopefully.

The other three kind of just dropped their eyes back into the fire.

"Not likely," Pops said sadly, "The word down at the bar is she was taken down two weeks ago. Seems like a couple of the fellows know it for a fact."

You could hear the wheels turning inside The Fugitive's head.

"A couple weeks ago? Who do they think done it?"

The Fugitive's query was followed by another battery of eye glances and shrugs before Pops answered:

"Well, you're the only one of the bunch that skipped town."

The sound of The Fugitive's heart dropping into his stomach was as palpable as a felled eighty-foot fir.

"I didn't do it."

More silence.

"I been down here for two weeks!" The Fugitive tried.

"It happened the day before that SWAT raid," Stoner countered.

"Are you sure?"

"Like I said, that's the word down at the bar," Pops averred sadly.

The Fugitive's mind was in hyper-drive, by now on to the theory that this was some sort of conspiracy conjured up by the law.

"D'ya think the Man is just makin' this up to try to flush me out?"

Pops shrugged. "All I know is they've been tailing me wherever we go."

"Me too," Stoner said, "They had a slick (an unmarked squad car) following me home from the bar last night!"

"You gotta watch it; they use two cars, you know," The Fugitive warned.

"You're tellin' me? I done ditched the first one by pullin' into a drive way, turnin' off my lights and duckin' in the seat. Then a helicopter come and lights up the whole neighborhood and a second slick drives by. But I din't move and they din't find me!"

The Fugitive shook his head, "Jesus."

"I hope you haven't called your mom," Chrissy said.

"Why's that?"

"Her phone's tapped. Every time someone calls she hears these little *clicks* over the receiver!"

Right about then I was wishing I wasn't at the party: this fugitive guy was obviously in very deep shit to warrant having his whole extended family under surveillance. That's about when Stoner set a suspicious bead on me.

"What's your real name, Rattlesnake?" he asked.

Before I had the chance to answer, The Fugitive interceded, "Don't you worry 'bout ol' Rattlesnake; he's good people. He could've ratted on me anytime he wanted."

"I just wanted to know what his name was."

"Well, maybe he don't need you to know his name: ever think of that?"

That was something even I hadn't thought of; that, by using the pseudonym of Rattlesnake, The Fugitive assumed I must be on the lam as well. In a way it was perfect; a détente of dirt of sorts, or so he thought.

I nodded a silent *Thanks* to him, across the campfire.

He nodded one back.

As I wandered through the darkness back to my tipi, I wondered if I should tell The Fugitive at some point just how often the Man storms the canyon; about last summer's raids by the FBI and Sheriff, and the bi-weekly fly-overs by any number of federal agencies. I probably should. And, while I'm at it, I should probably pad the figure considerably. I don't like this guy being down here. Someone's likely to get hurt.

JOURNAL ENTRY; 28 MARCH 1985:

The automobile insurance on the Cranbrook expired last night at midnight. I would've paid it, but I have only eight dollars to my name. Now, according to the California Penal Code, I am a criminal; an outlaw on the lam, a fugitive. Well, now, at least, I fit in.

It's been storming these past four days. First heavy rain, then heavy hail, now heavy snow. More than a foot of the fresh white has gathered up on the ridge tops, forcing Pops, Chrissy, and Stoner to stay in the canyon five nights instead of their intended one. The ironic drawback to this is the fact that the overstay has forced them to gnaw through all the supplies they had packed in for The Fugitive, and even what few canned goods Greenhorn had left behind. Compounding their collective woe, it seems they're now even out of alcohol; no small matter for two steady alcoholics (Chrissy and Stoner) and one profound drunk (Pops). Suffice it to say, tensions have been running pretty high up at The Comfort Zone. Suffice it to say, I've been keeping my distance.

In the four days since that first night I've visited them twice: once was to play dice (which they play constantly), the other, which was two days ago, to borrow The Fugitive's .22 rifle.

"What d'ya want it for?" The Fugitive asked.

"I was thinkin' of shootin' you all."

"Okay-doke," he deadpanned, handing over the rifle.

"Yeah, put us out of our misery," Pops added.

Chrissy's eyes started darting around the dice table as if we were speaking seriously.

"You goin' huntin', Rattlesnake?" Stoner asked, probably more for Chrissy's edification than his personal curiosity.

"Yep. Spotted some deer tracks this morning. Gonna see if I can't rustle us up some venison for lunch."

"Sounds great."

I then recalled Stoner telling me he was half Paiute. I figured I might as well drag him up Snakehead Point to see if he passed out: a little science fair project to see if Eros' hex still packed a punch with native blood.

"Wanna come?"

"Naw."

"You sure?"

"Yeah, I gotta whip these punks' asses in dice again."

Contrary to what I told them, I didn't go hunting. Far from it, in fact, for the only thing I contemplated shooting in those forty-eight hours was myself. I didn't, of course; partly because I was worried about my painfully surviving a .22 calibre wound, or even several (I actually pondered the possibility of shooting myself in my stomach, heart *then* mouth), and partly because I feared for the heartbreak it would cause family and friends. Also there to prevent me was a promise I once made to myself; that being that whenever I felt the urge to commit suicide, I would give myself a one-year stay of execution—one year to throw myself earnestly into life in a no-holds-barred quest for enlightenment. Well, that year wasn't quite up just yet. Another two moons. Besides, I wasn't all that depressed; just so dawg-gone *curious!*

Like I said, that was two days ago. When I wandered back into The Comfort Zone camp this morning, my arrival was met by four pairs of drooling eyes. But, once they saw that I had returned empty-handed, the drools hardened to frowns.

"No venison?" Stoner asked.

I shook my head, handing back the rifle. "Not even any squirrel."

Had I known just how hungry they were, and how much hope they had invested in my bringing back some game, I might have tried a bit harder; hell, I might have *tried* period.

JOURNAL ENTRY; 1 APRIL 1985:

The weather took a turn for the better since my last journal scribbling. Ever since the storm broke it's been so clear that I catch myself gazing up at the lush green firs backdropped by the impossibly blue sky, wondering if I'm not dreaming it. But it seems I'm not: it's all very real and very beautiful.

The break in the weather permitted Stoner and Chrissy to finally flee the canyon. That was two days ago. Good riddance. Two down, two to go. Pops stayed behind. When I asked why, I was made privy to the drunk driving hit and run arrest warrant which awaited him were he ever to leave the canyon. So, he too is in trouble with the Man—an outlaw, a fugitive. Birds of a feather....

In light of this new information about Pops, and the fact that it was, after all, April Fools Day, I hiked to the Comfort Zone's perimeter early this morning to pull a little April Fools prank on The Fugitive and Pops. My plan was simply to hide in the bushes, there above the gulch, and shout out: "Alright, boys, we got'cha surrounded. Come out with yer hands up!"—you know, just to see what they would do. But, as I stood there—hands cupped around my mouth, Bud at my side panting, *Do it! Do it!*—some little voice inside me suggested this mightn't be the prudent thing to do. So, I dropped my hands and returned to the tipi.

Getting on towards noon two raft-loads of river guides anchored in the pool below my tipi and dispatched emissaries up to make my acquaintance. Over the past week I've spotted five or so different outfitters making the voyage, only two of which—The River Rats and Whitewater Voyages—have mustered the nerve to stop and chat. The River Rats seem to be a rag-tag team of young macho guys out to tame the world, while Whitewater Voyages, my personal favorite, appears to be a tight ship of amazons (predominantly), out on the sole quest of making my nights restless.

Today, thankfully again, it was the latter outfitter who made the stop: Stephanie, Christine, Suzy, Kelly, Spark, some guy named Bill (who owned the company), and a few other jocks hardly worth mentioning. They informed me that the five companies I had observed were all vying for the two permits The Forest Service would issue next season granting rights to run this stretch of the North Fork commercially. Because of the inherent dangers of this "Giant Gap" stretch—what with its tumbling cataracts, sheer walls, and voracious holes—the Forest Service had never before permitted commercial trips here. But now, with the more maneuverable "self-baling" rafts whittling such previously "un-runable" Class VI rapids down to "barely-runable" Class V ones, the USFS was willing to consider it, but only to the two outfitters who proved themselves to be the most capable. And to this end, these outfitters and their teams of guides train tirelessly; flipping their rafts and taking harrowing swims, hurling themselves down Danger's gullet, all for a few shekels and the fleeting adrenaline fix. God bless 'em.

They fixed me lunch—a splendid buffet, with leftovers even for Bud—but they demanded something in return; they demanded *lore*. So, I granted them their demand, telling all that I've learned about this stretch of the canyon over the past ten months: I told them of the Maidu who first lived here, then of the goldrush folks; I told them about Slim, The California Goldminer, The Marijuana Grower and sweet Lolita; I spewed on about Steve Wallenda and the FBI bust; about the rattlesnake

I ate, the deer I couldn't shoot, and all the fish I had out-smarted; I even told them about the legend of Eros' Pyramid, and how I had come to learn of it, and how it was to blame for my learning of this spot in the first place. In fact, the only thing I didn't tell them was about the dangerous Fugitive living upstream a piece with his Pops. They didn't need to know that.

When I was all done, one of the amazons asked: "So, why are you doing this?"

"Why? Because I'm a writer, that's why!" I snapped, feigning anger as I directed her attention to my clackle-clacker, as if it should have been obvious.

"A writer, huh? So, you writing about this year in the wilderness of yours?" Bill asked.

"Maybe," I replied, cryptically.

"Well, if all those stories you told us are any indication, it sounds like it might be pretty good. What are you going to call it?"

"Well, I don't go in much for these pretentious titles you find these days. I wanted something straight to the point, something that would-n't lead the reader to think he was getting something he wasn't."

"Yeah, so what's it gonna be?" he pressed.

"Well, I was thinking of—and you tell me if you think it's a good idea or not—I was thinking about calling it, 'Marilyn and Elvis: The Awful Truth.' What do you think? It's not too *on the nose*, is it?"

"I think you oughta come guide rivers for us when you get out of here. That's what I think. What do you think?"

I swept my gaze across the regimen of amazons, their bikinis no match for my imagination. "I think you've got yourself a deal there, mister."

As the two rafts of amazon warriors and their scrawny men-boy slaves paddled off into the west, it dawned on me that this would be the perfect method to extricate my tipi and things from the canyon at the end of my stay: I'll just float it all out on rafts!

"There they go," I sighed wistfully to Bud, as we watched from the tipi terrace as the amazons' tanned muscles pulled their vessels through the first of the scores of rapids they would shame today. "There they go." Who could've guessed I'd be shacked up with one of them a year later?

Journal Entry; 5 April 1985:

I've been quiet again, haven't I, dear journal? Well, my excuse this time is that over the course of these past five days I have been surprised by three different visitors. It now seems we've come full circle; the solitude of winter has yielded to the society of spring.

My old buddy Jae was the first of the visitors. He arrived in his typical m.o.—a silent grin smeared from ear to ear and a backpack unbelievably over-stuffed with beer and grub.

"God bless you, Jae!" I said, unpacking for him.

"Did ya find religion, Bob?" he asked.

"No, but I found a couple of beers!" I answered, pulling two cold ones from near the bottom of his pack.

Ssppfftt! Ssppfftt!

My second visitor, an old pal named Pete, showed up the next day. This was Pete's first visit, and to celebrate, he brought with him his banjo and two bottles of wine: an '81 Chardonnay, and a fine March vintage Thunderbird.

"May I smell the cap?"

And thus the next two days were passed with Jae and I fishing the strong vernal currents while Pete played his banjo for us from the sunny banks.

My third visitor tumbled into the canyon on the heels of Jae and Pete's departure, the day before yesterday. It was late at night when he arrived, probably around midnight. The moon, of course, was full. From right out side the thin canvas of the tipi, probably not twelve inches from my soundly sleeping ear, came his thunderous Injun whoop. Bud instantly began thumping his tail against the earthen floor, for this third visitor was, of course, none other than The Marijuana Grower.

"C'mon in!" I shouted, climbing out of my sleepingbag and lighting a kerosene lantern.

Bud was wagging and whining so badly he would have peed his pants, were he wearing any. Since he wasn't, he just peed.

"Hello, Shithead," The Marijuana Grower said, greeting his former best friend with an affectionate nose-rub. Bud licked The Marijuana Grower's face so much, it was a wonder his skin didn't come off.

As for The Marijuana Grower, he looked pretty good, I guess you could say. This in spite of the obvious fact that he was once again obese.

"How much do you weigh?" I asked, right off.

"Two-forty-five," came his unashamed reply.

"That's, what, seventy pounds in five months?"

"Seventy-*five*!" he proudly corrected.

Other than his mass, not much else had changed in his life: he was still broke and homeless, and still hadn't a clue where life would lead him next.

"Didn't you make any money off last season's harvest?" I asked.

"Not really. Traded two ounces for a Nikon camera, and one for a piece-o-shit Plymouth."

"Plymouth, eh? A Cranbrook perchance?"

"No, but I was thinkin' of you."

"So, what did you do with the rest: you left here with about two pounds of bud!"

"Well, pretty much all of it I gave directly to Santa Cruz prostitutes."

"The barter system."

He nodded. "It's the only way to beat the tax man."

That was last night. Come this morning The Marijuana Grower was up before dawn and off to places undeclared. Since he had left his bedroll behind, I knew he was still in the canyon, which left little doubt in my mind that he had headed up the back side of Snakehead Point to plant some pot seeds in that marshy spot where his replacement plants had done so well last year. By late this afternoon, he was back at the tipi and ready to hike out of the canyon again.

"Welp, gotta go," he announced.

Since it had been some weeks since I had been out, I decided to make the hike with him; at very least to pick up some pancake mix stored in the Cranbrook, at very most to grab a few brews up at the Monte Vista Inn.

"Let me show you out," I told him.

The "force" was with me, up at the Monte Vista; I won three straight games of liars dice, so didn't have to pay for a single beer. Out in the parking lot, Bud and I bade The Marijuana Grower farewell.

"Bye," he said, ever so wryly, as he headed for his car.

"Bye," I replied, starting the Cranbrook's ignition.

He bump-started his car, then shouted out the window: "Probably won't be seein' ya."

"Probably not," I confirmed, driving off without out so much as a goodbye wave. As I may have mentioned, he and I shared a sense of humor that kind of mocked the severity of life; the fact that we probably *wouldn't* ever see one another again, only made the moment richer.

As The Marijuana Grower headed back down for the coast, Bud and I drove the Cranbrook back out to the ridge. I parked up at the trailhead, grabbed the bag of pancake mix, and headed back down the trail. By then it was probably close to eleven, with the full moon burning brightly overhead. En route, Bud flushed a skunk. It brushed past my legs as Bud chased it back up the trail. I shouted for Bud to call off his pursuit, but he blatantly ignored me. A few seconds later, the skunk let loose, teaching Bud a poignant lesson.

For the rest of the hike, so long as Bud was downwind of me, the air was sweet with the honeysuckle fragrance of manzanita bloom. Above, the stars were made faint by the moon's brilliance. The surrounding fir-lined ridges gnawed at the sky with their serrated horizons. Mining scars glowed like sheets hung out to dry against the utter blackness of the canyon's southern slopes, while all else took on various shades of gray to drab-olive, as they reflected the moon's cool cool smile.

When at last we reached the meadow, the azalea blossoms, and those of the pear and apple trees, shone like magnesium flares beneath the garish moonlight. But brightest of all in the canyon was the simple conical structure I call "home sweet home"; a site for sore eyes and weary legs—my tipi.

JOURNAL ENTRY; 7 APRIL 1985:

Now that spring is in full thump, green seems to be all we see these days: the forest-green of the firs, that glossy avocado green of the California bays, the almost black-green of the azalea leaves, the tender lime-green of the new pine needle sprouts, the frosty silver-green of the manzanita, the moss-green of the moss in the creek, the green-green of the grass in the

ROBERT P. JOHNSON

meadow. Fifty different shades of green! What could die in the spring?

"C'mon, Rattlesnake, stay for supper!" Pops demanded.

"Yeah, you ain't visited in over a week!" The Fugitive kicked in.

"Thanks just the same, fellas, but I eat over here too much as it is," I said as I poured my dice onto their table. "Don't want to wear out my welcome."

But Pops pressed on: "We got a bunch of sausage we gotta eat up 'fore it goes bad: hell, you'd be doin' us a favor!"

"Thanks anyway," I said, counting up my five hundred-point roll.

"Heck, didn't think my cookin' was that bad. Is it that bad, sonny-boy?" Pops asked The Fugitive as he shook his dice in his hand.

"Well, it's pretty bad, but not so bad that Rattlesnake should be turnin' it down like he is," The Fugitive posited.

Pops rolled his dice. "Hot damn, lookie there: four aces. Mark me down for two thousand, sonny-boy!"

As often happens, and perhaps more so in solitude, a tune will often get mired in ones head, sometimes to ensconce itself there for hours, sometimes for days. With little or no social stimulation to jar it loose, it's conceivable that such a tune could stick there indefinitely. Rumor around these parts has it that Joe Steiner had a tune stuck in his head for thirty-five years; with some going so far as to claim that, if you put your ear to his grave, you can hear him whistling it still. But, then again, I may have started that rumor... just now.

Anyway, throughout our marathon dice tournament this perfectly pleasant afternoon, The Fugitive has had such a tune stuck in his head. He's been whistling it almost non-stop. And if he ever did lapse in whistling it, say, for five minutes or more, Pops and I would catch ourselves, quite unintentionally, whistling it for him. It was just one of those things you just couldn't keep from doing. Still, no one brought it to any of the other's attention. In fact, I may have been the only one of the three to notice. The tune itself was unmistakable; the title song from the musical, *Jesus Christ Superstar*. But would The Fugitive whistle the whole song? No-o-o; just the opening fifteen or so notes—over and over and over.

"Say, do any of you know when Easter is? " Pops asked, without even knowing what made him think of it.

"It's gotta be one of these Sundays comin' up," The Fugitive surmised.

"You wouldn't think it'd be so hard to keep track of the days," I told them, "But some times I hike down on, say, a Wednesday and by Thursday I've already lost track."

"Humph, 'magine that," Pops mumbled, rolling and counting his dice again.

"Ain't it suppose to come early this year?" The Fugitive asked.

"You know, you may be right. I think it's this comin' Sunday, in fact!" Pops said.

"What makes you think that?"

"Well, when your mama dropped off this last load of supplies, she said to keep the ham and chocolate bunnies for Easter supper."

"Hell, we gobbled those up the first night."

"Yeah, well, that was Tuesday, so, let's see, today must be... Saturday?—no, today must be... No! *Yeah*—Sunday! Crimony, today's Easter Sunday!" Pops guffawed, slapping his knee.

The revelation stung us all.

"Well, I'll be god-damn," The Fugitive reveled. "No wonder I had that damn song stuck in my head!"

"Sweet Jesus on the cross: Easter Sunday," Pops said, shaking his head as if he had witnessed a miracle. "Now ya gotta stay for supper, Rattlesnake!"

"Yep, I reckon I do."

Had I but known just how bad supper was going to be, I certainly would have declined the offer. But, regrettably, I'm no soothsayer. Sliced green, under-cooked potatoes fried together with the spoiled Farmer John sausage, in re-used bacon grease, served on dirty, plastic plates and eaten with fingers: a veritable feast made as memorable by the food as by the company.

"Hey, I wonder if the pruno's ready?" Pops said, jumping up and moving, as quickly as I've seen him.

"The what?" I asked.

"The *pruno!*" he repeated, disappearing around the back of their cabin.

I swung my puzzled stare towards The Fugitive.

"It's a kind of wine desperate drunks make out of prunes and sugar and yeast, I think. We used to make it in Folsom in a plastic garbage bag. That's how Pops made his, 'cept he used fruit cocktail," The Fugitive explained.

"How long does it take to ferment?"

"A couple weeks; if it's done right."

"How long has Pops been brewing his batch?"

The Fugitive shrugged: "A couple days."

I had the sudden urge to shovel down a second helping of the rancid fried green potatoes, anticipating that my tummy's tender lining might need the additional buffer. But it was too late to act; Pops was already headed back to the table, carrying the large black plastic garbage bag which contained a gallon or so of pruno.

"Take this all of you and drink from it, for this is my blood; the blood of the new and everlasting covenant!" Pops sanctimoniously bellowed. He then raised the bag above him, nibbled off the lowest corner until a rusty-colored fluid began dribbling from it, and then sucked on the corner like a lamb at its mother's teat. After a fair sampling, he smacked his lips; still trying to decide if the vintage was up to his discerning approval.

"It ain't my best batch," Pops said, passing the bag to me, "but it should do the trick."

I prepared myself mentally, then raised the bag overhead. It tasted bad, with a tart effervescence that suggested a process barely half completed. Nevertheless, polite guest that I am, I swallowed my portion and passed the bag on to The Fugitive, who guzzled it down without any reservations.

"I think it could've used another few days, Pops," The Fugitive suggested, puckering on the aftertaste, then belching.

"Why, you don't like those tiny bubbles dancin' on your tongue?" Pops guffawed, raising the bag overhead for the second of his many doses to come.

As the pruno's plastic udder was slowly sucked dry, The Fugitive told us about life behind bars; particularly, on how easy it was to get heroin: "We'd just stuff a handball full of dimes (to be used for the pay phone) and pretend to accidentally hit it over the handball court walls, into another, sealed-off part of the rec yard. It'd come back over with a fix inside of it. No problem."

"Who was over the other side there filling the prescriptions?"

The Fugitive shrugged, "Could've been another inmate, could've been a guard for all we knew *or* cared."

Later, when The Fugitive mentioned that his post-pokey habit had cost upwards of $1000 a day, Pops came unglued: this was obviously the first time he had heard about the real costs of heroin addictions.

"A grand a day?" he fumed, "You goddamned little prick! Here ol' Pops is breakin' his ass for a nickel ninety-five an hour, and sonny-boy's out there pumpin' a grand a day of that horseshit into your veins?"

"That's right, Pops," The Fugitive confirmed.

"Well, you ungrateful sonuvabitch!"

Pops turned towards me: "Every goddamn Friday when my payday come, there he'd be; beggin' for a handout, *Can you spare a little cash, Pop's?* If I had twenty, I'd give him ten. If I had a hundred, I'd give him fifty! Even after I lost my job, I'd give him half of whatever I had, and never saw a red cent of it come back!" Pops turned back towards his son. "A thousand goddamn dollars a day, and couldn't spare a nickel for your old man!"

"Hell, Pops, when you got that monkey on your back, you can't think of nothin' 'cept Mister Needle and Mister Spoon."

But Pops wasn't listening: "Bustin' my ass, day in day out, to help out my sonny-boy whenever I could."

"Oh, now it's bustin' your ass, huh?" The Fugitive snapped back. "The only thing you ever busted your ass at was makin' sure you got it up on that barstool every night!"

"On a barstool! Is that where your mama told you I was?"

"That's where we knew you was! We used to sit up nights with mom until the cops finally dragged you home. Some role model. No wonder I turned out the way I did!" The Fugitive paused to spit into the camp-fire; a *dramatic* pause that spoke as loudly as his accusations. "Look at us now: a couple of derelict bums cowering out in the woods; a plastic shithole for a home; eatin' dogfood for our Easter supper. Like father like son, eh, Pops? Like father like son!"

With the flare-up between Pops and The Fugitive subsiding as quickly as it had begun, that was pretty much it for the evening's entertainment. And though tensions had run quite high at times, I never felt they were at risk of reaching *fightin' mad*. Rather, this seemed more a tired rerun of guilt-trips they had beaten each over the head with a thousand times before. *Fightin' mad*, after all, is attainable only in defense of honor, and these two had no honor left to defend.

Later, as stars began to appear overhead, the topic of conversation wound around to religion.

"How about you, Pop's; do you believe in God?" I asked.

"In God? Hell, yeah, I believe in God! I wouldn't go so far as to call myself religious, of course, but I know there's a God up there that watches over us, just as sure as we're sittin' here. There's a Devil too, and they both want our souls!" Pops assured us, sounding more like a practiced politician who knew the proper response than someone who had seriously pondered the issue. "How 'bout you, sonny-boy: you believe in God, don't ya?"

The Fugitive stared into the fire with sincere yet brief contemplation. In ten seconds he knew his answer: "Nope."

Pops looked rattled. "Not even a little?"

The Fugitive shook his head. "There ain't no God."

Pops swung the question back to me, as if hoping to prove The Fugitive wrong by a two-to-one vote: "What about you, Rattlesnake; do you believe in God?"

Being one who poses, basically, that same question to himself every day, you would think I'd have a ready answer. But, I didn't; because I don't. For Pops' sake, I pondered the subject until I could come up with as succinct an answer as I could: "I believe there's more to this life than meets the eye. I don't believe we just die and that's it. Some might call that God."

Pops seemed satisfied with my answer, though, under close scrutiny, it really didn't make much sense. The three-way tie—between theism, atheism, and agnosticism—seemed the perfect segue to a departure.

"Well, thanks for Easter supper, guys," I said standing to leave.

"Well, thanks for being our guest," Pops said.

"Alrighty, Rattlesnake, goodnight," The Fugitive added, interrupting yet another unconsciously whistled chorus of *Jesus Christ Superstar*.

The night was cool, as is the rule in the Sierra even on the hottest days. I was wearing only a torn t-shirt (silk-screened "Bud's Buds") bequeathed upon me by The Marijuana Grower his last visit, a pair of trousers purchased a year ago for 25¢ at a rummage sale, and a discarded pair of tennis shoes left behind by one of The Bros last summer. Having not planned to stay for dinner up there at the Comfort Zone, I hadn't brought along my sovereign-willed flashlight. Nevertheless, I was able to find my way home reasonably well just by following the somewhat contiguous path of stars overhead, which showed the way between the towering pines. As above, so below.

Approximately a quarter-mile upstream of the tipi, there's a vantage point above God's Pool which proffers a particularly sweeping view of a mile-long stretch of the river. I pulled up a seat, on a rock shaped like a Lazy Boy chair, to take in the vast night. By then the moon had risen enough so that its light shone on the higher ridges, but not so high that any of its light fell here into the canyon's bottom. As I sat there, looking about—from the inky ribbon of river coursing its way between glowing sandbars, to the blurry spill of stars which comprise the Milky Way, our galactic home, then even way out to the blackest reaches of deep space, then back again to my big toe protruding from a worn tennis shoe—it all, everything both near and far, began to feel, inexplicably, *equidistant*.

I've had this feeling before. If I had to describe it, I would say that it feels a bit like snorkeling in crystal-clear water. *Snorkeling* is the key word here; for while my eyes are wide open but staring hard at the pond's bottom, my air supply—my breath of the life force—feels as if it is being piped down to me from some higher, unseen clime far above the surface of this world. Admittedly, this is just a notion I have; a notion of the absolute.

ROBERT P. JOHNSON

Moon of the Shedding Ponies II

"There's no hope,
When you're a dope."
— Sri Baba Lu Bop

Journal Entry; 30 April 1985:

Today marks the eleventh month of my year in the wilderness. I should be giddy, but I'm not. I'm not anything; either happy or sad. Symptomatic of this ennui, I can't seem to drag myself out of the sleepingbag; I don't want to get up. This concerns me, but not too much.

A small bird—a Canyon Wren, I suspect—has found its way into the tipi through the smoke flap. It's chirping away hysterically. Perhaps prompted by the chirps, Bud has decided we've lingered long enough inside here. He rises from his rug beneath my desk, stretches, makes his way over to my cot, then sticks his cold, damp nose in my face. By now we know each other well enough to realize I have two choices at this juncture: either I can get up and we can go outside to piss and begin the day; or, I can scoot over a bit, to give him room to hop up on the cot and curl up beside me. I choose the latter, which seems fine by him: after sixty seconds he's sound asleep again.

The sun now spills over the ridge and into the valley. I only know this because the tipi's canvas had taken upon a warm, copper glow. It's subtle at first, the dawn, for the sunlight comes filtered through the needles and branches of the pines lining the eastern ridgetop more than a mile away. But after another minute or two it's far brighter and warmer, as the sunlight falls upon the canvas uncensored. I unzip my sleepingbag down to my feet to keep cool.

From here within the tipi I get a sense of what it must be like being a chrysalis hanging in its cocoon with the nudging sun falling upon it; an inspired caterpillar yearning to fly, a fledgling butterfly with humans in its stomach. Moments ago everything in the tipi was equally lighted, vague with dawn, but now all is marked with sharp contrast. The converging poles, seams, and ropes becomes as distinct from the translucent canvas as bones are from the flesh in an X-ray photograph. The lower part of the main canvas glows creamy-white, while the higher reaches take on an ever-deepening golden-brown coloration due to the smoke residue which gathers up there. Through the porthole-like doorway, I can see out to the vibrant green of spring. The tips of the rush and grasses, the serrated edges of the wild grape leaves, as well as the wings of the swarming ladybugs and sundry other darting insects, all appear

Robert P. Johnson

to burn with their own light sources as they reflect the crisp morning sun. The unquenchably delicate fragrance of the wild azaleas rides with the cool breeze slip-sliding from off the warming northern canyon slopes, passing through my tipi's canvas as if through a screen door, pausing to dally in my nose hairs for a moment or two, before continuing on with the flow, down to the cool river bed below.

A tipi *is* a cocoon.

Life *is* a metamorphose.

JOURNAL ENTRY; 5 MAY 1985:

I shouldn't let it bother me so. After all, aren't I the one who's always claiming that the world is perfect; that everything which happens, all good and evil, happens for a reason? Isn't this the basis of Christian forgiveness? Isn't this the wisdom of Zen? Wouldn't it be better then, even prudent, for me to just to take a step back and assume the role of the detached observer rather than allowing myself to get so emotionally entangled in this "illusory" planet?

This seems to be the dilemma which paralyzes many of our generation: eastern and, to some degree, western religion, as well as "new age" science, has asked us to accept the world as "perfect"; thereby challenging us to view all "threats" and "imperfections" and "injustices" as mere misconceptions we hold of our true selves. And yet, looking around, our eyes and ears and sense of smell and reason tell us that the planet is destined for environmental and/or political ruin. So, what to do? Camus posited that the only important question was whether or not to commit suicide. I beg to differ; positing that the only important question is, Is there any point in trying to save the world? This is just the quandary in which I find myself today: whether or not to take action against what I perceive to be a grave environmental atrocity, or just to sit back and accept it as inevitable change.

At issue here is something called "The Tahoe National Forest Draft Plan"; a systematic harvest proposal drafted by Louisiana Pacific Lumber executive John Crowell for the Reagan administration. This 50-year "plan" calls for the clear cutting of over half (300 square miles) of the entire Tahoe National Forest at a rate of six square miles, in forty-acre patches, per year. Included in this proposed harvest is this very stretch of the American River canyon, regardless of the fact that it was granted "Wild and Scenic River" status back in 1975, regardless of the fact that logging such steep canyons inevitably create irreversible erosion, and regardless of the fact that the requisite reforestation contracts are rarely fulfilled. (It's a common scam: the logging companies contract out for the planting of the replacement seedlings, granting the contract to the lowest bidder. The subcontractor in turn takes the money, plants a few seedlings around the perimeter of the cut, then skips town.)

When one considers that Reagan was born into a world with just one-quarter of the five billion people loitering about the planet today, it is easy to understand why he might perceive the world's wilderness as invulnerable and boundless. But the wilderness is far from being either; in fact, at our current rate of adding a billion people per decade to the population, it is likely that, in our lifetime, there will be no forests around that weren't planted by man; which, by definition, means there will be no "wilderness."

Perhaps what irks me most about this "Draft Plan," and the depletion of wild spaces the world round in general, is the *aesthetic* loss I foresee. That is, I fear for all those would-be Thoreaus who will not be able to take a sabbatical from society, simply because there will be no place to do it. And if the loss of a future Thoreau doesn't scare you, what about the prospective loss of a future Christ or Mohammed or Buddha? For didn't each of these men, while pursuing their unique paths, find it necessary to flee into the wilderness for a time in order to clear their heads of society's frivolities? What if there was no wilderness for them?

I have nothing more to say about this Tahoe National Forest Draft Plan. I have staked my position; prudent or not.

JOURNAL ENTRY; 15 MAY 1985:

I was shin-deep in the icy river working the sluice box. The Fugitive was working the sandbar. After filling two buckets with gravel, he carried them out to me. As I poured the first bucket into the top of the box, he sat himself on a suitable boulder and rolled a cigarette.

"So, Rattlesnake, I've been meaning to ask you something for some weeks now."

"Yeah? What's that?" I asked, helping the current wash the gravel through the sluice.

"Why d'you tell Pops that I told you that my name was Robert?"

"I figured you needed an alias."

"Yeah, well, I see the reasoning there, but why Robert? I mean, your name's Robert, and you told me that that Marijuana Grower's real name was Robert, and, I don't know, it just seems kind of confusing."

"Precisely; think of the confusion when the cops swoop into the canyon lookin' for a fellow named Robert."

The Fugitive squinted up at the canyon walls, trying to imagine the event. He then shook his head: "I don't know, it might work."

"Sure it will," I assured him, tossing the empty first bucket back to the sandbar, and picking up the second. I had to smile to myself: this fugitive fellow didn't have a clue of the real reason I gave him the name *Robert* as an alias, not yet anyway. "Sure it will."

JOURNAL ENTRY; 22 MAY 1985:

Nick tumbled into the canyon this evening just before dusk; the same Nick whose chimney sweep business I baby-sat in January. There was no surprise to his showing up; it had been planned for weeks. Nor was there any confusion as to his purpose for coming: Operation Pull-Out had begun.

Operation Pull-Out was the not-so-clever code name given to my extrication from the canyon; my final pull-out from this year in the weeds. To this end Nick had come to accompany me on an exploratory raft trip down through Giant Gap; the purpose of which was to determine whether it was feasible to float (rather than carry) my tipi and other belongings out of here. If our exploratory trip went well, we had a veritable flotilla of assorted rafts and inflatable canoes at our disposal, as well as an as-yet-unspecified number of Bros, to help pull off the operation this coming weekend. If it *didn't* go well, well, suffice it to say, my powers of persuasion would be put to the test once again as I try to convince The Bros to help me carry all my shit out of here, much as it was put to the test when I tried to get them to help me carry all my shit *into* here a year ago.

It's now late at night. Nick is snoring. Bud is snoring. The crickets are snoring. But the river; the river rages on. I lie in my cot, wide awake. I dare not shut my eyes for, each time I do, the same terrible visions haunt my mind: tempestuous rapids, stacked, like derailed boxcars, one atop the next for miles; sucking cataracts, free-falling ten, twenty, thirty feet, before smashing head-long into graveyards of jagged boulders; inescapable reversals, all frothy-white and bottomless; and, worst of any and all, the innocuous-looking, calm-but-swift stretches between boiling rapids, whose crevices are nonetheless capable of catching a dragging leg or arm and pinning you down with the force of the river, drowning you within an inch of the surface. And it doesn't help that I already know the names of these rapids: Mustache Rock, Locomotive Falls, Nutcracker, Cranky Bitch, The Grater, Dominator, and Dominatrix.... And it doesn't help either to know that an expert kayak-er drowned in Giant Gap not two weeks ago, and though his kayak popped up three days later, his body is still trapped—down there.

In all seriousness, I am terrified. I feel like a grunt soldier heading out on his last in-country mission before the end of his tour of duty. The threat posed by Giant Gap seems suddenly the logical culmination of that blasted tarot card prophesy given to me by The Marijuana Grower last year—*death*. Death—the tidy conclusion to my yearning for the divine.

JOURNAL ENTRY; 24 MAY 1985:

By the first hint of dawn, I was already up and stuffing my piece-o-shit novel manuscript, hand-scrawled journal, clackle-clacker, and sundry other "valuables" I couldn't risk getting wet, into my backpack in preparation for Operation Pull-out. With that done, I sloshed across the creek and began up the trail leading out of the canyon. Wading through the meadow's tall, lush grass, the valley floor sounded like a jungle with all the bird chirpings.

I reached the trailhead just minutes before the rising sun's rays. At the Cranbrook I exchanged my backpack for the tattered wetsuit that would try its meager best to stave off the river's cold during the raft trip through Giant Gap. En route back into the canyon, I paused to pick blackberries from the bushes near Joe Steiner's grave. So efficient had my morning been thus far, that I already had coffee brewing and black-berry corncakes flipping by the time Nick awoke.

"Rum-bubble-gum-ball," he chanted, as he emerged from the tipi rubbing the sleep from his eyes.

"Rum-bubble-gum-ball," I chorused.

Don't ask me how, but *rum-bubble-gum-ball* had become Operation Pull-out's official mantra; a prayer we offered up to the water gods—Neptune, Ynamia Ynamia, Joe Steiner, and George Cayton—a silly little superstition neither of us would cop to. It made no sense: but, then again, so little does.

We ate in humorless silence, the threat of the voyage looming as thick as the syrup we poured over our pancakes, our hope of surviving it as thin as our coffee.

"Do you want to call it off?" I asked.

Nick only laughed. And for good reason: Of course he wanted to call it off. Both of us did. What prudent man wouldn't? But he knew as well we couldn't; our macho pride wouldn't allow it. No, against better judgment, it was painfully obvious we were going to go through with this exploratory trip down through Giant Gap. Like the river itself, we seemed to have no say in the matter. *Rum-bubble-gum-ball.*

We slapped together two salami and cheese sandwiches apiece, donned our wetsuits, left a *To-Whom-It-May-Concern* note on my table informing passersby of our endeavor in case we were never heard from again, inflated our two two-man rafts, then carried them up to The Crossing, so that God's Pool—in some twisted homage to The Marijuana Grower's near-drowning so many moons ago—would be our voyage's first set of rapids.

By then the sun pierced the crystalline water at a steep angle. Nick checked his wristwatch. Ten a.m. We waded out into the pool and climbed into our rafts. They felt like toys. We might as well have been attempting the voyage in a pair of those yellow-plastic Donald Duck life-preserver rings. Oh well. We slapped our paddles together to signal the operation's commencement, chanting—just once, but in perfect uni-son—*Rum-bubble-gum-ball.*

The river has dropped considerably these last two weeks, from nearly 2,000 cfs (cubic feet per second) to 800 or so. This explains why no rafters have been seen lately; it's too low for them. In canyons such as this, more is better—more is safer. Nevertheless, Nick and I, stooges that we are, took the low flow as a blessing, assuming that it would allow us to portage the more dangerous rapids and thereby keep our thrashings to a minimum.

The initial two miles of river slipped smoothly beneath our boats. Even ominous Mustache Rock, which had flipped us in a trial run yesterday, we managed and, I dare say, rather skillfully. But these were still the relatively placid class II and III waters of Green Valley and not the class V+ of Giant Gap; a little fact that kept our hubris in check.

As we floated around The Outlaws Camp's curving sandbar, we came upon The California Goldminer, sitting, back turned to us, on a boulder and rolling up a cigarette. We held our silence until the river carried us to within ten feet of him, then let out a canyon-shaking Injun whoop that sent him clawing for the sky.

"Jesus frickin' Christ!" he cursed, until our rafts and wetsuits distracted him. "Where the hell do you two think you're goin'?"

"The Gap," I told him.

"The Gap?!" he shuddered. "D'ya know where the waterfalls are?"

"Nope."

"D'ya hear about the kayaker?"

"Yep."

"You'll be floatin' right over his body, ya know."

"Thanks, we'll keep that in mind," I said, as the current dragged us away from him and onto the tongue of the next rapid.

"Nice knowin' ya!" The California Goldminer shouted a last time.

Two short pools later we found ourselves being whisked through the fast waters of week-end warriors, Stanley and Milan Jones' claim.

"Hey, Stanley!" I shouted.

Stanley looked up from his sluice box, squinting at us like he wasn't certain we weren't just passing-through ghosts.

I was in the mood to tease: "It's me, Joe Steiner—Ghost of the River!"

A smile spread across his face. "Naw it ain't. It's Rattlesnake

Cutthroat Johnson!" He then shouted up to their deck, where his brother Milan was cooking breakfast over his two-burner Coleman stove: "Hey, Milan, lookie who's a-floatin' through!"

Milan gazed down through the steam of some frying bacon.

"Who is that?" he asked Stanley.

"It's that Rattlesnake fella."

Milan smiled. "Hey ya, 'Snake. Where ya off to?"

"Dunno. What's down here?" I answered, playing dumb as I pointed downstream.

"Hell! This is the river Styx, and down there's Hell!" Milan shouted back, waving farewell.

We waved back.

Stanley didn't: he just stood there—staring.

A tall, upright shard of rock, suitably named "Chimney Rock", serves as the official demarcation of the beginning of Giant Gap. If the Pearly Gates of Heaven has two pillars at its entrance, it's probably appropriate that the Gap has just this one, for not a boat-length afterwards does the river turn a hellacious and frothy white. Not five seconds after passing Chimney Rock, both our boats flipped and Nick and I found ourselves swimming. And this proved just the beginning: Cranky Bitch flipped us, as did Nutcracker, Locomotive Falls we wisely portaged, only to fall prey to The Grater, Dominator flipped Nick but not me, Dominatrix flipped me but not Nick, and Pyramid Ally, Pinball, Rock-'em-sock-'em barely let us sit atop our rafts at all. Verily, over the course of the next three hours, we were as often in our boats as we were tumbling in the violent water somewhere outside of them. And not helping our pace was the worrisome fact that my raft suffered three separate blow-outs. (Quite inexplicably, Nick's suffered none.) Upon earning my third blow-out, I paddled my air-less scrap of plastic towards the nearest scaleable bank and proceeded with yet another futile patching.

"Hey, Nick, we're out of glue," I told him, as I squeezed the last precious drops from the tube of glue.

"I guess you better not have another blow-out," he snapped, evidencing the stress of the journey with his curt reply.

"Now, don't get cocky. Your little S.S. Piece-o-Shit isn't going to take much more of this!" I assured him.

"Speaking of which: how much more of this do you reckon we have?" he asked, becoming conciliatory once again.

I looked upstream, trying to ascertain our mileage by the folds of the canyon, but the sheer walls made it impossible to see much beyond the previous turn. Turning downstream, however, the canyon was widening noticeably; a good sign.

"It's kind of hard to say, but it looks like we're pretty much through Giant Gap," I posited.

"Meaning?"

"Meaning, that out of a total fourteen miles, I'd guesstimate we've got five behind us with nine still to go."

"What about the rapids down there?"

"What about them?"

"Bigger, smaller, more, less?"

"Well, one rafter told me the rapids became few and far between after the Gap. Course, he also said they didn't flip until they got halfway or so. Apparently there's still plenty of class V water ahead."

Nick didn't seem encouraged by the news. As I dizzily blew air back into my raft, he squinted at the sun in an attempt to ascertain the time.

"I'll bet it's getting on three or four o'clock," he guessed.

I followed his gaze up to the sun, only to find it diving for the horizon like a fat kid after a box of Milk Duds.

"I thought you had a watch."

"I *did* have a watch, didn't I?" he said, perusing the un-tanned ban of skin circumnavigating his wrist. "Humph."

"Well, if it is three, that puts our progress at a modest mile-per-hour."

"Meaning we can expect to reach Iowa Hill Bridge by, oh, midnight or so."

"Well, then, I guess we had best keep at it," I surmised, staring trepidatiously at the churning current.

"Yep, guess so," he replied, glumly.

"Rum-bubble-gum-ball."

"Rum-bubble-gum-ball."

Over the course of the next hour the relentless fervor of Giant Gap subsided into long, lazy pools broken apart by mischievous but manage-able class III and IV rapids. One such pool dragged us past the sandbar where the kayaker's body had apparently been finally recovered, for there someone had fashioned a small cross from two pieces of drift-wood and stuck it in the sand. Another pool proved long enough for us to consume our (miraculously dry) sandwiches without feeling as if we were wasting valuable time. And a third pool dragged us through the first gold claim on the downstream side of Giant Gap—the Hutchinson brothers' claim.

"Hey, we're at Frank and Benny Hutchinson's claim!" I shouted back upstream to Nick. "Maybe we should stop and say *howdy*."

"Are you sure we got time for that?" Nick lobbied.

"Probably not. Then again, they might have some glue and patches, which we are definitely going to need."

"Alright: a brief *howdy*," Nick capitulated.

We moored our rafts on the south bank of the pool and hiked the fifty yards or so up to the (non-identical, twin) Hutchinson brothers' one-room, plank-wood cabin. I knocked on the door. Seventy-two years-old Frank answered the door, naked as the day he was born.

"Get some clothes on, Frank; you've got company," I suggested.

"Yeah, yeah—you're absolutely right," he muttered, still groggy from an afternoon nap. He turned towards his bed in an attempt to remem-ber where he last set his trousers. Spotting a bathrobe hanging from a nail on the opposite wall, he crossed towards it, chatting all the way: "Don't get much company these days, ya know—not since Benny died. He was the socialite of the pair."

"Your twin brother Benny died?" I asked, shocked at the news.

"Oh, you didn't hear?"

"No. I'm sorry."

"Wasn't your fault," he replied, with no attempt at humor.

"When did it happen?"

"Well, funny you should ask, 'cause I happen to know the exact *second* he died, even though nobody knew for a fact that he had until his body was found four days later!" Frank claimed, sans a trace of remorse.

"How was that?" Nick asked.

"Well, Benny had gone up to town for supplies, you see; this would be January fifth. I was layin' up in my bed 'cause he was pretty late in gettin' back. See, normally when one of us makes the hike we try to be back by sundown, but here it was, one in the morning, and still no sign of him. Anyway, the lights were off and I'm just layin' here in the dark, fumin' mad 'cause I'm thinkin' he's just up at the bar gettin' drunk, when I hear footsteps comin' up the trail to the cabin. Now, I know it's Benny 'cause he's got this kind of hobbly walk of his. Next thing, I hear the door here opening, then Benny walkin' in. I then hear him close the door and I'm thinkin' he's tryin' to be quiet so's not to wake me, but I'm mad so I says, Why don't ya turn on the light, Benny?—'cause I don't want him to think he's gettin' away with sneakin' in like that."

"And what did he say to that?" I asked.

"Nothin'! He just kept right on walkin' across the floor. So, figurin' he must be really drunk, even though that really ain't like him, so I says it again: Benny, turn on the light!—this time kinda yellin' it."

"And?"

"Still, not a peep: he just goes across to his bed and sits on it and starts to take off his shoes."

"Could you see him?" Nick asked.

"Not at all: it gets pitch black in here with the lights off. I could just hear him; ya know, the floor boards, bed springs, his shoes hittin' the floor and all that; plain as day I could hear him—just as I'd done most every single day since we moved down here way back in '62. Hell, I even felt the breeze of him walkin' past my bed!"

"So, what did you do?" I asked.

"Well, we got electricity, see, from that generator and those batteries out back; they power our refrigerator, tv, and these two lights here," he said, pointing about the cabin. "So, I reach up and flip on one of the lights, and, lo and behold, no Benny!"

"What d'ya mean, no Benny?" Nick asked.

"He wasn't there; not on his bed, not in the cabin—not nowhere!"

"So, do you think you were just imagining that you heard him come in?" I asked.

"Not on your life: that was Benny's *ghost* that I heard. I swear to God it was! Right then I looked over at the clock, and it said 1:05, and that's when I knew he had just then died—January fifth, 1:05 in the morning.

Like I said, four days later they found his body, at the bottom of a 300′ cliff up in the switchbacks on the hike back in."

After expressing our condolences and thanking Frank for the patches and glue, we left him at his cabin and headed back down to the river. By the time we saddled back into our rafts it must have been already past five in the afternoon.

"What do you think of Frank's story?" I asked Nick.

"I try not to think when I visit this canyon," he replied.

We dug our paddles into the slow-moving water.

"Rum-bubble-gum-ball."

Another two miles of long, languid pools, pinched at the ends by half a dozen uninspired rapids, brought us to Fords Bar. It was probably 6:30 by then.

Technically speaking, Fords Bar is the river's first vehicle access point, the caveat here being the fact that its long, steep, switchbacking dirt road is rarely used, let alone maintained, making it an unlikely bet to have weathered the heavy runoffs of '82 and '83. Compounding matters is the fact that private property owners up on the ridge have sealed the road with no less than three chained padlocks and a stout iron gate up near the top, thus rendering the road anything *but* a vehicle access these days.

The next few rapids after Fords Bar were tough class IVs. Nick and I were getting colder with each wave that splashed over our bows, gunwales, or sterns, and the sun, even when it wasn't hiding behind a ridge, was by then too low in the sky to warm us.

"This sucks," Nick muttered, as we teeth-chattered our way through a long section of tall, haystacking waves.

"Yeah, this sucks," I averred.

One of the waves had its way with me, flipping me like a peso and ripping my raft from my clutches. While tumbling underwater my knee struck a submerged boulder; not so hard as to injure it, but hard enough to make it all too apparent the idiotic risk we were taking. When I bobbed to the surface I saw that, though Nick too had been flipped by the wave, he nonetheless was able to hold on to both our boats. I swam down to him, latched on to his private little flotilla, and sidestroked us both to a bank.

"Nick, while I was underwater back there, I had a revelation."

"You were an altar boy; I suppose you're entitled," he deadpanned.

"Aren't you going to ask what it was?"

"I already know what it was: you had a revelation that we should abort the expedition 'cause Fords Bar is the last trail or road out of here until we reach Iowa Hill Bridge, which ain't for another, what, seven miles or so."

"You're a very intuitive guy, Nick."

"Maybe, but do you know what?"

"What?"

"I'm an intuitive guy who lost a shoe somewhere in that last set of rapids."

"So?"

"So, you're gonna have to hike out, find a four-wheel drive, and come back and get me."

"But, even if I can get the gate opened, I don't know that the road isn't washed out!"

"Well, then send a helicopter for me."

"Are you crazy?—only criminals get free helicopter rides out of here."

"Then, I dunno, tell 'em—Oh, hell, it's a long hike, you'll think of something!"

I stripped off my wetsuit down to my cut-offs and wet tennies, took a long drink of river water, bade Nick a confident *See-ya-soon, baboon,* then headed up the north bank of the river, back up to Fords Bar, then up and out of the canyon via the uncertain Fords Bar access road.

With the terror of the river behind me I could at last enjoy what had been a beautiful day: the beauty of having adrenaline pumping like electricity through my veins for the last eight hours, the beauty of having survived tenacious Giant Gap, the beauty of having thoroughly exhausted myself by climbing out of the canyon twice in one day, and paddling or swimming seven miles of ravenous white water. What a day! What a gift!

I hiked the road's steep switchbacks then, upon reaching the ridge, jogged the four or so miles out to the tiny town of Gold Run ("Population 6" the sign reads). By the time I reached Interstate 80, the cars were already turning on their headlights. I stuck out my thumb. Funny, no one seemed to want to take the risk picking up a sweaty-looking guy wearing only cut-offs and worn-out tennis shoes. I pulled in my thumb, turned east, and commenced to jog up the interstate—illegal, but what did I care?—for another four or so miles, through the town of Dutch Flat and up to that of Alta.

It was just after nine o'clock when I finally reached my father's house. And right about when I arrived, so too did Nick's brother Vid—driving up in his spanky-new four-wheel drive.

Coincidentally, or perhaps, providentially, or perhaps, for anyone with a lunar calendar, predictably, the moon was again full. All this year I can't recall it being anything but full: like an unyielding girlfriend, it seemed always "that time of the month."

Vid's 4x4 made it almost too easy for us to drive back into the canyon and retrieve Nick from Fords Bar. The road, it turned out, had survived the run-offs and the property owners didn't seem to have a clue that their stout and triple-padlocked gate lifted readily off its hinges. Oh well.

In that the moon was full and bright, Nick, Vid and I decided to hike back down to the tipi that night. En route out to the trailhead, Nick and I were able to convince Vid that Operation Pull-out's planned flotilla would not only be risky, but also much more laborious than merely carrying the tipi *et al* back out of the canyon. With that settled, we left all the rafts in the cars, filled the void in our backpacks with beer and grub, and began back down the trail.

We arrived back down at the tipi right around midnight, there to find Jae and Bud (who had managed to chew his way off his rope up at The Fugitive's Comfort Zone) waiting up for us beside a modest campfire. As the others sucked down beers, I pulled down the tipi, folding its canvas sections into neat bundles in preparation for the final exodus. Using the now-obsolete tipi poles now for fuel, we built the campfire into a roaring bonfire: after all, I had survived the Death prophecy—just cause for celebration.

Right now, it's got to be sometime after one in the morning. I'm lying here on my cot, staring up at the moon and stars, feeling more physically exhausted than I can ever recall. And come tomorrow, Saturday, I plan to do absolutely nothing but continue to lie here. Jae, Vid, and Nick, Mac, Karp, Mitch, Alex, Wayne, and the rest of The Bros, when they arrive, they can do whatever they please; hike, swim, fish—whatever. But not me: I'm just going to lie here, sip beers, if my pals are so kind as to hand me some, and watch the river flow past. That's all I'm going to do. Goodnight.

ROBERT P. JOHNSON

Moon of Making Fat II

"I have learned this, at least, by my experiment: that if one advances confidently in the direction of his dreams, and endeavors to live the life which he has imagined, he will meet with a success unexpected in common hours. In proportion as he simplifies his life, the laws of the universe will appear less complex, and solitude will not be solitude, nor poverty poverty, nor weakness weakness. If you have built castles in the air, your work need not be lost; that is where they should be. Now put the foundation under them."

— HENRY DAVID THOREAU

JOURNAL ENTRY; 30 MAY 1985:

Bud and I hiked back into the canyon today for the very last time. We had spent the past few days uptop felling young lodgepole pines; these, of course, to be used for the new tipi poles, so I could sell the tipi at the soonest opportunity. With my bowsaw I cut the requisite seventeen trees from a thicket so dense that competition for light and soil would have soon killed them regardless. Next, I trimmed their branches and husked their bark with my hatchet. In all, the task was a lot easier than I had imagined. In fact, had I known how easy it would be, I wouldn't have bothered dragging all the original poles into the canyon in the first place; rather, I would have simply cut new ones from the thicket of firs near the meadow and be done with it. Live and learn.

The purpose of today's visit was two-fold. First, there was still the main section of tipi canvas to be packed out, since none of The Bros or I had room in our packs for it last Sunday. Second, but actually foremost, was the none small matter of my premeditated, surreptitious abandonment of Bud on The Fugitive. This would have to be handled with extreme tact so as not to arouse suspicions—of *either* parties.

"Hey, ya, Robert," I called out, as I entered The Fugitive's Comfort Zone camp, intentionally using the alias I had given him for this very reason.

"Hey there, Rattlesnake. I see you survived Giant Gap," he shouted back.

"Barely," I said, pulling up a log beside his breakfast fire.

Pops stumbled out of their black plastic cabin, scratching the sleep from his tangled gray hair.

"Mornin', Rattlesnake."

"Mornin', Pops."

"I passed through your camp the other day; look like you're all moved out."

"Yep, just got the one last load to pack out."

"So, what's next for ya?" The Fugitive asked.

"Well, I plan on heading back up to Tahoe this afternoon; look for a job, a place to live, that kind of thing. To that end, I was wonderin' if you guys wouldn't mind looking after Bud for a week or so; you know, 'til I get settled."

Something in the tone of my voice caused Bud to drop the otherwise ever-present stick from his mouth, crane his head around, and look me square in the eyes. He could hardly believe his ears: for here I was, spewing the very pitch his previous three owners had spewed, nearly verbatim, before me: *I was wonderin' if you wouldn't mind looking after Bud for a week or so; you know, 'til I get settled.* The gall!

"Sure, we'll look after him for ya," The Fugitive said, with a knowing grin.

"It'll be a pleasure havin' ol' Bud around!" Pops added.

"Thanks," I said.

I then gave Bud's head a pat; a subtle, little *see-ya-next-week* pat rather than a long, drawn-out *farewell-forever* one. It was all I could do not to break down sobbing, drop to my knees and hug him to death, and I think they all—The Fugitive, Pops, *and* Bud—knew it.

"Well, bye," I said, tipping my hat and turning for the trail.

"See ya, Rattlesnake," they replied.

It is now some vague hour in the afternoon, as I put my final hike from this canyon behind me, a plodding step at a time. I pass a thigh-high escarpment of broken rock and catch myself holding my breath in anticipation of The Ambassador's ever-invigorating buzz of rattles. But, as I pass beyond the danger zone without The Ambassador deigning to make an appearance, I am awash with disappointment; an emotion which reveals to me that, over the course of four seasons and as many meetings, he has gone from reviled foe to respected neighbor. And, somehow, I will miss him.

Reaching the halfway cedar, I pause to turn towards the canyon. The low sun casts long shadows across the tiny valley that has been my address for the past year. I have paused here in an attempt to take it all in; to soak up the whole experience as if with a sponge and drag it out of here with me. But that's impossible: you can't take it with you.

I send my loudest Injun whoop out across the void. After several seconds it echoes back faintly, like an already-fading memory.

A couple days ago I had built some flimsy racks out of scrap lumber, and bolted them to the Cranbrook's front and back bumpers so I could transport the tipi poles back up to Tahoe. When I finally reached the trailhead, the Cranbrook was awaiting me, shiny-new tipi poles and all.

I swung the heavy pack from my back directly onto the Cranbrook's backseat. Released from the burden, my shoulders seemed to float. A sudden breeze raked across the ridge, causing the towering pines to creak and sway. The leaves of the California bay trees spun from their limbs like fishing lures. Firs lifted their skirts and sighed. Once again, there was something special about the day at which the wind could only hint. The world still bustled with... there's no way other to describe it... *ennui.*

I took my position behind the Cranbrook's rear bumper and began to push it towards the gentle downhill in order to bump-start it. No sense trying to start it the conventional way; the battery wouldn't be up to it. Once gravity began to pull the massive 'Brook on its own, I ran up to the driver's door and hopped in. I fished through the debris in the ash-tray until I found the car key, which I then stuck into the ignition switch, and turned to "on". For awhile, I just let the Cranbrook coast; both because I wanted it to pick up more momentum, but also because I love the sound of it, sans engine noise, crunching the twigs and pinecones that littered the dirt logging road.

In that brief period, I began pondering my immediate future: In an hour or so I'd be back up at Tahoe. Being this late, the bank would be closed, meaning my total life savings of eight dollars would be held captive until morning since the Automated Teller Machine deals only in twenties. In the coming week, I'd probably sleep in the Cranbrook or crash on friends' couches while I looked for work and, sometime there-after, a place to live. Normally, the contemplation of such daunting tasks would depress me, but for some reason, today, now, I feel irra-tionally optimistic. Indeed, if I've gained anything by this year in the wilderness, it seems I've acquired an inexplicable faith that I will be provided for. Curiously, I still don't know if I believe in God or not, but I've come to trust Providence.

Once we reached the bottom of the downhill, I shifted from neutral to second gear and popped the clutch. The mighty flathead-six explod-ed to life.

THE END